THE
TRUTH
OF THE
MATTER

My Life In and Out of Politics

BERT LANCE

with *Bill Gilbert*

SUMMIT BOOKS

New York · London · Toronto · Sydney · Tokyo · Singapore

SUMMIT BOOKS
Simon & Schuster Building
Rockefeller Center
1230 Avenue of the Americas
New York, New York, 10020

10   9   8   7   6   5   4   3   2   1

Library of Congress Cataloging in Publication Data

Lance, Bert
The truth of the matter : my life in and out of
politics / Bert Lance with Bill Gilbert.
        p.   cm.
    Includes index.
    1. Lance, Bert.   2. Politicians—United
States—Biography.   3. Carter, Jimmy.   4. United
States—Politics and government—1977–1981.
5. Jackson, Jesse.   6. United States—Politics and
government—1981–1989.   I. Gilbert, Bill.
II. Title.
E840.8.L32A3   1991
973.926'092—dc20
[B]   91-25016
                                                  CIP
ISBN: 0-671-69027-2

Photo credits:
1: courtesy of the Governor's office, State of Georgia
5, 8, 9, 10, 11, 12, 13, 14: Official White House
Photos
7: courtesy of Marty LaVor © Photo
16: courtesy of R. Long Photography

Acknowledgments

No book is written without the help of others. In our case we extend special thanks to several people who made this book possible:

Kim Leighton, who preserved some of the memories in these pages several years ago because of the possibility that there might be a book in the future;

Dominick Anfuso, senior editor at Summit Books, his assistant, Cassie Jones, and their editor-in-chief, Jim Silberman, for their confidence in our work and their skill as editors;

Russell Galen, our agent and a vice president of the Scott Meredith Literary Agency in New York, for representing us with professionalism and success, as always.

Bert Lance and Bill Gilbert
July 1991

First and foremost I dedicate this book to my wife of more than forty years and my childhood sweetheart from the sixth grade on. Without her love, support, trust, belief, understanding and, most of all, her total faith and trust in Jesus Christ, I would never have survived the trials and tribulations inflicted on me and my family. LaBelle has been the source of my strength and for all she means to me, I shall always be grateful.

In addition, I dedicate this book to our four sons, Tram, David, Stuart, and Beverly, and their families. They have brought so much joy into our lives, especially our eight grandchildren.

Finally, I would be remiss if I did not also dedicate this book to my dearest friends, Mack and Nita Robinson, Ed and Susie Elson, and Jimmy and Rosalynn Carter for years of friendship and support. The Carters have occupied a very special place in my life and "the truth of the matter" is that all the fun you are about to read about would not have been possible without them.

*That man is a success who . . . has filled his niche and
accomplished his task,*

*Who leaves the world better than he found it, whether by a
perfect poem or a rescued soul,*

*Who never lacked appreciation of earth's beauty or failed to
express it,*

Who looked for the best in others and gave the best he had.

—ROBERT LOUIS STEVENSON

Contents

Memories

The scenes and emotions are burned into my memory:

- A man most people never heard of, named Jimmy Carter, standing in the shade of an oak tree on the campus of a small college in Georgia in 1966.
- The election of the same man, one of my closest friends, as President of the United States ten years later in one of the most stunning achievements in the history of American politics.
- My shock and pride eight months later as I lay on my bed, physically and emotionally spent after an entire summer of broiling political controversy, and heard my wife say to the President, "I want to tell you one thing—you can go with the rest of the jackals, and I hope you're happy."
- Eighteen straight months of running for governor while unable to sleep lying down because of a ruptured disk in my back.
- The sight of eighteen TV crews the first morning of my trial on charges of banking violations and the lesser number of those folks on hand when I was found innocent four months later.
- The luncheon on the deck of Walter Mondale's Lake Tahoe cabin the weekend before the 1984 Democratic convention, when my son warned Fritz to stick by me if any leftover mud from the "Lance affair" started getting smeared around when he named me his campaign chairman.

- The hurt and abandonment I felt when boos and catcalls greeted me as I walked onto the convention floor in San Francisco.
- Listening with pride as Jesse Jackson united the 1988 convention more than Mike Dukakis did.
- My sense of peace as I walked onto the floor of the 1988 convention without being booed as I had been four years before.

To reflect on a career encompassing such sharp contrasts produces not one emotion but a whole range of them: joy and sadness, relief and concern, pride and bitterness. I admit to having felt all of these at one time or another, depending on the matter at hand, but on balance I am struck by one overriding feeling—an awareness of the irony of it all.

There was a rich amount of irony in the story of Jimmy Carter, coming from out of nowhere to be elected President but then failing to win reelection. I was a witness to those years. There was added irony in what Jimmy told the voters all through the 1976 campaign and then what happened after he got to Washington. He told the people he was an "outsider" who could go to Washington and straighten out those folks up there, and they elected him. But then he was criticized for being unwilling to cooperate with the "insiders."

There was irony in the fact that some Americans persisted in believing that I was convicted and sent to jail despite my vindication by a jury. (Some folks think I'm still there.) And there was irony, and worse, in Ronald Reagan's campaign promise to eliminate the budget deficit by 1982 when he ran against Jimmy in 1980 and his decisions, once he got himself elected, that raised the deficit to an all-time high.

There was irony in Walter Mondale's boldness in deciding to select a woman as his running mate in '84—and then picking one who couldn't help him. There was irony in the contrast between Jesse Jackson's image as a pulpit-pounding black preacher and his 1988 presidential campaign, when he was the leading candidate in spotlighting drugs, day care, catastrophic health insurance, and so many other issues, and making sound recommendations on how to deal with them.

The list goes on, and as it grows the exhilarating triumphs, the stinging defeats, the infuriating frustrations, the pride of accomplishment, the laughs—there were many—and the tears—there were enough of them, too—all come back to me.

And the irony of it all.

1

The Man, the Governor, the President

JIMMY CARTER was standing in the shade of a big oak tree on the campus of Berry College in Rome, Georgia. It was 1966. I hadn't met him before, but we were both at Berry for a meeting of our regional planning and development commission to discuss the future of our area, the Coosa Valley, where my hometown of Calhoun is located.

Near Calhoun was the last capital of the Cherokee Indian nation, New Echota. Between 13,000 and 17,000 Cherokee were living there in 1836 when the federal government ordered them off their land and to a new, distant territory called Oklahoma. Thousands of them died in making that journey, and their route forevermore has been called the "Trail of Tears."

One hundred thirty years later, we were discussing the economic future of that area. I was there because of my concern for our region's economic development. Jimmy had been the first president of the statewide planning commission. He was running for governor, even though as a member of the Georgia State Senate from Plains, he was not well known outside his own town.

From the articles I had read about him in the papers, I wanted to meet him. I liked what he was saying about what he wanted for the people of Georgia. His philosophy was the same then as it was when he was governor and President: "Government ought to be as good as the people it serves."

I liked that. So when I saw him at Berry College, I walked over and introduced myself. "Mr. Carter, my name is Bert Lance. I want you to know that I like what you've been saying about the state and its future."

It happened at an outdoor barbecue at the conclusion of that conference. It was a typical southern setting, with picnic tables, soft drinks, and down-home country cooking. Jimmy comes from the flat-lands of southwest Georgia; Calhoun is two hundred miles away in the mountains of north Georgia, but as we talked we learned we had much in common—both of us were from small towns, both of us dreamed as kids of going to sea, both wanted to go to the Naval Academy (which Jimmy did), both of us wanted to serve the people of Georgia in a significant way, and both of us were practicing Christians.

I came to Calhoun as a ten-year-old fourth-grader in 1941. War clouds were darkening on America's horizon, but for the Lance family the future was bright. My father, Dr. Thomas Jackson Lance—Jack—had been appointed superintendent of schools for Calhoun.

For Dad this was the latest in a line of successes in the aca-demic profession. He began his career as a high school principal in Hopewell, Georgia, and then taught English at Young Harris Col-lege in the Blue Ridge Mountains of northeastern Georgia and at Richmond Academy in Augusta. He served as superintendent of schools in Waynesboro, Georgia, from 1930, the year before I was born, until he returned to Young Harris College as president. He serve there until 1941.

For my father to enter the teaching world was not remarkable. Most of the Lance men were farmers, preachers, or teachers, and I thought as a boy that I might follow him into teaching. That would have been an outgrowth of the careers of both my father and my great-grandfather, who was a Methodist circuit rider in the Blue Ridge Mountains in the nineteenth century. He told my father many a story with vivid descriptions of helping to open the American frontier all the way from Virginia to California as a preacher on horseback.

My great-grandfather was a strong orator and a staunch protector of his followers. One of his favorite subjects was his efforts to relieve the misery of his parishioners by bringing them medical and financial help. He was especially vigorous in opposing the sale of alcohol, which led to so many problems in frontier days.

The moonshiners making their own alcohol warned him to stay out of their way and to stop building opposition to them. They didn't want any Bible-quoting preacher breaking up their racket by turning public opinion against them or, worse yet, getting the law after them. But my great-grandfather wouldn't back off. No Lance ever did. He kept on helping the members of his flock, at the same time warning them about the dangers of what today is called alcohol abuse. After one of his strongest sermons, a gang of moonshiners ambushed him in a creek near his home and killed him by slitting his throat.

I always admired my great-grandfather for his sense of public service and for his stubborn refusal to back down in the face of threats when he knew he was right. And I always admired my father for the same devotion to the public and for his strength of character.

My early years were spent on the campus at Young Harris. My parents had four children: Jack Jr., Bob, Alice Rose, and me, the baby. There was joy in our family, but there was an early tragedy, too.

Jack was a strong, active sixteen-year-old who was also a member of the Boy Scouts. After a scouting meeting one evening, he became ill in his room and collapsed with a cerebral hemorrhage. He was dead in only a matter of hours.

My parents saw my birth as an example of the Christian belief that whenever God shuts a door in your life, He opens another one. But Jack Jr.'s death was not the only tragedy to befall my parents. Thirteen years later, my other brother, Bob, was killed in the Atlantic during World War II.

Life at Young Harris College was the perfect combination for a preteen like me. To the happiness of life in a small southern town in the "Old South" were added the cultural opportunities that came with being a college president's son: receptions and dinners; an introduction to fine reading; and stimulating conversations that piqued my interest in new subjects like history and the world beyond my own little universe of school, church, baseball, and bike riding.

IN ONE of those storybook tales that sounds like something out of a Doris Day musical, I met LaBelle David immediately after we moved to Calhoun—at the reception welcoming the new school superintendent and his family to Gordon County. The reception was held at the David Cabin, a farm owned by LaBelle's grandfather, Austin Banks David.

It was a summer fish fry, and LaBelle was one of the hostesses for the young folks. She was responsible for introducing me to other people my age and making me feel at home. Today she admits that she slipped me away from her sixth-grade competition by showing me the rest of her granddaddy's farm, though all I kept thinking about were the fried fish and all those side dishes and rolls and desserts back on the picnic tables.

It was love at first sight—of course puppy love at first, but it became the real thing as the days and weeks turned into months and years. Today, a half-century after that fish fry, our love is still the real thing.

LaBelle and I attended Calhoun Elementary School together, a red brick two-story schoolhouse just off Wall Street, our town's main street. The bricks from that building, which was torn down years ago, now form the walls of our home on our farm, Lancelot, outside Calhoun. We were in almost every class together, worked on school activities together, went out together, and went to church and Methodist Young Fellowship together.

Our close relationship didn't remain a secret very long. In our seventh-grade English class, our teacher intercepted a mash note we were passing between us and stuck it up on the bulletin board. From that time on I have followed a policy of full public disclosure to prevent such embarrassments.

LaBelle remembers the first Christmas present I gave her: a beauty set of perfume, lipstick, and rouge by Evening in Paris. I accumulated the vast sum needed for the purchase, $8.50, the old-fashioned way—I earned it. I worked in the Calhoun drugstore as a soda jerk after school for ten cents an hour.

I was introduced to sports, and the valuable lessons about life that you can learn from them, the same way all kids were in those years. The Little League hadn't been formed yet, so my first exposure to athletics was plain old sandlot baseball on the corner lot.

Usually there was only one ball available, but we made it enough. The cover would be chewed up by the rocky fields five minutes after it was new. When the cover began to come off, we'd re-cover it with black tire tape. And if we happened to crack a bat in those years before aluminum bats, we pounded a couple of brads into the split, covered it with more tire tape, and kept on playing.

Some of our fall activities, including football, were curtailed for a few weeks every year during World War II because of the "manpower shortage." With so many of Gordon County's young men off to war, it became the responsibility of us preteens and teenagers to help pick the cotton crop. There was one major fringe benefit: school would close for those weeks.

Harvesting the cotton was a necessity in those days. In the Old South, the entire southern economy, not just our own county's, depended on cotton. The financial survival of families all across the South was tied directly to cotton, plus soybeans and peanuts. The South has made remarkable economic progress since World War II, and the most notable advancement is in the way our economy has become diversified so we are no longer gambling our very survival on the success of each year's cotton crop.

We were paid for our back-bending work—ten cents a pound. Each of us was issued a heavy cotton bag by the field boss. We'd loop the bag's strap over our shoulder and head down long rows of cotton balls that seemed to stretch forever. It was a combination of groups, which became typical as the war went on—kids and adults, all shapes and sizes, rich folks and poor folks.

This wasn't like one of those Doris Day scenes. This was more like something from Stephen Foster. The line of cotton pickers moved among the plants, back and forth, singing school songs and hymns and the top tunes of the Big Band era, bending and picking, bending and picking, from dawn to dusk, taking a break for a drink of water as often as the field boss granted his permission.

During those war years, the life of every American changed. In Calhoun, when we weren't picking cotton we did what communities all across the nation did: we held scrap drives to collect used paper and metal and even cooking fat to donate to the war effort. In school we had air raid drills to practice ducking under our desks or evacuating the building and anything else that was recommended in those days as a course of action in the event of an enemy air raid.

For Dad, the war added one more major responsibility. It was enough that as superintendent of schools he was responsible for all the children in the county school system, but now he had to supervise these wartime precautions as well.

However, all the cotton picking that I did and all the added wartime responsibilities imposed on my father were barely a ripple in our lives compared to the shock and tragedy of my brother Bob's death. He was, in the language of the day, "killed in action" while serving as an officer on the U.S.S. *Buck*. Now LaBelle and I had one more thing in common. Her brother, Banks, also died at an early age.

Bob's death had a sharp impact on me. I always looked up to him as little brothers do to their big brothers, especially when their big brother is eighteen years older. I took great pride in my brother, especially his appointment to West Point and his later graduation from the University of Georgia after he decided he didn't want to stay at West Point for his entire college career.

Bob was teaching English at Young Harris when the Japanese attacked Pearl Harbor. He met his wife, Mary Anderson of Jacksonville, Florida, when she was a student in one of his classes—which was exactly how my parents met.

Dad met Mom in 1913 in one of the Latin classes he was teaching at Young Harris, where he also taught Greek. Dad could read, speak, and write both Latin and Greek. Male teachers couldn't be so bold as to be seen in the company of one of their young female students at the turn of the century, so their only contact was in the classroom.

When that certain chemistry developed, he visited her one night long enough to pop the question and give her a respectable period of time to consider her answer. Because they couldn't be seen in public under society's rules in that more puritanical era, he worked out a code of communications for the next day in his class. He told her he would ask at the end of the class if anyone had any questions about the upcoming exam. She should ask one question about the test if she was accepting Dad's hand in marriage and another if she was rejecting him.

Dad got the question he wanted—and thus the answer he wanted, too. They were married at the end of that semester. On their wedding day, they traveled by horse and buggy to Hayesville, North Carolina, where Dad was scheduled to deliver a commencement address.

Then, in the very next generation, Bob met his future wife in the same way, although he did not have to resort to such complicated methods to get Mary's answer in those days of more direct communication.

Shortly after the Japanese attacked Pearl Harbor, Bob enlisted in the Navy. He was a communications officer on the U.S.S. *Buck*, a destroyer on patrol duty in the Mediterranean Sea. While escorting a convoy of six liberty ships from Sicily to Algeria, the *Buck* attacked and sank an Italian submarine and captured forty-five members of its crew. There was a picture in the paper of the *Buck*'s commanding officer speaking to the commander of the sub, and we had the thrill that families back home always yearned for: we got to see Bob in the picture.

We were able to recognize him even though it wasn't a sharp photo. One of the other officers with the two commanders was holding his right hand over the watch on his left wrist. That was one of Bob's habits. There was no question about it—that was Bob in that picture. Seeing him there was one of the big thrills for his kid brother back home in Calhoun.

Shortly after that, our home was filled with the excitement anticipated in millions of homes all over the nation. The family's serviceman was home on leave—or "furlough" if he was in the Army. Bob came home on a short leave in September 1943 when the *Buck* completed its mission of escorting smaller ships to the United States, and it was a happy time all around. We were able to see Bob again, and he got to see his three-week-old son, Robin.

All too soon, Bob shipped out again. Not long after, we experienced the horror dreaded by everyone and felt in 400,000 American homes during the war: a knock on the door and a telegram saying the government regretted to inform us that Bob was missing in action.

We found out later that the *Buck* was on convoy duty in September and October of 1943, supporting the invasion and occupation of Italy. On October 9, while on patrol off Salerno, it was hit in its forward section by one or two enemy torpedoes. The damage from the hit was so devastating that the command to abandon ship was sounded. The destroyer was abandoned in three minutes. One minute later, it sank. Bob was not listed among those who escaped.

I've never forgotten that tragic time. The experience made no sense to me and left me with strong feelings generated by war. While my parents remained stoic because of their greater acceptance of the horrors of war, I felt anger, dismay, and hatred toward the Germans for starting the war. In my twelve-year-old's logic, they had no right to kill my brother. I wanted them punished, and if the war was still going on when I became old enough, I was going to help dish out some of that punishment myself as my personal revenge against them.

Our problem was compounded by the uncertainty of Bob's case. We knew only that he was missing in action. The reality was that there wasn't a million-in-one chance anyone could survive that explosion. Still, the human spirit clings to every hope, and we hung on desperately for as long as we could to the shred of comfort represented by the fact that his death was not yet confirmed.

After a period of months, we finally accepted the undeniable. Mom hung a gold star on a white flag with red trim in our front window, the national symbol that a member of that household had been killed in the line of duty. Bob left his young wife and their infant son. I didn't have my brother-hero to look up to anymore, and my parents, blessed with four children, now had only two.

IT WAS in high school that LaBelle and I formed our habit of becoming involved in community affairs. I was on the football and baseball teams. LaBelle was one of the school's cheerleaders. I was editor of our school newspaper, and LaBelle was our "society editor." I was president of the senior class, and LaBelle was our secretary-treasurer. I was voted "most likely to succeed," and LaBelle was chosen as "Miss Gordon County."

When that trying time of separation came for us, when high school sweethearts follow separate paths to college, the emotional stress was minimized because we were going to college within a few miles of each other in Atlanta. I enrolled at Emory College and LaBelle went to Agnes Scott College. In the spring of our first year of college, fate intervened in our lives.

LaBelle almost died from appendicitis while on a camping trip with some of her classmates and college advisers at Lake Raburn in the Blue Ridge Mountains. I sent her camellias, which were always her favorite flower, and then visited her as soon as she was able to see anyone. I brought her a rose, which was reflection of my own taste in flowers as much as hers. (I have always been a lover of roses, and today I grow a whole variety of them in my garden on the farm. It remains one of my most enthusiastic activities.)

LaBelle's appendicitis attack told me something. We had always been each other's best friend, as we are today, and high school and college sweethearts, but her sudden illness made me realize that she meant more than that to me. We grew even closer as a result of that scare. I gave her my Sigma Chi fraternity pin when we were sophomores, and in the September before our senior year we were married in Calhoun Methodist Church, where we have worshipped together every Sunday since childhood, below its stained-glass windows of Christ as the Good Shepherd, teaching children and praying in the Garden of Gethsemane.

LaBelle's grandfather gave us the biggest helping hand any adult can give to young people—a chance in life. He had come to town in 1900 after working at a bank in Adairsville, ten miles south, and built Calhoun First National Bank into a thriving business and a keystone of our local economy. Concurrently, but not coincidentally, Calhoun became one of the leading centers of the carpet industry, a role which it continues to play today.

He also gave me one of the other valuable gifts a parent or grandparent can give to their children or grandchildren—their time. He taught me his ways as a country banker, practices and values which I then applied myself as my banking career got under way. His attitudes became my attitudes because I saw how much he helped individual people and our whole town.

He held a deep trust in people and used his knowledge of someone's situation and character in deciding whether to grant a loan,
instead of basing his decision on a person's collateral—and I always
followed the same philosophy.

"That's the key to country banking," he used to say. "I know a
man's face and his character. I know his folks. I know he's got a farm
and he isn't going to leave town. I know I can trust him, and I know
just how much I can loan him."

He started me at the bottom as a teller, and as my enthusiasm for
the banking business grew, so did my career. By the early 1960s I was
president of the bank, the youngest bank president in America, thanks
to the opportunity LaBelle's grandfather had given me ten years before.

Our lives were even more exciting at home. We were blessed with
four fine boys, and with each of them we experienced the kinds of
traumatic events that bring you even closer to your children and make
you appreciate them more, if that's possible. Our firstborn son,
Tram—Thomas Bertram Lance, Jr.—was hospitalized nine times before overcoming a fragile infancy. Another one of our sons, Stuart,
almost died after swallowing rat poison as a baby. Our son Beverly
suffered five hundred yellow jacket stings as a boy and hovered between
life and death for three days. Our second son, David, almost lost his
life after a routine tonsillectomy. When LaBelle wrote a book of her
own in 1978, no wonder she called it *This, Too, Shall Pass*.

But the positives far outweighed the negatives. We were delighted
with family life and our four sons. I got away from the bank at every
opportunity to be with LaBelle and them. We did everything we could
together. I coached them in Little League baseball, refereed high
school football, and volunteered to be the master of their Cub Scout
pack. LaBelle served in the PTA and in various church activities for
our sons and their friends.

This involvement in community activities with our sons had an
effect on me that was both satisfying and stimulating. It satisfied the
desire I had inherited from my father and great-grandfather to contribute something to my friends and neighbors, and it sparked a determination to do even more, in a more meaningful capacity, whatever
that might prove to be.

That determination led me, unwittingly, to Jimmy Carter.

I MADE it a part of my work at the bank to become involved in any
undertaking that came to my attention that might help the economy of
Calhoun and Gordon County. Our economy in north Georgia had
been mired down far too long, going back to the ravages to the cotton

crop caused by the boll weevils during the 1920s and continuing
through the Great Depression of the 1930s. Unlike most other communities, World War II did not prime our economic pump. The
young men who were needed to work our fields and harvest our crops
were drafted into the armed forces, and others left our rural area for the
inflated wartime salaries in the cities.

When our generation came along, Gordon County and the rest of
north Georgia needed help badly. Our economic slump had lasted for
forty years. The difficulties stemmed from the predominantly agricultural economy that typified the Old South, the South of my boyhood.

We had more time than money. Industrial jobs were few, and
money was short. The region was struggling to build a stronger economy, but there was no economic diversity. Everything was dependent
on cotton. That was still true when I started working at the Calhoun
bank in 1950.

Our county was still rural. We had ten cotton gins—there are
none today—and the bank's assets were small. The big local industry
was bedspreads, a cottage industry, with the women making spreads by
hand in their spare time. You could drive down Route 41, the main
north–south road then, and see bedspreads for sale, hanging on
clotheslines. You could buy them right off the line.

Then something happened. The multineedle sewing machine
was invented. Now the women could turn out far more spreads than
they had ever dreamed possible. That, in turn, spawned a huge carpet
industry, which remains one of the mainstays of our region's economy
today. People could make throw rugs, and the tufted rug became a
major product. Yarn became cheaper with the development of nylon
and other synthetic materials. A new day was dawning, and we had to
act to seize it.

After I had been at the bank for a few years, it was clear to some
of us that we had to do something to get out of our economic doldrums
and take advantage of the new economic opportunities being developed through the carpet industry. In the mid-1960s, we formed an
association of thirteen counties and thirty-nine cities into the Coosa
Valley Planning and Development District.

Our efforts—a combination of business and government working
cooperatively for everyone's benefit—produced almost immediate results in obtaining critically needed funds for water and sewer facilities,
roads, health care, and other public services and facilities. The district's board of directors was composed of local elected officials, but
many of us from the private sector participated in the organization's

activities and events to lend the full support of the business community. In the first five years of this innovative approach, employment in our region jumped 20 percent.

Those early years at the bank provided me firsthand education in the need to create jobs to stimulate any economy, whether it's local, regional, or national. I wanted to use our bank's collective assets and resources to do that. I never missed an opportunity to develop new industry and create new jobs.

I learned from those years, and from the expansion of our regional economy in the ten years since, that an economy is directly dependent on the creation of jobs. Any national administration must be convinced of this fact of life and must pay attention to job creation as much as to any other domestic concern.

Jimmy Carter was a young state senator at that time. He was an enthusiastic supporter of this cooperative approach and was a leader in forming the same kind of organization to serve the region in and around Plains. Jimmy was elected its first president and later headed Georgia's statewide planning agency.

He understood the economic needs of our state, and this understanding informed his perspective on the civil rights issue dominating the affairs of Georgia and every state in the nation during this period. To both of us, the moral and legal questions aside, it just plain made good sense to support the civil rights struggle, because it would improve the financial ability and future of the entire black population. That would produce a stronger economy for the entire South, and that would be an enormous improvement for everyone.

My philosophy as a banker always was that any time someone gets a job, or a better one, the marketplace functions better. Applied to the civil rights battle, this meant that opposing the efforts of Dr. King and others harmed your own growth and development, whether as a community, a state, the entire South, or the nation. In addition to being morally wrong, it was bad business.

Yet the opposition was strong. However, the people who understood the dynamics of the civil rights cause, and its promise of economic improvement for all—not just for black people—moved quickly and decisively to support it. Jimmy Carter was one of those supporters.

Out of his experiences as a state senator working to advance the state's economic development and his support for the civil rights movement came his increased desire for public service, the same kind of desire I was feeling. That's what put each of us on the path to our chance meeting—or was it destiny?—at Berry College.

•   •   •

THE TWO OF US stood under that tree for a long time, talking about making our state government more responsive and effective, something we Georgians hadn't been treated to for a long time. We felt an instant kinship, an uncanny mutual understanding that has endured the years and through any disagreements we had when he was governor and President.

The most consistent, predictable theme in every campaign Jimmy Carter ever waged and every office he ever held was his insistence that government be responsive to the people it serves. When he felt that the state government in Georgia had grown fat and excessively political, unresponsive and uncaring where the needs of the people were concerned, he decided to take matters into his own hands and get himself elected governor.

He never wavered in his determination and commitment to bring the people the kind of government that is as good as they are. His strong points and his weak ones were the same both as governor and as President: commitment to provide a strong, enlightened, moral administration; determination to make the right decision regardless of its political consequences to him; willingness to read everything and be a well-informed governor and President; and unwillingness to cultivate political favor with the members of the state legislature or Congress.

All of us were happy to do more than our share in maintaining legislative relations for Jimmy in Georgia; but that's never enough. The members of the legislative branch need to see the chief executive himself, to be invited to have lunch with him in private, and to see him come to visit them on their turf. Jimmy Carter never did those things.

Jimmy always had trouble dealing with the Georgia legislature. Nothing came easy to him, and having Lester Maddox, a cantankerous segregationist and former governor, as his lieutenant governor didn't help, because of the lieutenant governor's constitutional role as presiding officer of the state senate. Maddox and Carter went back and forth at each other all the time.

Finally it became too much for one of Carter's close friends in the senate, Ford Spinks, who became Jimmy's point man there. I used to have lunch with Carter in the governor's office often, and Ford wanted to join us and plead with Carter to extend the hand of cooperation to the senate to a greater degree than he had in the past.

Lunching in the governor's office was no great treat. When you find yourself at that level of state or national government, the human reaction is to think, Man, this is great! I'm going to have a private lunch with the governor! This is really the top!

Well, if that was the top, I'll take one of the lower floors. Lunch with Governor Carter used to consist of an old, dried-out sandwich that his secretary, Mary Beazley, would go out and get for us. She'd come into the governor's office while we were talking and say, "What would you-all like for lunch?"

I'd ask her to get me a ham and cheese and a Coke. If I happened to be feeling expansive that day, I'd ask her to add a bag of potato chips to my order.

Then a few minutes later, Mary would return with your old dried-out sandwich and hand it to you and say, "That will be two dollars and seventy-eight cents."

So much for the thrill of lunching in the governor's office.

I don't know whether Ford Spinks was aware of the ambiance in the governor's office when he asked me to make it a threesome, but he knew Jimmy listened to me. The legislative leaders often used to call on me for moral support. Their attitude was, "Look, you have this special relationship with Carter. We don't know what it is, but whatever it is, if you're there when we take this subject to him, you'll keep us out of the stew."

When Ford said, "I'm going to talk to him about this relationship business," I told him, "Ford, I'll come. But I'm going to tell you something—you're getting ready to get yourself chewed out."

Ford looked sort of puzzled and said, "What are you talking about?"

"I'm telling you that your friend the governor is not going to take kindly to your telling him how to deal with the legislature."

But Ford insisted and said, "Well, I'm going to tell him."

I said, "Okay—but that's not the better part of wisdom."

So we had our lunch—another old dried-out sandwich—and finally Carter says, "What do you want, Ford?"

Senator Spinks says, "Governor, I've been in the senate a long time. And you served in the senate yourself. I've been observing you lately in the way you've been dealing with the senators and the members of the house. Governor, you aren't paying enough attention to them. You aren't stroking them enough. You aren't inviting them down to your office to chat and pass the time of day. Governor, you've got to love those folks more."

I was slinking down lower and lower in my chair as Ford went on.

I was watching Carter's forehead. He has a vein that throbs when he's getting mad, and that thing was going, *Pow! Pow!*

Then Carter says, "Ford, I want to tell you that as long as I'm governor of this state, don't you *ever* tell me again what I ought to do and what I ought not to do with the legislature."

So I said, "Enjoyed lunch, Governor—c'mon Ford, let's get outta here."

2

A New Georgia

My CLOSE ASSOCIATION with Jimmy began as soon as we met in 1966. I was happy and proud to help him when I could in his campaign for governor and to raise funds for him when I could spare the time from my job as president of the First National Bank of Calhoun. He kept crisscrossing the state, meeting people one-on-one, shaking hands, smiling that toothy smile of his and telling people that the state government was no longer responding to them and he was going to correct that. He said it needed to be modernized, that there were too many boards, commissions, and agencies, that it should be reorganized.

Carter didn't make history in that first campaign, but he did make progress. Like the rest of the United States, Georgia was caught up in the explosive civil rights controversy of the mid-1960s, and it showed its effects at the polls. Lester Maddox, an avowed segregationist who refused to serve blacks in his restaurant, was elected governor, but not by the citizens of Georgia themselves. The race was so close it was thrown into the Democratically controlled legislature, where Maddox won election. Next door in Alabama, the governor was another segregationist, George Wallace. The attitude of the times prevailed.

Jimmy didn't let the victory by Maddox in '66 stop him. He simply kept right on running for governor, every day for the next four years. He gave more than a thousand speeches and shook 600,000 hands. By 1970, Carter was where he wanted to be—leading the race for governor.

Even the most committed of us have our human side, and Jimmy did, too. Shortly after his strong fight for the governorship the first time around, he and Rosalynn were blessed with the birth of their daughter, Amy. I sent him a note telling him that the press was saying he looked like one of the Kennedys—and now he appeared to be acting like them.

Jimmy was a formidable campaigner. In addition to his skill at projecting himself in personal meetings, he was taking all the right stances on the issues. He was a moderate to the moderates, a conservative to the conservatives, and a liberal to the liberals. He was all things to all voters, a great trait to be able to project—and it got him elected.

Carter had to do some healing as a candidate. The business community supported his leading opponent, Carl Sanders. Carl had served as governor from 1962 to 1966, and he was a good one. I liked and respected him, and so did a lot of other people. Georgia was a progressive state under him.

Jimmy faced the question of relations with the business leaders of the state head-on, meeting with them individually and in small groups, again projecting himself in a way that either won them over or at least neutralized them so that they would not go out and fight against him.

The business community did not oppose Jimmy's candidacy. The people, on the other hand, supported him enthusiastically. He was elected governor as a popular, he's-one-of-us personality.

To MY SURPRISE and puzzlement, the governor-elect asked me to become the state highway director. I didn't know a thing about that department of state government, but that didn't stop Jimmy. It turned out to be another of the many parallels between his governorship and his presidency—when he named me his director of management and budget in Washington, I didn't know anything about that job, either.

Jimmy viewed the state highway department as the very essence of what was wrong with the state government. It was too fat, too political, too arrogant, and too everything else. He wanted to make it better so it—and he—would become the shining example of the high quality of government that he had committed himself to bringing to the people of Georgia.

It was one of the first examples of just how seriously Jimmy takes his campaign promises. He showed the same faithfulness in Washington, even when keeping such promises worked to his political detriment. In this first case, it almost did the same thing in Atlanta.

Jimmy campaigned long and hard on his pledge to clean up the state highway department, and he said he would start by firing the highway director, Jim Gillis, who also happened to be the most powerful political leader in the state of Georgia. Gillis had been director of the department for twenty-three years, and his situation was like that of J. Edgar Hoover as director of the FBI. Presidents would come and go and try to get rid of Hoover, but none of them ever succeeded. It was the same with Jim Gillis. A couple of governors even got to the point of firing him, but then they'd reappoint him because they found they needed his political clout with the state legislature.

After Jimmy defeated the Republican nominee, Hal Suit, he asked me to take the highway job. I told him, "If you're foolish enough to ask me, I'm foolish enough to take it." That was November 23, and complications developed immediately.

Jimmy knew full well what he was getting into where Jim Gillis was concerned. He had this promise to keep, but first he met with the members of the state highway board, who run the department outside the control of the governor. There he ran into a major lobbying effort on the part of Gillis supporters.

They told Jimmy he needed Gillis because of the help he would bring in dealing with the legislature, especially during Carter's first legislative session. They also pointed out that another of Jimmy's main campaign promises—to reorganize the state government—would be a whole lot more possible with Jim Gillis running interference for him in the legislature.

Jimmy began to think maybe they had a point. But then some of the members on the highway board who opposed Gillis spoke in blunt terms about Carter's promise to the voters. They told him his governorship would be destroyed at the outset if the citizens felt he was waffling on his promise or breaking it altogether. They said people would accuse him of vacillating or worse, and they would lose all confidence in him and anything he would say in the future.

That was all Jimmy needed to hear. He stood firm, even in the face of renewed pressure from the Gillis side, and used all of his own clout as a new governor to get Gillis out of office.

My appointment was subject to confirmation by the state highway board, and at least one of the members seemed to share my evaluation of myself as one who didn't know anything about the department. At my hearing, he asked me what I knew about roads.

I told him, "The only things I know about are people and money, and that's all there is anywhere."

When he pressed me for specifics, I said, "I have a very simple philosophy. Roads should be built on the basis of needs, not on the basis of politics." I was confirmed shortly afterward.

IN HIS FIRST HOUR as governor, Jimmy Carter made one of the most profound commitments of his career, placing himself on the path to the White House, at the confidential request of a man unknown to the public.

This irony contains several others.

In the 1966 gubernatorial campaign in Georgia, Jimmy was one of the three Democratic candidates in the primary, running against Ellis Arnall, a respected former governor, and Lester Maddox. On the Republican side, Bo Calloway was the only real contender. It was a close race on the Democratic side, and Jimmy did better than most people expected. I worked my hardest for him, and I was terribly disappointed when he didn't make the runoff. He didn't miss by much, but Maddox and Calloway became the nominees.

There were a lot of disaffected Democrats who couldn't bring themselves to vote for Maddox, and many Republicans joined them in writing Arnall in on their ballot. The Republicans' thinking was that they could take votes away from Maddox. There was a well-organized write-in campaign in Arnall's behalf. That made it a three-way vote and complicated the election, with the result that the vote in November was so close there was no clear majority. Under the state's constitution, the election was thrown into the Georgia House of Representatives.

The legislature was controlled by the Democrats, so Maddox, despite strong disapproval by so many voters, was elected governor. Jimmy immediately began working to get himself elected governor four years later.

It was what I call "cockroach politics"—it's not what they eat that's the problem, it's what they mess up. In states like Georgia, where you don't have party registration and where the controlling party is the Democrats, Republicans engage in cockroach politics from time to time to mess things up. That's what they did in Georgia in 1966.

During the Democratic primary that year, a student activist named Terry Adamson became heavily involved in the Ellis Arnall campaign. While I was involved in a gubernatorial campaign for the first time, working in Jimmy's behalf, Terry was also involved in his first, working for Ellis. Student activism was getting up a full head of steam on America's college campuses in 1966, and Terry was just the student to help that movement. He was an energetic and creative young man who opposed the war in Vietnam and got himself involved in other causes.

Ironically, Terry had been my second-baseman when I coached Little League baseball for my sons. I say ironically because we certainly didn't end up working on the same team. As a Justice Department official in 1977 Terry read the announcement of my indictment to the news media in Washington. In 1988, his wife, Edie Holliday, was the attorney for the George Bush campaign, and she was the first woman counsel for the Treasury Department. She is now an assistant to President Bush in the White House.

In 1966, Terry was so anxious to help Arnall get elected governor that he flew around the state making speeches for him—with his own pilot. The pilot, a native of Savannah named David Rabhan, was a retired Air Force colonel who owned a nursing home.

Four years later, Terry introduced Rabhan to Jimmy Carter, and Rabhan became the pilot for the Carter gubernatorial campaign. I saw him frequently during the campaign, and so did others like Jody Powell and Hamilton Jordan, who joined Jimmy's drive to the governorship that year. All of us still remember that Rabhan never changed in appearance. Every time any of us saw him he was dressed the same way: a blue jumpsuit, cowboy boots, and a clean, shiny head. Today he might be mistaken for an aging "skinhead."

He baffled me. I saw Rabhan at different political functions with Carter and never could figure out the relationship between the two. He never said anything. He was a stoic personality who never did anything but donate his own private airplane and his services as a staff pilot to Jimmy for his campaign. I never understood the attraction between the two. I still don't.

One day late in the campaign, as they were flying back to Plains after still another appearance, Carter asked Rabhan if he could do anything for him as governor. Rabhan said, "Yes. In your inaugural speech, you can say that the time to end segregation is now."

Carter wrote it down on a flight map in the plane.

TIME PASSED, and when Jimmy won the Democratic nomination it was clear he was going to be the next governor of Georgia. The folks in Georgia just weren't about to elect a Republican as governor at that point in the state's history.

Jimmy agreed with Rabhan's concern about ending segregation. Asking him to make a statement in his inaugural address was only asking him to say what he had felt all his life anyhow.

So he did—and he instantly became a national political figure, not just an unknown new governor in the South. In his inaugural address, he told his audience:

> I say to you quite frankly that the time for racial discrimina-
> tion is over. Our people have already made this major and difficult
> decision. No poor, rural, weak or black person should ever have to
> bear the additional burden of being deprived of the opportunity of
> an education, a job or simple justice.

That kind of statement came easily to Jimmy Carter. He wasn't engaging in any political posturing when he made it. In fact, it took a certain amount of guts to make a statement like that in Georgia twenty years ago, but he did, even though he knew he would immediately lose every vote from the Maddox supporters and from other groups, too.

Jimmy had a portrait of Martin Luther King, Jr., hung in the state capitol. He named black people to the state board of regents, and one of the four security men who traveled with him was a black patrolman. In all of these statements and actions, Jimmy was merely speaking and behaving as he always had done on the subject of racial justice. No one should have been surprised at that statement in his inaugural address or at his actions or appointments.

After all, this was the same man who flat-out refused to join the White Citizens Council back home in Plains, the only businessman to take that stand—and in his own hometown, where he and his parents had spent their lives. If that's not courage, then somebody has to define it for me. And this was the same man who once drove all night, interrupting his gubernatorial campaign, so he could be at his church to vote in favor of integrating the congregation.

The week after Jimmy delivered his inaugural address, *Time* magazine ran his picture on its cover, heralding a new day in southern politics. Joe Kane, who has headed *Time*'s Atlanta bureau for most of the years since, wrote the article that propelled Carter into nationwide political prominence overnight.

There is an irony there, too. Joe went on a sabbatical from *Time* in 1989, in accordance with the magazine's policy of encouraging its writers and executives to do something else from time to time to continue their professional development. Where did he work during his sabbatical? On the campaign staff of Andrew Young, who was running for governor of Georgia. The same white man who wrote the article about Carter's commitment to a fully integrated South went to work nearly twenty years later to get a black man elected governor of the same state.

To BORROW THE TITLE from Jimmy's book, *Keeping the Faith*, we kept faith with the people of Georgia. We reorganized the state highway department into the Georgia Department of Transportation, because our concern went far beyond just building highways. We reduced the department's payroll from 9,500 employees to 6,500, without any bloody mass firings. We did it through attrition: when somebody resigned or retired, we tried to get along without filling that position, and in most cases we were able to manage without a replacement.

We implemented zero-based budgeting, requiring every agency to justify its entire budget every year, to defend current programs, expenditures, and staffing, not just those new ones being proposed. We surrendered control over hundreds of millions of dollars previously controlled by the commissioner of highways and put it into the state's general treasury so it could earn interest instead of being kept in political bank accounts.

We discovered that the highway department had $100 million in cash that Gillis had been able to scatter around to the various banks throughout the state, which gave him enormous political influence all over Georgia. We stopped that practice immediately and instead instituted a central cash management system which earned $14 million in interest for the state in our first year.

And while we were doing all these things, we were improving our service to the people and making the department responsive to them. We increased the amount of road-building contracts from $95 million to $400 million.

Our efforts were not without some surprising challenges. Lester Maddox, who didn't do anything about the conditions in the state government in his four years as governor before Jimmy, kept barking at everything Jimmy did, making as much noise as a junkyard dog. He reached some kind of a high or low point when, obviously having run out of things to complain about, he called a press conference to charge me with the high crime of sending a highway department airplane to Sea Island to pick up my golf clubs. It's hard to imagine a more laughable reason for a press conference, but that's what old Lester did, and sure enough, the press showed up.

The truth of the matter, of course, is that I never did any such thing, but that wasn't Maddox's real concern. He wanted to keep embarrassing Carter and hassling him at every turn with whatever trumped-up wild charge he could dream up—and then run against him in 1974. Jimmy knew what Maddox was up to. I knew it. The whole state of Georgia knew it.

But the folks in the media, who presumably knew it, too, obviously thought they were on to a major political scandal in the Carter administration, just as their counterparts in Washington tried to prove later and failed. They brought their notepads, microphones, and TV cameras and asked me about this allegation of such a grave nature made against me by the former governor.

I stood on the front steps of the highway department and told them in solemn tones, "Governor Maddox can do what he wants to, but you go back and tell him that I have a long-standing practice of never flying on the same airplane with my golf clubs."

Then I turned and went back inside. End of scandal.

There are some things in this life worth worrying about and others that aren't. That one wasn't. In politics, if you allow yourself to get drawn into a silly nonissue like that, you'll spend most of your time putting out brushfires of things that never were, instead of doing the productive things you were elected or appointed to do.

AT THE TIME Jimmy took office in Georgia, the state government had ballooned to three hundred agencies, hog-tied by duplication, archaic activities, bureaucratic procedures that took too long and cost too much, and arrogant attitudes. The reorganization plan enabled Jimmy—and future governors—to make any changes they wanted, subject only to veto by the state legislature or constitutionally elected officers.

For those nonbelievers who scoff at the thought that one vote can make a difference, consider this: The opportunity to do something about these failures in serving the public was made possible because our reorganization bill was approved by one vote, on a roll call.

In four years, Governor Carter knocked down those three hundred agencies to twenty-two.

Jimmy was a creative executive. One the best examples of the vision and leadership he brought to the governorship was his program called "Goals for Georgia." He brought together the senior business executives from the business community to examine the state government thoroughly and to advise us on how we could make it better. The way he went about it was impressive and effective.

He recruited these executives from their corporations on a loan basis. Each department head had several corporate executives assigned to his department, one directly to him. These were folks from Georgia Power and Coca-Cola and other major corporations and utilities. They served without compensation from the state. The program was a huge success because the loan executives did an outstanding job for the people of the state in advising us how best to reorganize each department and agency.

In my case, my loan executive objected to the constitutional mandate that gave the department full control over the money from the tax on motor fuel. He thought that was a bad deal for the department, even though it assured us of a permanent source of revenue and made us an independent agency of government. He pointed out that the department's share of taxes wouldn't keep up with the growth of the state budget and its revenues.

It was a lost cause, because that arrangement is a sacred cow in Georgia and remains in effect today. He was right in his thinking, though. As the state's revenue increased, the income from the fuel taxes didn't keep pace. The department received a greater amount of revenue, but its share of the overall state budget dropped. Even though his recommendation would never fly, it was the kind of insight and experienced, objective analysis that Carter liked as governor and later as President.

JIMMY AND I had fun while we made progress, and that was another promise he kept. We flew around the state together frequently. On one of our first flights, we took a helicopter to the opening of a shopping center on Atlanta's Perimeter, the highway that goes around the city, what other cities would call a beltway or a circumferential.

As we were flying back to the office, we looked down at the spectacular sight of the prosperous Atlanta skyline. It was a magnificent January day in 1971, and Jimmy said to me, "Sometimes when we're flying like this, I look down at Atlanta and see what's happening there, and I feel the strong desire coming to seize the opportunities and challenges of being governor and put my imprint on the future of Georgia. You and I are going to have a lot of fun doing those things."

He made frequent references after that to the fun of what we were doing. But when we found ourselves in a crisis, as we did from time to time, I couldn't resist needling him and saying, "You're going to have to define what 'fun' is because I don't believe we share the same definition."

Jimmy was right about that, too. It was fun, and from the fun of the work and the pleasure of working together, the bond between us grew even stronger. Folks around Atlanta and the rest of the state began saying that Carter and I had a peer relationship. They weren't really sure what or why it was, but word had it that I was the one person who could speak candidly to the governor and still keep his respect and support, and vice versa. My respect for Jimmy continued to grow, but I never stopped being completely honest with him on any subject where I thought he needed to hear the truth from somebody who had nothing in mind except the best interests of the people and of Jimmy himself.

As soon as Carter took office as governor, we began meeting nearly every morning in his office to review the news of the day, not only the items I had to report to him from the Department of Transportation but anything else that I thought he ought to know about—dealings with the legislature, stories in the news media, and any other developments. I was happy to perform this extra role for my friends, even though it meant I had to leave my home in Calhoun at 4:20 every morning and drive seventy-six miles to Atlanta.

I remember one morning in particular. It began the usual way. I knocked on the door of the governor's office and Jimmy called out to me to come on in. He was reading the paper when I entered the room, and he kept right on reading it.

I waited, and then I waited some more. He never did look up from that newspaper. I shuffled my feet. I coughed. Nothing got his nose out of the paper. After five minutes of that nonsense, I steamed out of my boss's office and stormed across the street to my own office. Later in the morning I sent a note by messenger back across the street to the chief executive:

> Governor, I came in this morning because I thought there was something important about the department that you should know about. I stood in front of your desk for five minutes or so, and now I have a basic question I need answered if I'm going to continue as director here.
>
> I'm about ready to quit and go back to Calhoun, but if I stay, you're going to have to advise me as to how you want me to communicate with you. Do you want me to use personal visits, the telephone, or smoke signals? Whatever avenue you want me to take, please let me know and I won't waste your time and mine standing in front of your desk.

A few minutes later, Jimmy called me on the phone and apologized sincerely. We never had any questions about communicating after that. As a result of that incident, he understood that when I wanted to talk to him, there was a time element involved, that I was ready and able to report to him on something that had just happened or I had just learned about. That exchange on the day he kept reading the newspaper was another great stride in our no-holds-barred relationship in which both of us always spoke with complete candor about what was on our minds.

WHEN THE FIRST Arab oil embargo was imposed, Richard Nixon was President and Jimmy was governor of Georgia. Carter was convinced immediately of the severity of the situation, and he wasn't going to stand by idly and watch state officials and citizens waste energy.

One of the first things he did was to replace the larger state cars with Chevrolet Novas. I thought it might be a slight case of overkill, but that was Jimmy. He is so conscientious that he wants to feel he's doing everything possible about a problem, and in this case using smaller cars was simply something that he thought the state government should do.

You don't look much like a governor when you drive up in a Nova, but that didn't bother Jimmy. It didn't really bother me, either, but something else did, and I told him about it. It had to do with my six feet, five inches and 245 pounds.

I said, "You just did that so I can't go with you anywhere, because I can't fit into one of those things. There ain't room in there for you and me both."

He denied the charge.

While Jimmy was setting the example by reducing energy in every way he could think of, he became a one-man vigilante squad. He'd be riding down the road on the way to a meeting or to give a speech, and if he and his driver spotted somebody violating the new fifty-five-mile-an-hour speed limit, he'd have his driver pull them over. Then he'd get out and give them a stern lecture.

One night while he was driving back to the governor's mansion he passed the Trust Company of Georgia, a venerable institution that had just built a fine new office building in Central City Park in downtown Atlanta. The building was ablaze with lights.

The next morning he scribbled a note to his friend Billy Sterne, the chairman of the board of the Trust Company, and told Billy he wasn't doing his part. He told him flat-out to turn out those lights.

Well, in his zeal, Jimmy doesn't always allow for how other folks might feel, especially if they don't believe they have to snap their heels and obey his every wish. Billy Sterne was one of those folks. He wrote a quick response to the governor explaining that the lighting system in his new building was computerized and the company would use more energy in turning the lights off at night and back on the next day than it would by just leaving them on. Then he told Carter bluntly that this was the company's basic decision and that's how it was going to be, notwithstanding any smart, know-it-all letters from the governor.

There were other ways in which I thought Jimmy overdid it at times in his conscientious attempts to be alert to the public's every concern. For example, while Jimmy was governor, a road near Billy's house in Plains was just about the only one in town that wasn't paved. That just didn't make any sense at all to me. We were paving the roads in every town. The one near Billy's house should have been paved, just like all the others. Why have one unpaved road in one town?

Jimmy was determined to avoid any hint of favoritism toward his hometown or his brother. So, out of fear that he might be accused of granting favored treatment to his town or his brother, he granted Billy a penalty instead. What he seemed to be saying was, "Paved roads all around, except for my town or my brother."

If I had been governor, I would have gone right ahead and paved that road, and if folks in the media or in the opposition party said anything, my answer would have been simply that everybody else was getting paved roads, and I wasn't going to make any one person a second-class citizen because he lived in my town or happened to be my brother.

THE CIVIL RIGHTS battle was in full force when Jimmy Carter became governor, and he supported it vigorously and consistently, even with George Wallace serving as governor right next door in Alabama. On the evening news Americans saw the cops turning police dogs and fire hoses on blacks, but Carter was able to keep the lid on things better in Georgia because he provided the kind of political and moral leadership so necessary throughout the nation during those divisive times.

The issue was brought to his desk in ways you wouldn't expect, such as the complaint by black members of the Georgia legislature that we didn't have enough black engineers in my department. There was an obvious answer: There weren't any black engineers available.

The few blacks who were engineers were working for IBM, AT&T, and Xerox. We even had trouble attracting white engineers when we had to compete against the salaries and fringe benefits of Fortune 500 corporations. The scarcity of blacks in the engineering field in general made it all the more unlikely that a black person would call us up looking for a job or respond to our recruiting program.

Carter and I met more than once with the leading black legislators, including Julian Bond and Richard Dent. We discussed the problem and our eagerness to attract black engineers to my department and black professionals to every department of Carter's state administration. The legislators understood the contributing factors and appreciated the honest efforts we were making. Eventually, we began to turn things around. But that was an example of enlightened political leadership by Carter. He didn't stonewall those folks in their concerns about the lack of black engineers. He told them he agreed with them and was trying to do something about it and asked for their understanding and support in his efforts.

That's the kind of intelligent, systematic performance Carter provided as governor and President. Jimmy understood better than almost any other key figure in those years that the South was maturing through the civil rights struggle. He knew that the economic change under way through such forces as the development of the carpet industry in my own part of Georgia was in turn producing the political change represented by the civil rights movement.

Despite the mistaken impression that some might have, the fact is that economic change produces political change, not the other way around. As the South moved away from its dependence on cotton and developed a diversified economy, things got better for everybody. When more jobs were created, black people began demanding an equal opportunity to be hired for them. The civil rights fight was for more than just the right to sit in the front of the bus.

Economic change was the original impetus in that movement, and the political forces followed. The shift in southern society from segregation to integration, from separate-but-equal to a truly equal status for all people, and from whites' complete indifference to the black population as a market to their recognition of blacks as a market important to business all came about as a result of the increasing diversity and expansion in the southern economy.

When that economy grew in strength through its diversity, the political factors came into play. Political leaders then had to respond to the political concerns in the same way that the business leaders had responded to the business concerns. Once again, as always, economic forces were the forerunner of political change.

Carter understood all of this. He knew that if the South had remained almost solely an agricultural economy based so heavily on cotton, the civil rights movement never would have succeeded because there would not have been enough pressure for it. And he knew that because the shift away from a strictly agricultural economy was occurring across the South, the political and moral issues of the civil rights movement would have to be supported and advanced. To Carter, and to me too, the reasons for supporting civil rights came down to two:

1. It was right.
2. It was good business.

ABOUT THE CRAZIEST experience I ever had with Jimmy in either Atlanta or Washington—and that's covering a lot of ground—was the day when we awarded the biggest construction bid in the history of the state of Georgia.

All of us in the Georgia Department of Transportation were working hard to show our new responsiveness, professionalism, and integrity. We showed this in different ways. The best example was in our resurfacing program.

We began to conduct our resurfacing projects at night in populated areas so as not to disrupt the flow of daytime traffic. It cost more money to do it that way, but I was convinced that the cost was justified, not only in sparing the people such inconvenience but also in showing them that the state government really wanted to do a better job for them.

With this buildup of good will, we then took on our biggest project ever, the widening of I-85 starting just outside downtown Atlanta and moving out to the Perimeter. We went out of our way to let the good citizens of Atlanta know that we were about to provide them with a great improvement in their daily lives.

On the day the bids from the highway contractors were to be opened, there were a lot of folks in our building. The bid was to be awarded that Monday in the auditorium on the fourth floor. We had increased the department's ability to solicit and award bids, with the result that we were dealing with many more contractors. That, plus the lucrative cost of this project, brought a larger crowd than usual to the building that Friday.

I was across the street meeting with the governor and his political adviser, Charlie Kirbo, when I glanced at my watch and saw that it was almost time to award this bid. I also remembered being told that morning by Morene Whitworth, my secretary, that one of the highway contractors from Rome, Al Ledbetter, wanted to see me.

I called Morene from Jimmy's office and told her I was going directly to the auditorium for the letting of the bid. Then I excused myself from Carter and Kirbo and dashed back across the street into the Georgia DOT building, passed my office on the right, and turned to the left toward the elevators next to the front door.

When the elevator arrived and the door opened, out raced Al Ledbetter, heading toward the back door of the building. I barely had time to call to him by name. "Al!"

He stopped abruptly, and I said, "I thought you wanted to see me today."

He said, "I'll see you later." Then he continued to hurry toward the door and out the building.

Just at that moment, another elevator arrived. The door opened, and there stood two of my employees and Clyde Shepard of Shepard Brothers, a major highway contracting firm in the Atlanta area and the biggest contractor doing business with our department. It was one of those eerie meetings where you have the nagging feeling that one of you is in the wrong place at the wrong time.

I stepped in, and the atmosphere in the elevator was the strangest I've ever sensed. Clyde Shepard was almost out the back wall of the elevator, he was trying so hard to avoid me. He was hunkered down apparently trying to look invisible. He seemed to think that if he got his back flat enough against that wall he would disappear altogether.

I said hello to my two employees, and I knew immediately that something was wrong. They became discombobulated. They pushed Down instead of Up to go up to the auditorium. As we went down to the basement, Clyde turned white as a sheet.

I turned to one of my employees, Ken Maxwell, and asked, "Ken, what's going on?" Whereupon the strangest conversation of my life followed.

"Mr. Lance, you're not going to believe this—but I've been hijacked."

"You've been *what*?"

"I've been hijacked."

"Well, I've heard of airplanes being hijacked and ships and cars, but I never did hear of an employee being hijacked. Let's get upstairs and find out what you're trying to tell me."

After we reached the fourth floor, I asked Maxwell to repeat what he had said.

He explained, "Well, Mr. Lance, I was walking down the hall with the bids in my hand getting ready to get on the elevator, and Al

Ledbetter came down the hall and jerked his bid out of my hands and ran."

Instead of going into the auditorium, I put Ken and Clyde Shepard back on that elevator and took them back down to the first floor and right into my office.

I turned to Shepard and said, "Now, Clyde, I want to know exactly what happened."

He was just as nervous as Ken. He said, "I ain't involved, Commissioner. I didn't have anything to do with this, Commissioner. I was just an innocent bystander, Commissioner." He was sirring me up on one side and down the other. I thought he was going to have a heart attack.

Then the story began to unfold as Clyde told what happened. It involved not only Clyde but his brother, Harold, who was a partner in the company.

Clyde always stood in the same spot in the letting room, next to a post in the back. His story began at that spot. "I was standing back there by the door, where I always stand. You know where that is, Commissioner."

"Yes, Clyde. I know."

"To tell you the truth, Harold was sitting there in the letting room next to Bob and Al Ledbetter. Now you know, Commissioner, that we're bidding on that project. And the Ledbetters are bidding on it. Well, they started talking about the bids and Bob and Al said to Harold, 'What was your bid?'

"And Harold told them what we were bidding—$18,700,000. Well, Commissioner, Bob and Al nearly died."

It turned out that the Ledbetters had posted a performance bond like all the others, and they realized suddenly that they had committed a major oversight, one that might bankrupt them. They forgot to include what are called "clearing and grubbing costs," the expense of cleaning up the right-of-way along the highway, removing trees and shrubs and other items before the construction can begin. They knew that once the bids were opened, they would win the job because their price would be so much lower without those costs included.

However, they also knew there was no way on earth that they could do the job for what they were bidding, something like $3 million below the others, so they were in the Catch-22 position of bidding for the job and no longer wanting it. They knew that once their bid was read and they got the job, we would hold them to their price—and they'd lose their shirts.

They knew that the best way to prevent that from happening was simply for them to retrieve their bid.

Al ran out of the letting room, and Clyde stopped him coming by the post where he was standing and asked, "What's the trouble, Al?"

Al said as he dashed by, "I've got to get my bid back."

Then Clyde followed Al running down the hall. They met Ken Maxwell at the elevator with the bids in his hand. Al jerked the bid right out of Ken's hand, punched the elevator, and was running out of the building, bid in hand, when I came onto the scene.

After hearing the play-by-play account from Clyde, I told him, "This is serious business. I don't know what all it involves, but I've got to talk to the governor and the attorney general. This is a close legal point as to when a bid becomes the property of the state."

So I went back across the street to the governor's office and said to Jimmy, "You told me when we came down here that things were going to be strange, but I've got to tell you that the strangest thing you can ever imagine just happened. We've just had a bid hijacked."

Carter exploded with "What!"

I told him the story and he exploded again. He said, "I'm going to blast the highway contractors."

I said, "For goodness' sake, don't do that. I've got enough problems already just dealing with the situation as it is."

I called to Arthur Bolton, the attorney general, who ruled that a bid becomes the property of the state when it is opened. His ruling saved the Ledbetters. We wrote new specifications for the project because the Shepard bid had been exposed, rebid the job, and eventually Clyde Shepard and his brothers, Dan and Harold, were awarded the contract.

There was no publicity about the incident because we moved so swiftly. To this day the story is largely unknown in Georgia. The highway was improved, and all lived happily ever after.

But there's a P.S. to the story, which once again shows Jimmy Carter's intelligence and ability to think quickly. Many months later, Jimmy phoned me from the governor's office to say, "For the first time since you've been commissioner of DOT, I've had some criticism of you."

I replied, "And I'm sure you can't wait to tell me about it. It's what you've been waiting for since you put me in this job. Who's it from?"

"Bob Ledbetter. Come on over and let me tell you about it." I figured Jimmy was about to hang me high.

He told me that Ledbetter had called him with a complaint and then had come down to see him at Carter's invitation. Bob had immediately taken off on me and my performance, saying I wasn't treating contractors right.

Jimmy went on. "I listened to all the things he said and told him I was there to hear him out." It was clear to me that Jimmy had enjoyed his own performance with Ledbetter, and now he was enjoying telling me all about it while I suffered in the chair across from him.

After Ledbetter had finished with his bill of particulars against me, Jimmy had told him, "Bob, I appreciate your coming to see me, making the effort to come out here to the mansion. I find it very interesting that you would come and make these criticisms known to me.

"I have to tell you this is the first criticism I've had of Lance since he's been over there in the department. And to tell you the truth, there hasn't been any criticism of the department either, except that I do recall at some point not too long ago some damn fool hijacked a bid."

Jimmy said Ledbetter's only comment was, "Thank you, Governor. I'll see you later."

WE BOTH enjoyed a good belly laugh over that postscript to the hijacking story. To the best of my knowledge the subject has never come up again between Jimmy and Bob, who by now have known each other more than twenty years.

As we were sitting in his office that afternoon and my friend the governor was telling this story with such delight, I could see he was proud of what he considered the perfect squelch—and it was. But to me his put-down had a certain significance, too. It showed Carter's great ability to remember things, file them away in his computerlike mind, and recall them in a split-second to use with devastating effectiveness at the most opportune moment.

The next week after that crazy episode, I called Ken Maxwell into my office and told him with a straight face, "Ken, I've just decided on new procedures for handling our bids so we don't get a repeat performance of what happened here Friday. We're going to requisition you a .45 pistol to carry down the hall with you, and we're going to handcuff the bids to you. The next time some crazy fool tries to hijack a bid, he's going to have to take you with him."

Maxwell looked at me sideways, still suffering from Friday's effects, and asked meekly, "Commissioner, you don't mean that, do you?"

Those folks in that department never quite knew how to take me anyway. They were the best, hardest-working, most loyal workers you could ask for, and the folks who worked for me at the Office of Management and Budget in Washington were, too. I don't care how much bashing Reagan did of federal employees in his eight years as President—and he did as much as he possibly could—the government workers I met and worked with in Atlanta and Washington were public servants in the highest sense of the term, working hard, taking abuse from folks like Reagan, and making a whole lot less money than they would have by doing the same work in private business.

But those engineers in Atlanta, as great as they were, never could understand this big ol' boy from north Georgia who was now their boss. I'd ask the right question but for the wrong reason, so they thought I knew more than I really did. And while they were throwing around all those terms that engineers like to use, they were way over my head, but they didn't know it.

They were so serious in their work at times it blunted their sense of humor, so they didn't know when I was kidding. We had a staff meeting every Monday morning, and I told them once, "I always wondered before I got down here why you engineers smoke a pipe. I've found out since I've been here that there are two reasons. One, it gives you time to think when somebody asks you a hard question. You tamp on that pipe and puff around on it while you're trying to think of an answer. The second and more important reason is that you are all so damn afraid you might smile one morning that you keep that pipe in your mouth so you won't ever have to worry about smiling."

ANOTHER HIGHWAY episode wasn't funny. On the contrary, it may have been the single incident that prompted Jimmy Carter to run for President.

One of our most important highway projects turned out to be the decisive experience that convinced Carter of the need to bring the federal government back under control. Ronald Reagan got much publicity in 1980 when he promised to "get the government off the backs of the people," but the truth of the matter is that Jimmy Carter tried it first.

The issue was Interstate Route I-75, the road that stretches across Lake Allatoona forty-five miles north of Atlanta. The lake is an impoundment of the U.S. Army Corps of Engineers. Five years before Carter became governor, the U.S. Department of Transportation approved an application from the state government to build a network of three bridges taking I-75 on a path twenty-seven miles long across Lake

Allatoona. That would make it possible to complete the interstate north of Chattanooga.

When Carter and I took office, that stretch still existed only in blueprints. One month into my job I learned that the route which had been approved five years before had to be reevaluated by the Nixon administration and the secretary of transportation, John Volpe. New federal environmental protection laws prohibited the use of federal funds for building interstates that crossed recreation lands, which I-75 would do in running across the lake.

Volpe, a former governor himself in Massachusetts, promised us he would make a decision within two weeks. More than two months later, we still hadn't heard from him, so the highway board fired off an angry telegram demanding that Volpe explain the delay. The board also directed me to contact Attorney General Bolton about suing the federal government.

In the midst of this, I flew to Washington for a face-to-face meeting with Volpe, and what I learned there had a profound effect on both Carter and me. Here was this cabinet member, presumably empowered with some authority, banging his fist on his desk in frustration and assuring me he was doing everything humanly possible to get the information he needed before he could make his decision. It was clear that his hands were tied by the bureaucracy he depended on for his information, and maybe by political considerations as well.

Publicly, Carter was blaming "blind bureaucratic stubbornness" and "a narrow, restrictive view of approval" for Volpe's delay. But Jimmy wasn't voicing his complaints without a certain amount of pleasure. He had always been anti-Nixon, and criticizing Nixon in public was an opportunity that he wasn't going to pass up.

Their relations, even then, could well have been a factor in the delay being caused by the federal government. The bad vibrations between Nixon and Carter most assuredly came to bear on a later incident, when the feds singled out Georgia and two other states for sanctions because our billboards supposedly were too close to our highways. As a result of that cheap-shot one-upmanship by Nixon and his people, $8 million in federal highway funds for Georgia were delayed.

When Volpe finally made his decision on I-75, he ruled against us. He cited environmental factors, which were receiving far greater emphasis then than five years earlier at the time of the original federal approval. The ecology movement had come of age. Carter never had a problem with giving proper emphasis to environment considerations, and neither did I. But we did have a problem with the federal bureaucracy and its lack of responsiveness to the fifty states.

We revised the proposed route for I-75 and eventually won Volpe's approval—fifteen months, eight hundred accidents, and more than twenty deaths later.

Jimmy and I had identical reactions to that whole bitter experience: The federal government had to be brought under control. It had to be made more responsive to the American people. The man for that job was Jimmy Carter.

3

A New South

THE 1972 CAMPAIGN was a disaster for the Democratic party as far as the presidential election was concerned. George McGovern made a shambles out of the race by positioning himself too far to the left and managed to get himself soundly whipped by Richard Nixon. In the process, he also managed to get his party soundly embarrassed.

But for Jimmy Carter it wasn't a total loss. He received visitors all year long at the governor's mansion—candidates who were seeking the support of this bright new face on the national scene, this enlightened and progressive southern governor. McGovern came by, and so did Scoop Jackson, Ed Muskie, Hubert Humphrey, and the rest.

The candidates were looking out for themselves, but they weren't hurting Jimmy, either. Some Democrats were saying he would make a good running mate for the winning candidate, and we didn't discourage that talk. Our thinking was that any national exposure Jimmy got then would help him when he announced his candidacy for President, a decision he was well on the way to making by the time of the '72 campaign.

Then, on election night itself, a tragedy occurred in Georgia, and again Jimmy showed that he had what it takes to make a good President.

I was in Calhoun getting ready to watch the election returns on TV, knowing that the presidential news would be nothing but bad. It was around eight o'clock. I had decided to stay home because there was no reason to plan any gala election night parties if you were a Democrat that year, not with McGovern running.

It was an awful night, with heavy rains and high winds, the kind of night when tragedies seem to happen. Just as I was settling down, the phone rang. It was my office calling to tell me that a freighter had just crashed into the Sidney Lanier Bridge at Brunswick. The ship had ripped out 150 feet of the bridge and its pilings. Eleven people were dead, and nobody knew how many more were missing because it wasn't known how many were on the bridge when the barge crashed into it.

The Sidney Lanier Bridge is a huge structure—a drawbridge—and people were lined up on it waiting for the ship to pass through. Some were out of their cars and standing on the bridge as they watched the ship approach. It was a horrible thing. Some plunged right into the river moments after standing there. Others slid down the paved surface of the bridge straight into the water to their deaths.

Jimmy was at Sam Nunn's election headquarters in Atlanta watching the returns. It was the night of Sam's election to the Senate, where he has served the people of Georgia and the United States so well for eighteen years. His election that night was one of the few bright spots for us.

I called the state pilot and had him pick me up in Calhoun, and from there we flew to Atlanta and picked up Jimmy. We arrived in Brunswick shortly before midnight. They were still searching the river for bodies.

Jimmy's presence on the scene in only a few hours after the tragedy, on election night at that, sent a reassuring message to all Georgians that they had a governor who cared and who was capable of dealing effectively with a disaster.

He projected that same kind of reassurance at other times as governor and later as President. When a damaging tornado swept through Gordon County in my part of Georgia, Governor Jimmy Carter was there. When the nuclear reactor plant at Three Mile Island malfunctioned and caused an emergency, President Jimmy Carter was there. He has always been quick to grasp the seriousness of a situation, and quick to respond by showing his concern and taking charge of things. People could always count on his concern, his presence on the scene, and his ability to direct operations like the capable executive he was.

The emergency at the Brunswick bridge involved the same kind of questions prompted by the collapse of a highway bridge during the San Francisco earthquake in 1989. We needed to know how many people were on the bridge when the barge hit it, and we needed to find those who were still in the water, dead or alive.

Working with our management team, Jimmy and I made arrangements with the police and the Navy out of Charleston, South Carolina, to begin rescue operations. We talked to witnesses to determine how many other vehicles might have been on the bridge. For two days I rode a minesweeper as we combed the river.

Jimmy had to return to the governor's office the next morning, and I had to deliver a speech in Augusta, so we left early, but Jimmy wanted to be sure the operations in Brunswick continued properly. He told me to go back there and stay as long as there was any hope at all of saving lives, finding more bodies, or just showing the people that their state government cared. I spent three or four more days there.

The disaster was a tragedy for so many people, but there was a positive side to it for the state government. The job done by Jimmy and everyone under his supervision in coping with that crisis helped restore public confidence in the highway department. We had reorganized it and changed its name to Department of Transportation, but our handling of the disaster at Brunswick was proof that the department was no longer bureaucratic, arrogant, unresponsive, and highly politicized.

If you asked people in that part of Georgia today how we could have handled that situation better, I think they would tell you we did about as good a job as anyone could have. Our performance was a real milestone in proving that the changes we had made, which the people of the state had asked for in electing Jimmy, were real and were producing results right before their eyes.

JIMMY CARTER has always been capable of shocking me, and he dropped one of his biggest bombshells on me in the fall of 1972. We were touring the state in a series of prelegislative meetings when he sent one of his assistants, Stock Coleman, down to my hotel room one night with the simple message, "The governor wants to talk to you for a few minutes."

I went dutifully down to his room and saw him lying on the floor, which didn't surprise me. He likes to do that. It's a farming trait, and he's an old farm boy. When farmers need to rest in the field, the only way they can do it is by lying on the ground.

That's why it was never unusual to see Jimmy in that position—and it made no difference whether he was a private citizen, a state

governor, or President of the United States. When he felt like lying on
the floor, that's exactly what he did.

After I sat down, Jimmy said, "Let's talk about Georgia and its
future. I want you to think about running for governor."

My reaction was immediate. "Man, you're just as crazy as you
were when you asked me to come to the highway department. You
ain't got any sense at all."

The state law at that time prohibited a governor from succeeding
himself, and besides, Jimmy was already thinking about frying bigger
fish, so he wanted to be sure the person who succeeded him could be
trusted to carry on what he had begun. He was thinking that I would
continue those changes. But he was thinking something else, too: if I
could get elected governor, Lester Maddox wouldn't.

Jimmy simply never got along with Maddox. He considered him
an unreconstructed segregationist who preached hate, practiced it, and
used it for his own selfish political gain. He knew Maddox in a second
term would destroy every advance that Jimmy had accomplished for
the state. Carter had every reason to be proud of what he had achieved
for the people of Georgia in his four years as their chief executive—
streamlining the state government, purging the politics and the politicians from the highway department, stimulating Georgia's economy,
introducing zero-based budgeting, trying to cleanse the state of racism.
Jimmy didn't want this out-and-out demagogue to come back into the
governor's mansion and trash all of those improvements.

There was another element in Jimmy's logic. If Maddox had been
elected governor again, Jimmy would have felt considerable difficulty
in trying to run for President in 1976. Defeating Maddox in '74 was the
overriding concern in Carter's life as his governorship approached its
end.

Carter was also smart enough to know that if Maddox got himself
back into the governor's job, he would have the publicity forum that
every governor has. Given his ability to generate publicity even without a forum, Maddox could have been a humiliating thorn in Jimmy's
side if Jimmy was running for President while this redneck followed
him all over the country saying he had been a lousy governor and
would make a lousy President, too.

Lester Maddox was fully capable of that kind of behavior, and
Jimmy knew it. If Carter wanted to think seriously about running for
President, one of the first things he had to do was to see to it that
somebody defeated Lester Maddox—and shut him up.

So I campaigned for eighteen long, extremely hard months, and for nine of them I was unable to sleep in a bed at night because of a ruptured disk in my back. The only sleep I got was in a lounge chair, because I couldn't lie down.

That campaign had its moments, with shocks and laughs that still stand out in my memory, even with an aching back. There were fifteen candidates, a ridiculously high number. Six or seven of us were bona fide candidates including David Gambrell, whom Sam Nunn beat in 1972 for the U.S. Senate seat; George T. Smith, who had been a lieutenant governor and is now on the Georgia Supreme Court; Bobby Rowan, who is now on the Public Service Commission; and George Busbee, who won—able, well-qualified folks. The rest constituted about the strangest assortment of gubernatorial candidates you ever did see.

The strategy for each of us was to make it to the runoff election. Nobody was going to win that primary with fifteen candidates taking votes away from one another, so if you just made it into the runoff you could worry about winning the election there. And the rest of us knew that one statistic wasn't going to change: Lester Maddox was going to win one-third of the votes in the primary, no more, no less. He was going to make it into the runoff. The question was who among the rest of us would be there to compete against him.

The press traveled with me frequently. One morning, I was flying down to make several appearances in Fort Valley in central Georgia, Sam Nunn's part of the state. Reg Murphy, the editor of the *Atlanta Constitution*, flew with me so he could write a story for his paper about what it was like to spend a day campaigning with candidate Lance.

After we landed at Fort Valley, we headed toward the car we would be taking to tour that area. Never one to pass up the possibility of a handshake that might lead to a vote, I spotted a man digging a ditch near the terminal building, went over, and introduced myself. I told him I was running for governor and said I needed his vote.

He was a plumber, working on some pipes down in that ditch, digging the hole deeper when necessary. I was confident that Reg would be impressed with my grass-roots, press-the-flesh style of campaigning, showing myself to be a true man of the people. The plumber seemed to recognize either my name or my face, because he said, "Oh, yes—I have something I want to show you. I've read about you and I know you're a banker, so let me show this to you."

He reached into the pocket of his overalls and pulled out a thick roll of gold coins. It must have been worth forty or fifty thousand dollars. He apparently always carried the roll with him, and the fact that he was wearing overalls and digging a ditch didn't seem to him to be at all inconsistent. Instead, he told me how interested he was in the future of the Georgia economy.

It was the last reaction you'd expect when you shook hands with a man digging a ditch.

Then we headed to the Blue Bird Bus factory, where they manufacture school buses, and later we toured city hall. But Murphy couldn't resist the temptation. With all the different stops that day, his column in the *Constitution* after that trip was about the plumber and his roll of gold coins in his overalls, proving once again that things— and people—are not always what you might expect.

About four o'clock the next morning, I hit the campaign trail again, heading out in the predawn darkness for Randolph County, down in deep southwest Georgia near the Florida line, where Cuthbert is the county seat. After we landed at Cuthbert and I checked in with my campaign office, I found out that Reg had been kidnapped not long after we returned to the Atlanta airport the night before. The case became a major national story. A man named Williams was eventually arrested, tried, and convicted for kidnapping Reg and holding him for ransom.

I called Jimmy in his governor's office to make sure he was informed. Murphy had written some bitter columns about Jimmy, going back to the governor's race in 1970, and their testy relationship—and that's putting it mildly—continued right into Jimmy's presidential campaign in 1976, when Reg wrote a column with this headline:

JIMMY CARTER'S RUNNING FOR WHAT?

After Jimmy was elected President, Reg gave him an engraved plaque of that column.

Carter's problems with Murphy—and vice versa—were well known in Georgia, so when I mentioned to Jimmy that I was going to call Jack Tarver, the publisher of the Atlanta papers, to see if there were any new developments in Murphy's kidnapping, Jimmy said, "You be sure to tell Jack that I didn't have anything to do with it."

Hal Gulliver, at that time the associate editor of the *Constitution*, which had endorsed my candidacy, wanted to make the same all-day tour with me that Murphy had made. So I took him along, determined to show him what a campaign was really like and what a vigorous, hardworking candidate I was. We went to south Georgia, to Whigham, Cairo, Climax, and other towns near the Florida line, about as far south as you can go and still be in Georgia. That was the home territory of George T. Smith, one of the other candidates, so I campaigned long and hard to try to win some votes away from him. Then we covered the rest of south Georgia, came back up through middle Georgia, and were going to have covered the entire state by day's end. I was determined to wear Gulliver out, just to dazzle him with my campaigning.

Our schedule called for us to end up late in the day in Monroe. The community was a mill town at that time, with a large textile business and several "mill villages"—the textile counterpart to company towns in coal regions. I was to go door-to-door, shaking the hands of everyone who answered the door.

I walked up the steps onto the front porch of one house and approached a fellow sitting in a swing. It was a beastly hot July day, and I was dressed in a tan gabardine suit with a necktie and white shirt, trying to look as gubernatorial as a man can when he's running up and down steps, shaking hands vigorously, crossing the street to catch another unsuspecting voter, always hurrying—all of this while the temperature is in the nineties with humidity to match. The man was half dozing in his swing when I approached, tapped him on the shoulder, and said, "I'm Bert Lance, and I'm running for governor. I sure would appreciate your vote."

He said, "Well, I'll be damned!"

That was the extent of his reaction, but Hal Gulliver made sure he wrote that quote down in his notebook for his column later.

As we approached another residence, I saw the lady of the house in her backyard, watering her vegetable garden with a hose. I walked up to her and said, as usual, "Hello, I'm Bert Lance, and I'm running for governor—and I need your vote."

She turned toward me, and I saw the most shocked look I ever saw on anybody's face, and as soon as I did I knew right away what was going to happen next, and there wasn't going to be a thing in the world that I could do to stop it.

That lady faced me to see this celebrity standing right there near the tomatoes and green beans in her vegetable garden, and that hose was pointing right at me. She got me squarely in the front of that gabardine suit and white shirt. In her momentary shock, she stood half paralyzed, and the nozzle from that garden hose bobbed up and down, from my head to my toes. She got every inch of me. There wasn't a dry thread in that whole suit.

Well, sir, she got flustered at what she had done, I got flustered at it too, and we spent the next several minutes with her apologizing and me telling her to think nothing of it. While all this was going on, Gulliver was rolling in the grass, dying with laughter at what was happening to this poor candidate for governor.

I always wanted to go back to Monroe and find out if that lady voted for me. But I think she did, because she felt so bad about what she did to me. That experience established one of Lance's Cardinal Rules of Campaigning: Never go up to a voter who is holding a garden hose and ask him or her to vote for you, because what will happen next is unavoidable, and your image will suffer a temporary setback.

I spoke to a civic organization in Monroe that night, with my suit and shirt now only damp instead of dripping wet, and then Hal and I headed for the airport and our flight back to Atlanta. Along the way we passed a Little League baseball field. Seeing an opportunity to shake a few more hands, I told our driver to pull over. I wanted to walk around and talk to the cluster of parents who were watching their kids play ball.

Hal couldn't believe the lengths I was willing to go to, so he asked me, "Haven't you had enough?"

I said, "You never can tell. One vote might be the difference."

I got out and worked the crowd—what there was of one—and then climbed back into the car to resume our drive to the airport. Halfway there, Hal bolted up in the backseat and hollered, "Just a minute, Lance! Stop the car! You've made a terrible mistake! You have to go back to that game!"

I was as shocked as I was puzzled. I said, "Gulliver, what in the world are you talking about?"

He said, "You missed the second baseman!"

THROUGHOUT MY CAMPAIGN I was viewed as the candidate Jimmy Carter had anointed to succeed him, which of course was true. Some of Maddox's supporters called me a two-for-one candidate—vote for Lance and get Carter free.

My close association with Jimmy didn't help. At the end of his term as governor, he wasn't tremendously popular. He had fought too many people on too many issues and spent too much of his political capital. The political observers were saying he couldn't have won reelection, and I think they were right. But Jimmy also had his supporters, because he had done so many good things as governor, so I went after that pro-Carter vote and concentrated on his accomplishments when I talked about him.

I did something else in my campaign: I supported proposals for a state financial disclosure law for political candidates. Before the primary in August, I voluntarily issued a financial disclosure statement. It is another irony that in trying to be open and forthcoming, I probably cost myself the election.

The Democratic primary, which is always close in Georgia, neared its finish with George Busbee and me running a close race, maybe even neck-and-neck. George beat me out in a photo-finish—four days after Nixon resigned and Gerald Ford became President. It has been speculated, and I think with some validity, that the overwhelming public attention to events in Washington distracted Georgians from the message and appeal of my own campaign just enough to help Busbee force a runoff with Maddox.

At that point, the overriding question across the nation and even around the world was whether our government was going to be able to survive what many considered to be a full-scale constitutional crisis. The United States had never been through any experience like that. With Nixon's resignation and the rise of Gerald Ford to the presidency, there was almost unanimous agreement around the country that this nation was extremely fortunate to have a leader like Ford, with his years of leadership in the House of Representatives, on hand to step into this breach in our national government. The news media concentrated on it, and every political commentator wrote or spoke of how fortunate the United States was to have a person of this experience, leadership, calmness, and integrity ready and able to lead us out of what Ford himself called "our long national ordeal."

George Busbee's background was analogous to Ford's, on a more limited scale. He had been in the Georgia House of Representatives for eighteen years and was seen as a stable, calm sort of man with a record of having served the public well as a member of our legislature. The obvious comparisons were made in the Georgia news media and elsewhere over the four days between Ford's swearing-in and the Georgia primary.

I remain convinced to this day that if Nixon had resigned earlier or later, I would have been elected governor. We had a last-minute advertising campaign ready to hit TV and the papers, plus other plans to make things happen our way in that final week, but everything was knocked in the head by all the talk about whether the nation was going to survive and the comparisons between Ford and Busbee.

Whatever the reason was, Busbee beat me by 1 percent.

The returns came down to the margin of victory in Savannah,

where I also lost by 1 percent because I didn't carry the black vote there. That's another irony. In 1988 I was described in the news media as Jesse Jackson's closest political adviser, but in 1974 I lost my campaign for governor because of the black vote against me—made possible by the active involvement of Julian Bond and other black leaders in support of Busbee. Busbee was able to win the support of the black community in and around Savannah. There were always ways to win that support by making a bunch of promises to black people. I refused. I assume Busbee did not.

I didn't enjoy losing, but I wasn't going to sit in the corner and suck my thumb—not with Lester Maddox still lurking around. I went to work for Busbee. There was too much at stake not to. His campaign was successful, he was elected, Jimmy's program stayed intact, and Lester Maddox was forced to return to private life against his wishes. The good folks of Georgia had once again shown their sound judgment.

FROM HIS FIRST DAYS in the governor's office, my respect for Jimmy as a leader grew to such an extent that LaBelle and I hosted a party for him in Atlanta on his forty-seventh birthday on October 1, 1971. I presented him with a set of commemorative coins representing every state in the Union, and I remember telling him in front of all the guests: "This gift represents your dominion over one state as governor, but from what I've seen, at some point in the future you will have dominion over all fifty states."

That was the first time anyone publicly mentioned the possibility that Jimmy Carter might be President some day. He had been governor only nine months. And to show I really meant it, when Jimmy and I went to Chicago the next year, I bought a book for him in a bookstore. I told him he might find it useful in the future. The book was by James David Barber. The title was *Presidential Character*.

Jimmy, of course, was thinking the same thing. We kept thinking about it and talking about it between ourselves and with others. At the same time, Watergate was a worsening disaster for the Republicans, so 1976 began to look like a Democratic year.

We were going through the same mental processes that John Kennedy said he experienced. JFK once said he felt it was presumptuous, maybe even arrogant, to think of himself as the future President of the United States—until he asked himself, Why *not* me? Carter, in effect, worked his way through that same line of reasoning. He announced his candidacy for President on December 12, 1974. By the time his term as governor ended, he was working hard on the first stages of his unbelievable bid for the White House.

During the early days of his presidential campaign, he asked me to help him obtain a speaking date at a business seminar in New York. The event was going to be hosted by my friend, Eliot Janeway, an economic consultant who is respected in the business community and in demand as a speaker and adviser to businesses and business organizations. Jimmy had completed his term as governor, but he was still unknown to many people, especially those outside Georgia. However, some of the folks in the business community had heard of him because he was said to be *anti*-business. He thought this seminar conducted by Janeway would be the perfect setting to put the fears of the business community at rest.

The arrangements were made, and I'll always remember the shock I felt when Jimmy stood up and said right off the bat to that room full of suspicious, high-powered business executives: "My name is Jimmy Carter. I'm running for President of the United States, and I do not intend to lose."

4

The Spirit of '76

JIMMY'S DECISION to run for President was based at least in part on his feeling that everything he saw in the Nixon administration was exactly what he abhorred about government at any level. Carter saw what he considered dishonesty, bureaucratic unresponsiveness, and a deep-rooted lack of concern for the public good.

His experiences with them and what he saw in Nixon's Washington reactivated Jimmy's commitment to the people from his first days in Georgia politics: "I'm going to give you a government as good as you are."

The Nixon experience had a profound and lasting influence on Jimmy. His training ground for observing and analyzing the office of President was the Nixon years. After what he saw as governor from 1970 through 1974—the two years before and after Watergate, culminating in Nixon's resignation in August of 1974—his commitment to serve the public in any way he could deepened. Everything he said and did in his 1976 presidential campaign was a reflection of the Nixon experience. Jimmy Carter didn't run against Gerry Ford in 1976. He ran against Washington.

As the leading Democratic candidates of the 1972 presidential campaign—McGovern, Muskie, Humphrey, Jackson, and Mo Udall —paid their courtesy calls to the white-columned governor's mansion in Atlanta and sat on the porch in rocking chairs to solicit Jimmy's support, Jimmy began to ask himself the same question John Kennedy did following the Democratic convention in 1956: Why *not* me?

When Bob Strauss was elected chairman of the Democratic National Committee following the McGovern fiasco, Jimmy and Hamilton Jordan convinced him to appoint Jimmy as chairman of the Congressional Reelection Campaign Committee. Strauss could not foresee that this was another step in the evolution of Jimmy Carter, one that would help give Jimmy a leg up toward a run for the White House.

It wasn't a case of Strauss thinking of Carter for that job. Jimmy thought of it himself; he knew it would be a great opportunity for him. He was determined and self-disciplined as chairman, just as he was in everything else, and all during this time he was moving toward his next goal with that complete, unblinking concentration and commitment that he applies to his every endeavor.

When you think about it, his appointment was a real windfall. He learned the rules of the Democratic party inside out. He structured an election campaign for the party within those rules. He was still serving the second half of his governorship, and when the time came for him to begin his own presidential campaign he had educated himself fully on how to use those rules to his advantage and to the detriment of his opponents. He learned the process, and then he became a victor of the process he had just chaired.

The press built him up as the promising, progressive young candidate who made a mark in his four years as a governor and played a key role in organizing the Democratic party for a successful showing in the congressional elections of 1974. They kept building him up, and by mid-1976 it was too late to tear him down, even if anybody wanted to. By the time we left for the convention in New York in mid-July, the nomination was his.

ON THE FIRST three nights of the convention at Madison Square Garden, LaBelle and I sat in what the folks of north Georgia would call the "Plum Nelly" section. Down home we say we're in the mountains, plum out of Tennessee and nelly out of Georgia. So we were plum nelly at Madison Square Garden, about as far back in the Garden as you can sit while still being in it.

I didn't take a visible role in Jimmy's behalf during the convention. Instead, I kept in contact with him and with Jordan and Powell and talked to others who might be able to help Jimmy's candidacy in one way or another. And I kept in close touch with the Carter family, because they were still working for the nomination, too—his wife, Rosalynn, his mother, Miss Lillian, and his brother, Billy.

When we moved into the national arena that year, the first conscious decision I made was that I was no expert on specific issues, so I wasn't going to damage his prospects by getting into the middle of things I didn't know enough about. Jimmy had plenty of people around him who knew a whole lot more about specifics than I did. But I knew a lot about Jimmy Carter, and we had our peer relationship that everyone else around him recognized and respected. They knew I could advise him more effectively than others on what to do and what not to do, because he listened to me on that peer basis, knowing that I had a thorough knowledge of his strengths and weaknesses and how to apply them. I also knew a little something about people, politics, and the news media, so I decided to direct my services to those three critical areas.

As the convention moved through the nominating process and Jimmy's hour of victory in being chosen as the presidential nominee of his party approached, the speculation grew about the selection of a running mate. There was the usual jockeying for position and the stories on the nightly news and the whispered conversations in the hallways and on the floor of the convention, but I deliberately stayed away from the vice presidential question.

Over the years and especially during the primaries that year, I developed a closeness with many members of the news media, one that endures to this day. I happen to like most reporters and columnists. I get along well with them, and I think that in general they do a fine job and provide an invaluable service to the democratic process of this republic by making an informed citizenry possible, with the exception of certain personal experiences which I'll get into later.

Because of my closeness to certain members of the news media, I didn't want to know Carter's private thoughts about a running mate. The folks in the press know that I always answer every question from them that I can. If I know something and they ask me, I tell them. It would be the same thing with the vice presidential speculation, and I didn't want to damage Jimmy's decision-making process and cause some bad feelings somewhere in the party by blurting out the wrong thing to a reporter.

I stayed out of meetings of the Carter high command on the subject, which was an easy sacrifice for me to make because I don't like meetings anyhow, but my own choice as the man on the ticket with Jimmy would have been John Glenn. Some of the other names being tossed about were Scoop Jackson, Frank Church, Adlai Stevenson, Jr., and Walter Mondale, all of them prominent names, good Democrats, and people capable of running a strong campaign.

If anybody had asked me, I would have told them who my preference was—John Glenn. He was a good Democrat, someone capable of running a strong campaign, and goodness knows he had name recognition. Not only was he well known, but he was known for the best reason of all in presidential politics: he was a genuine American hero. And he was from a state that has a large number of electoral votes—Ohio. Jackson was from Washington state, Church was from Idaho, and Mondale held Hubert Humphrey's old seat in the Senate, representing Minnesota.

Jimmy decided that the best choice was Mondale, and that suited me. I didn't know Mondale well at the time, although we have since become good friends and I have tremendous respect for him, despite what the folks around him did to me in San Francisco in 1984.

I learned about his selection when the rest of the Carter organization did, right before Jimmy made the public announcement. I wasn't surprised that he chose such a widely respected candidate, and that his short list included nothing but quality people. That was typical of Carter, making the decision that he felt was best for the country.

However, in the years since, I have developed a political theory about the selection of vice presidential running mates. Under this theory, Mondale was the wrong choice. The reasons don't have a thing to do with Walter Mondale as a person or his ability. In fact, they are a tribute to him. Many people will take violent exception to my reasoning—but that's what makes all of us political experts.

My theory arises out of a frequently overlooked reality: People who are astute enough as politicians to win the presidential nomination of their parties are smart about a whole range of things, but when it comes to picking a running mate, their inexperience often affects their selection. It happened to Carter—but it didn't happen to Bush. He's too experienced.

Under my theory, Mondale was a mistake because his presence in the vice presidential position made Carter fair game in the eyes of the Washington power structure within ninety days after his inauguration. Fritz's presence in the new administration's number-two position guaranteed that Jimmy's presidential honeymoon was going to last only a minimum number of weeks.

Why? Because the power folks on Capitol Hill and in the news media, the AFL-CIO, the U.S. Chamber of Commerce, and the

National Association of Manufacturers were a whole lot more comfortable with Mondale than they were with Carter. After a period of time that was only long enough to be polite about it, they had no reluctance to start jumping on Jimmy about anything at all.

They didn't care what happened to Carter, because they'd rather have Mondale in the White House anyhow. And if their attitude and abuse made Carter a one-term President, that would be all right too, because then Mondale would become the heir apparent to the leadership of the Democratic party.

By this same reasoning, George Bush scored one of the political strokes of genius in the history of this country in 1988 by picking Dan Quayle for the number-two spot on his ticket. The astuteness of that political decision is almost beyond calculation, and if Bush made that one by himself, which I believe he did, then this ol' boy gives him an A-plus in practical politics.

The one prevailing concern in Washington today is that nobody wants anything to happen to George Bush. And that feeling is shared in other world capitals, too, including Moscow, London, Paris, Tokyo, and Beijing. Bush made his choice, and he knew it was a roll of the dice. But he survived the early heat, and now he is sitting in the catbird seat, secure in the knowledge that no thinking member of either political party or the media wants to see any manner of harm come to him.

Look at the grave concerns expressed when Bush developed health problems in May 1991. The public was nervous that Quayle might be acting President for a very limited time. The man simply enjoys no confidence with the public. He provides as much material for Johnny Carson and Jay Leno as Donald Trump and Zsa Zsa Gabor. The country is not ready for him, and he's not ready for the country.

Bush could have selected Bob Dole, Jack Kemp, Howard Baker, or any one of a member of other well-qualified candidates, and he would have been elected President easily. But then Bush would have had a harder time in the presidency because the critics would have been more willing to go after him without his insurance policy to protect him against disaster.

His choice even gives him an antidote to help cure his one lingering ailment, the Iran-Contra affair. We will never know what Bush's role was in that scandal. Nor will we find out easily whether reports now surfacing on public television and elsewhere on what really happened in October of 1980 are true: whether Ronald Reagan's people made a secret deal to begin selling arms to Iran through a third country in exchange for the return of the hostages—but not until Carter's defeat.

Why will the truth on these gigantic questions be so hard to determine? Because nobody wants Bush to be caught up in them. Hearings may come and hearings may go, such as the confirmation hearings on Bush's nomination of Robert Gates to head the Central Intelligence Agency, but one fact dominates these events: Certain powerful people in Washington aren't going to let anything happen to Bush as long as the man who would succeed him is Dan Quayle.

During Oliver North's trial in 1989, you didn't see any orders coming out that showed the Bush administration was determined to get to the bottom of this scandal. You saw everything on the subject being protected by the Bush administration under the guise of national security or presidential privilege, and nobody challenged the administration to any great extent. That's because nobody wants to harm Bush to the degree that he becomes politically wounded. He'll be criticized for waffling on abortion or not doing enough to help the victims of Hurricane Hugo or flip-flopping on his pledge about "no new taxes," but the criticism won't do serious harm to his political standing because the establishment doesn't want to risk the consequences—a President Quayle.

Dan Quayle is George Bush's insurance policy. Bush is immune against almost any development. Was his choice of Quayle in the best interests of the country? Who knows? If Bush lives, it won't make any difference anyhow.

I don't endorse this as the preferred way for presidential nominees to pick their vice presidential nominee. But history, including history as recent as 1988, suggests that the theory behind this reasoning has been applied by nominees. It also suggests that some nominees who have not applied it have come to an unhappy end.

There is no way in the world that George Bush could have thought that Dan Quayle was qualified to be President of the United States. Maybe he convinced himself that Quayle could grow into the office if necessary and that he could become a great servant of us all. But at the time that Bush made the decision—and regardless of who thought up the idea, the decision was Bush's—it was a raw political decision, based on Bush's intimate knowledge of how our political system operates.

Bush, most likely, would deny vehemently that this was his reason for choosing Quayle. He would tell you he picked him because he was the best person for the job—not just the best *man* but the best *person*—that he has complete confidence in Quayle to help him carry out his programs and to continue if anything should happen to him.

Bush understands the agenda factor. There is always a multitude of agendas being advanced in this nation, by folks in different positions of power in the political and business establishment. When we elect a President who is not a product of that establishment, if he has chosen a Vice President who *is*, the establishment will declare open season on that President the minute he swears to preserve, protect, and defend the Constitution. He will be subjected to every allegation and criticism anybody can think of, and it makes no difference whether the pressures and unkind treatment come from the news media, the establishment, the poor folks, or some other group.

But if we have a President who is a part of the establishment and a Vice President who is not, the kind of attacks that Carter was subjected to right from the start won't materialize to the degree of heat and bitterness that Carter received.

Jimmy was criticized often and severely from his first days in the White House. He was called weak, indecisive, vacillating. He didn't have that Quayle protection. It was the hallmark of his administrations in Atlanta and Washington that he did what he truly believed was in the best interests of the country. So Walter Mondale was his choice for Vice President.

So what happened? As soon as he took office and proposed a national energy policy—*bam!* He was criticized for being silly and overreacting to a problem that most Americans, including the media, didn't understand or even care about. As soon as he said we ought to sign a treaty returning the Panama Canal to the people of Panama— *bam!* As soon as he tried to do something about the inflation problem he inherited from the Ford administration and its buttons that said "WIN—Whip Inflation Now"—*bam!*

Every time he turned around, he got clobbered, right from his first days in office. It had to do in part with the confidence felt by the establishment in limiting the Carter presidency to no longer than necessary, knowing that someone they felt comfortable with, Walter Mondale, was in the on-deck circle.

If Carter had a Dan Quayle as his Vice President, the attacks against Jimmy never would have developed to the extent that they did, so harsh and unrelenting right from the start and throughout his four years as President. Those folks pushing their own agendas would have been more careful to keep Carter in office. But Jimmy didn't have the protection that a Quayle gives a President. As unpopular as Harry

Truman was in his final two years in office, America's leaders didn't mistreat him for his entire term, but they did it to Carter.

Selecting a vice presidential candidate on the basis of these purely political considerations is a dangerous and cynical practice for anyone who wants you to think he possesses the qualities you prefer to see in your President. But the theory holds up, whether we like it or not.

Here's another example: The minute Richard Nixon became vulnerable to impeachment was when he selected Gerald Ford to be Vice President, succeeding Spiro Agnew. The whole time Agnew was in that position, Nixon could hold out indefinitely against the pressures that eventually led to his impeachment.

Nobody wanted to see Agnew succeed to the presidency. Nixon was safe as long as Agnew remained, but Agnew crossed him up by being exposed in his own scandal while Nixon was still trying to ride out the Watergate storm. When Agnew was uncovered, Nixon was stripped of his security against impeachment or resignation.

The history books show that Nixon was forced from office less than a year after Agnew was. Why? Because of the force of the Watergate snowball, but also because the media and the political leaders of this country knew they could live with Gerald Ford as President, now that Agnew was out of the way.

The theory works again when you apply it to Lyndon Johnson's choice of Hubert Humphrey in 1964. What happened? Johnson didn't run for a second term. He got too much grief from the establishment, because those folks would have been a whole lot more comfortable with Humphrey in the Oval Office.

Carter decided, in typically honest Carter fashion, to pick the best man for the job. He knew full well that Walter Mondale was more popular in Washington than he was, and that he could end up being at least embarrassed, and maybe worse, over four years of exposure in Washington while his Vice President kept smelling like a rose.

People shouldn't think for one minute that presidential nominees make their decisions based on the best interests of the nation in the normal definition of that term. They have their own definition, and it's a perfectly understandable one. They are convinced that the best interest of the nation is for them to be elected President.

They have their own confidence in their ability to run the country and to stay out of trouble while they're doing it, or they wouldn't be running for President in the first place. So they reason that they can pick anyone as their running mate because it will help them win election, which is what America needs in their opinion, and they will be able to preside over the affairs of the nation without needing a whole lot of help from their Vice President anyhow.

If that means a George Bush has to pick a Dan Quayle, that becomes sufficient justification in Bush's mind.

Bush also factored public reaction into the equation. That was the calculated risk. The Republicans were willing to gamble up front that the American people would not see the choice of Quayle as a reason to vote against Bush. They won the gamble, which is even more proof that they did a far superior job of reading the attitudes of the voters in 1988 than the Dukakis crowd did.

ON THE FOURTH NIGHT of the convention, we enjoyed the honor of being invited to sit with the Carter family in Madison Square Garden. The pride that you feel when you see one of your closest friends stand in front of a red-white-and-blue throng in one of the most famous arenas in America and accept the nomination of his party to be President of the United States is beyond description.

I was bubbling over with happiness for Jimmy and his family and confidence in the future of the nation and the Democratic party. I was sure he was going to win. And I was convinced that President Jimmy Carter was destined to accomplish great things in leading the nation forward, just as he had achieved so much in leading Georgia forward.

Then, on the next morning, a significant vignette in our intertwined lives took place on the sidewalks of New York.

I was walking to the Americana Hotel on Broadway, where Jimmy was staying, to have breakfast with Jack Nelson, a Washington reporter for the *Los Angeles Times*. As I turned the corner in front of Sheraton Center, I saw Jimmy walking in my direction.

But I saw in an instant that the man headed my way wasn't just my friend any more. He was surrounded by Secret Service agents and a pack of radio, TV, and newspaper reporters, all of them clamoring for a glimpse of the nominee or a word from his lips.

At that precise moment, our relationship changed. In a twinge of sadness, I realized that our homespun friendship was gone, or was at least about to take a different form.

Jimmy wasn't just a friend any more, one I loved dearly. Now he was a man who had an even chance, maybe better, of becoming the nation's next President and the leader of the free world. It wasn't that Jimmy would change—but there was going to be a difference.

Before he could spot me, I walked across to the other side of the street and stood in the shadows of a building alcove while he and his entourage passed. He didn't see me.

Then I remembered what day it was: July 15, 1976, ten years almost to the day we met under the oak tree down home in Georgia.

5
The Night We Fired the Cannon

FROM THE OUTSET of the campaign in 1976, Jimmy agreed with me that he needed to extend an olive branch to the leaders of the business community. He was well aware that he was viewed as antibusiness. We wanted to change that attitude. Maybe he couldn't fully win them over, but we wanted at least to try to neutralize them so they did not mount a major campaign against his candidacy and eventual nomination.

One of Jimmy Carter's great strengths is that he knows his weaknesses. That's no mere play on words or an attempt to be cute. It's a fact. He has in his makeup the ability and the willingness to look at himself objectively and to recognize what he does well and what he doesn't, where he is strong and where he needs improvement. He doesn't always take the corrective action that you might like, but nobody else does either.

That was why he had me arrange his appearance before the seminar in New York put on by Eliot Janeway. And in August I thought we should try to do even more in that direction. I suggested that we build on that first step in New York by hosting an all-day session with the biggest names in American business.

I was confident that, with his exceptional ability to win folks over in small groups, Jimmy could at least blunt the criticism being voiced against him in some parts of the business community. Maybe not everybody in that Fortune 500 crowd would vote *for* him in November, but if they got to know him, in an environment that we could control, maybe then at least they wouldn't be *against* him. And maybe we could impress them enough so they wouldn't speak negatively about him to others.

Jimmy gave me all of two days' notice to go ahead and get it done. So I pulled together thirty-two of the nation's most high-powered business executives: Ed Spear of U.S. Steel, Reg Jones of General Electric, Jay Pritzger of the Hyatt hotel chain, Graham Claytor of Southern Railway, Irv Shapiro of Du Pont, and others. We met for most of the day—Labor Day—at the Airport Hilton in Atlanta.

The tactic seemed to work. Those folks went away impressed with Jimmy, whether they agreed with him or not. And we not only blunted the criticism of him, we even got some active support from members of the group. Irv Shapiro became our liaison with the business community for the rest of the campaign. It didn't hurt Jimmy one bit to have the head of the Du Pont Corporation speaking to businesspeople around the country in his behalf. Graham Claytor was another one who did a lot of talking for us. He became a strong associate of Jimmy's. After the election, he left Southern Railway and became Jimmy's Secretary of the Navy.

One of the big pluses about the Carter candidacy in 1976 was that he really didn't need to be coached. You didn't have to unscrew his head and try to pour in a bunch of knowledge that he didn't have before and might not be able to remember. We didn't have to prop him up for "sound bites" on the evening news. He had a commanding knowledge of the subjects that were going to be issues of that campaign. He didn't need any three-by-five file cards from anybody.

He had his own very definite ideas about what it would take for him to be elected President and how he was going to accomplish it. He knew those things right from the start and was very secure in his candidacy. There were things he felt strongly about, and nobody needed to tell him to feel that way, and nobody tried to change his mind.

One example is human rights. He didn't come to feel the way he did on that subject just because of the campaign or his subsequent election. Human rights wasn't after-the-fact with him. What he had to say on that issue, and the strong worldwide role he played in its advancement during his presidency, grew out of how he had always felt, and he knew he was going to make it one of the legitimate topics of debate during that campaign.

Ronald Reagan was a born-again, Ronnie-come-lately politician on the subject of human rights. But not Jimmy. It is a matter of record that Jimmy was always one of America's strongest advocates of human rights. He has proven in his ten years since leaving office that he still is, and he is entitled to some of the credit for the waves of change sweeping over so many lands today in the cause of human rights.

Dr. Arthur Burns, the economist, was never a big Jimmy Carter fan, but two years after Carter left office Dr. Burns shocked me by telling me there was one area in which he thought history would judge Jimmy kindly. I told him I was surprised that he rated Carter highly in even one category.

Burns told me, "I truly believe that his stand on human rights will mark him as a man of great courage and will rate him a great President in that regard."

Jimmy's strong position on human rights during his 1976 campaign and throughout his political career always impressed me as a reflection of both his high moral conduct and his foresight as a leader. There was no particular urgency for him to sound his call to the American people and to all the other nations of the world, but he felt strongly that it was something that needed to be done and he was willing to be the leader who would do it.

He was convinced that he was right and that he should take the leadership position in the nation and in the world. He didn't care whether other folks and other world figures agreed or disagreed. As far as he was concerned, anyone who disagreed was simply wrong, and that was no reason for him not to take a strong position during his '76 presidential campaign in behalf of bringing human rights to all the people of the world.

That sense of his own responsibility to lead bore fruit when he achieved his monumental feat of the Camp David Accord between Menachem Begin of Israel and Anwar Sadat of Egypt. As with other of his accomplishments, Jimmy Carter never received the recognition he deserved for what he accomplished at Camp David against all odds—and against all advice that he was risking serious damage to his presidency. He stood up and took the initiative and brought about the accord between those two feuding nations—and he should have won the Nobel Peace Prize for it.

JIMMY'S BROTHER, Billy, had one of my favorite reactions to Jimmy's candidacy for the presidency. He was much maligned by the news media, who set him up as the token redneck in the campaign because Jimmy is a southerner, but Billy Carter was no redneck at all. He was a learned, informed man who read at least four books every week on every subject he could find, plus newspapers—including the editorial page—and newsmagazines. Billy was no fool. He knew what was going on, more than a lot of the folks who criticized him the most.

He was instrumental in Jimmy's victory in 1976, just as he had been in the gubernatorial victory six years before. Jimmy never could have been elected governor if Billy hadn't been willing to stay home and manage the peanut business so successfully. And Jimmy definitely wouldn't have carried Texas, and the nation, in November if it hadn't been for Billy.

He went to Texas, which is always a crucial state for the Democratic nominee, and took on Cesar Chavez, the leader of the United Farm Workers, successfully throughout the state. There was widespread opposition among farmers to Chavez's attempts to unionize their workers, and while the folks in the media were beginning to make Billy look like a buffoon and a redneck, he was out in Texas campaigning as hard as anyone for his brother. He kept hammering away at Chavez and his movement.

It is a truism of twentieth-century American politics that no Democrat can be elected President without carrying Texas. Billy knew this as well as Jimmy did, and he dedicated himself to doing something about it. I campaigned in Texas for Carter too, not as a speaker at campaign rallies but by meeting with local and state business leaders to try to minimize their opposition to Jimmy. In the process, I was able to witness Billy's contribution to his brother's campaign. I campaigned in Lubbock and El Paso and saw the impact Billy was having on the Texas people. You can imagine how many hundreds of votes Billy won for Jimmy every time he mentioned Chavez and told those Texans, "If the son of a bitch came on my land, I'd shoot him."

Billy was the unsung hero in his brother's election. Jimmy won Texas, and Billy is the one who created that opportunity for him. He never got any credit for it, for the simple reason that the news media never gave Billy any credit for anything.

You get an idea of his smarts from his comment to reporters during the campaign: "I got a mother who went into the Peace Corps at the age of sixty-eight. I got a sister who's a holy roller preacher. I got another sister who rides motorcycles and wears helmets. And I got a brother who thinks he's going to be President of the United States. I'm the only sane one in the family."

JIMMY CONSTRUCTED his own game plan for winning the presidency through his own thinking and suggestions from Rosalynn. (Hamilton Jordan also gave considerable help on strategy.) He always sought

Rosalynn's advice on the major decisions in his career. He was ridiculed for this during his campaign and his presidency, although I never could understand what was wrong with a man talking things over with his wife. Most folks I know think that's an admirable trait.

Apparently Ronald Reagan feels that way. But Jimmy was the one who was ridiculed for it. When Rosalynn suggested that Jimmy make a commitment to improving mental health services and facilities, they were ridiculed because she was involved. The media said she was interfering in Jimmy's administration. How can you criticize someone for wanting to do something about our mental health programs?

After the convention, Jimmy went back to Plains to wait for the Republican convention to go through the process of nominating President Ford for a full term. There wasn't any sense in trying to compete for time every night on the evening news while that was going on. Jimmy took a hiatus of several weeks when he was able to get some rest and prepare to kick off his campaign at the traditional time—over the Labor Day weekend. He could afford to be optimistic. He was leading Ford in the polls by thirty-three points, benefiting from his own superior performance in the campaign and from two negatives that were heavy baggage for Ford to carry in 1976.

One was the economy. People remember that we had double-digit inflation during the Carter years, but they seem to have forgotten that we had it during the Ford years, too. The Ford administration tried everything it could think of to reduce inflation, including silly buttons that said "WIN—Whip Inflation Now"—and nothing worked. The cause, of course, was the same one that produced economic troubles for Jimmy: the skyrocketing price of oil. The Arabs slapped their first embargo on the world in 1973 and the effects reached serious levels while Ford was President, from 1974 through 1976.

When the OPEC nations jumped their prices, the price of everything else jumped, too. There wasn't a whole lot a President could do short of war, and Ford rejected that option, as Carter did later. So we had to suffer through those years of galloping inflation, caused in large part not by Ford or Carter but by the Arabs. The only person who benefited from that was Ronald Reagan.

The second heavy piece of political baggage Ford had to carry in 1976 was something of his own doing: the Nixon pardon. When Ford pardoned Nixon only one month after he became President, many Americans were furious. He may have done it for the most noble of reasons—to spare us a lengthening of what he called "our long national ordeal"—but the political reality was that when he pardoned Nixon in 1974, he lost a boatload of votes for 1976.

Those were two of the reasons why Jimmy was enjoying that thirty-three point lead in the polls as he reduced his pace during the publicity buildup to the Republican convention. An earlier poll, taken for *Time* magazine in late June by the public opinion firm of Yankelovich, Skelly and White, revealed what became an irony four years later: if the Republicans had nominated Ronald Reagan in 1976 and the election had been held at the time of the poll, Carter would have defeated him by twenty points.

But Jimmy's lead began to disappear at an alarming rate. It plunged ten points in a hurry. The plunge became a problem of growing concern to all of us. We couldn't just sit there and watch that lead evaporate. We had to do something to stop the hemorrhaging.

I got Jimmy on the phone over in Plains and told him, "You have to make a couple of things happen so you can stop your decline. One is that the only media pictures coming out of Plains are of the groups you campaigned *against*—liberals, labor unions, and special interest groups. If there's one more picture on network television of Ralph Nader umpiring a softball game between you and the news media, you might as well forget about the election because nobody's going to vote for you.

"You're sending the wrong signals. You need to get that crowd out of there, and you need to be what you've always been—an outsider who's going to change things."

Jimmy took my advice. The wrong folks left Plains and the right ones stayed. His lead in the polls stabilized.

IN ADDITION to Hamilton Jordan, Jody Powell, his pollster, Patrick Caddell, and his media consultant, Gerry Rafshoon, Jimmy had help from another major source in 1976—maybe the man who helped him the most in the day-to-day conduct of his campaign. That was Charlie Kirbo.

Charlie is a special kind of man, the kind of commonsense human being and brilliant lawyer you'd want both as your friend and as your adviser. And to Carter he was both.

The two met in the early 1960s. Jimmy had been appointed to a vacancy in the Georgia senate representing Plains, but lost in a close primary in the next election. He and his advisers were convinced he had been cheated out of his party's nomination. Jimmy and his supporters felt that a crucial ballot box had been stuffed with votes for his opponent, but the Democratic establishment turned thumbs down on the request of this young upstart from Plains to throw out the results of the election.

So Jimmy got up early one morning, as he always does, and drove 150 miles to Atlanta to see Charlie Kirbo, having been referred to him by Griffin Bell, who became Jimmy's attorney general in Washington, and one of Jimmy's cousins, Don Carter, a newspaper publisher in Macon. Charlie got Jimmy his day in court, and talked in his folksy, down-home way about chicken thieves who are clever enough to cover their tracks but are thieves anyhow. The judge ruled in Jimmy's favor just in time for him to win the general election and take his rightful place in the Georgia senate at age thirty-seven.

Therein lies another irony. The governor in that episode was Carl Sanders, who had appointed Jimmy to that seat in the first place, only to be defeated by him when they ran against each other in the 1970 primary campaign for governor. But the irony doesn't end there. I'm convinced that if Sanders had beaten Carter in that gubernatorial race, he would have been the southerner who was later elected President. It is a political fact of life that certain people can be elected in certain places, but not elsewhere, even within their own regions of the country. To say that a particular candidate in a southern state, for example, could have been elected in any southern state doesn't necessarily follow. By the same token, to say that a southern governor could have been elected President in 1976 because Carter was doesn't necessarily stand up either.

Jimmy was elected governor in Georgia, but it is not certain that he could have been elected governor in Alabama at that time. Maddox could have been elected governor in Alabama, but not in Florida. Wallace could have been elected in Georgia or Mississippi, but not in Tennessee.

A look at the southern political figures of that time indicates, at least to me, that one southern governor who could have been elected in every southern state was Carl Sanders. For that reason, it has always been my feeling that if Carter had not been elected governor in 1970, and President in 1976, Sanders would have—maybe not in 1976, but at some time in that era.

Jimmy owes his start in political life to the fine legal work Charlie Kirbo did in his behalf when they contested the results of that primary race for the state senate, and he has always been quick to recognize Charlie's role in his success. During the '76 presidential campaign, Jimmy said to reporters, "Going to see Charlie Kirbo that day was probably one of the smartest things I ever did in my life."

Three years after my toast to Jimmy on his birthday, when I suggested that he would one day have dominion over all fifty states instead of only one, Charlie was beginning to say the same kind of things to Jimmy. Charlie told a magazine interviewer that by the fall of 1974 Jimmy had definitely decided to run for President, but was hesitant to make his announcement, so Charlie applied a gentle prod.

Charlie says one of Jimmy's concerns was that people might make fun of him for presuming to run for the highest office in the land. "So one day, I remember, we were talking about it, and he started in again on how high-heeled it was going to look when he actually did it, and I said, 'Jimmy, one of these days you're just going to have to raise up on your hind legs and tell them you're fixing to run.' "

Kirbo says Jimmy agreed, so Charlie added, "Well, then, why don't you just go on and do it?" So he did. I wasn't present at that conversation because I was just finishing up my own campaign for governor, but I can believe every word of Charlie's account. That's vintage Carter. He wanted to be sure—not just pretty sure but *really* sure—before making his decision. Then, having made the decision, he stuck by it and made a success out of it. It was the pattern he exhibited throughout his public career.

Over their years together, Charlie became one of Jimmy's closest friends and advisers. He didn't go to Washington with him, but throughout Jimmy's years as governor and presidential candidate, he served Jimmy well with loyalty and good advice.

He helped Jimmy, and others, by being able to simplify things. He liked to illustrate his points using the plain old mule. Charlie was a big admirer of mules and even owned one himself. He told James T. Wooten of the *New York Times*, "Now I regard the mule as a unique specimen. I don't mean in a biological sense. I mean in the sense that a mule is not fixing to do anything he hasn't decided is the thing he ought to do. That's not like a lot of folks, you know.

"Folks tend to do things and then think about whether they ought to or not—and folks, as you know, tend to get in trouble sometimes. But you take a mule now. He very seldom gets into trouble."

He showed the *Times* his modesty by explaining that the victory in court enabling Jimmy to win election to the Georgia Senate wasn't due entirely to Charlie's own legal brilliance. "The fellow who stuffed the box wasn't all that smart," Charlie said. "He forgot to take out the real ballots, so there were about 100 or so too many for the precinct—and most of the extra ones seemed to express the wishes of folks who were either deceased or had left town for one reason or another."

There was additional evidence pointing to a lack of astuteness on the part of the folks who were exercising their civic responsibilities a little overzealously in that election. The 100 phony votes found in that ballot box were in a stack—with a rubber band still wrapped around them.

Charlie claims that as a result of the Carter court case, "they passed a law that disqualified anybody from voting who'd been dead for more than two years."

With his down-home logic and philosophy, it's too bad we didn't have Kirbo with us in Washington.

ON ELECTION NIGHT, LaBelle and I hosted a dinner for some of our friends. Among them was Jimmy Roosevelt, the former congressman who was FDR's son. He entertained us with stories of his own election nights spent with his father at the family estate in Hyde Park, New York, and in Washington when FDR was being elected governor of New York and President four times.

Our home in those years was in the Buckhead section of Atlanta. The house had been used for the reception on the night of the premier of *Gone with the Wind* in 1939. It is a lovely, large home and was a perfect place to wait for the news that Jimmy had been elected President.

Jimmy Roosevelt had strong sentimental ties to Georgia. FDR went to Warm Springs as often as he could for its waters' soothing effects on his polio-stricken legs. He died during one of his visits there, on April 12, 1945. Many Americans have seen that famous photograph of an accordion player named Graham Jackson playing "Going Home" with tears streaming down his face as the casket began its journey to Washington and eventually to Hyde Park.

When Carter kicked off his campaign at Warm Springs in September, Jimmy Roosevelt and his brother, FDR, Jr., were both there. At our election night dinner, as we were showing the Roosevelts around the house, we opened the doors to one of our rooms. There stood Graham Jackson, with his accordion, and he began to play "Going Home." There were watery eyes all around.

THERE WAS a near riot that night at the World Congress Center next to the Omni in Atlanta. Jimmy's supporters gathered there to watch the returns, and the size of the crowd reflected his enormous local support. It was almost a contradiction in politics, but this man who probably couldn't have been reelected governor enjoyed tremendous support from the same people in running for President.

Jimmy was next door at the Omni with Rosalynn watching the

returns himself, and I was moving back and forth between the two buildings after our dinner with the Roosevelts. The center became so packed with Carter supporters that the fire marshal closed the doors and refused to let any more people in, and that's when the problem started.

The folks outside started storming the doors. They had worked hard throughout the campaign to help their man get elected, and now they wanted to be a part of the history of the night. Not only that, the occasion was a fund-raiser to reduce Jimmy's campaign debt, so these people had paid for tickets that entitled them to admission.

It was a bad scene. That mob was angry, and I could understand why. They were getting ready to knock the doors down and take over the building when somebody asked me to go out there and try to quiet them down. There wasn't any particular reason to pick me for that role, and it was an honor that I would have been happy to decline, but maybe they thought the sight of a man six feet, five inches and 245 pounds might have a calming effect on the crowd.

I hollered to them as well as I could that we were working on the problem, that I agreed with them they should be allowed inside, and they would be, just as soon as we could make enough space for them. That seemed to do the trick just long enough. Not too many minutes later—but just in the nick of time—the doors were reopened and everybody got inside and was happy.

I paid a price for my intervention—I lost my voice.

After that, we left for home. It was a good thing, too; I needed to get away from the crowd. Those folks had worn me out. But we took care of some business on the way.

The *Atlanta Constitution* has a small cannon, bought years ago by Henry W. Grady, one of the original visionaries of the new South, when he was editor of the paper. Mr. Grady began his own tradition of firing that cannon on election night any time a Democrat was elected President, including all four nights when FDR was victorious.

Jimmy Roosevelt and I went down to the *Constitution* with Hal Gulliver and Jack Tarver, the paper's great and long-time publisher, and put the cannon out in front of the building on Marietta Street. We took great delight in firing that cannon, booming to the world the news that a Democrat and a true son of Georgia and the South was going to be President of the United States of America.

WHEN SOMEONE close to you, someone you've believed in and worked hard for over a period of ten years, is elected President, you are immediately struck by an awareness that you are helping to make American history. The Secret Service expands the size of its detail protecting the nominee the minute he becomes President-elect. The media horde grows even larger and louder, which you didn't believe possible. As chaotic as every minute is during the campaign, it is even more so now.

The atmosphere isn't the only thing that hits you between the eyes and tells you you're writing the history books of the future. It's also the profound importance of everything you're working on. Before, you were helping the nominee to take stands and make promises, pointing with pride and viewing with alarm. Now you're helping him to pick the next secretary of state, to decide how he wants to supplement the last budget of the outgoing President, and to send a message to foreign leaders all over the world reassuring them that he wants to maintain good relations with them.

Everything the President-elect says or does is on the top half of page one of the *New York Times* and the *Washington Post* and is the top story on all the network evening newscasts. And the President-elect isn't the only one who gets quoted and finds himself producing an impact during the transition period between the election and the inauguration. Bob Strauss tried to warn me about that, but I didn't believe him.

Bob is a thoroughly delightful combination, one of the smartest leaders of the Democratic party and one of the most enjoyable. Every telephone conversation with him, every visit with him, is an occasion when I learn something and have a good time, too. Bob became President Carter's special trade representative to foreign governments, and during the transition period he taught me a lesson about speaking on behalf of the President or President-elect that I never forgot.

I was waiting to go on the air as the guest on the Sunday public affairs program "Face the Nation." Despite such an intimidating title for a TV interview, I was relaxed and looking forward to the opportunity to mobilize support early for the programs of the new President. Strauss came into the CBS studios on M Street in Washington, in the last few minutes before the "on the air" red light was due to flash on. He walked over to me and said in a helpful tone, "Now, Bert—whatever you do, when you're on this program, don't make any news."

I laughed and said, "Bob, you know I'm not going to make any news. How can I, when I don't know anything?"

Strauss wasn't convinced. He repeated his warning.

During the show, the moderator, George Herman, asked me about taxes. As the new director of management and budget, I said, "It appears to me that the economy needs to be stimulated. And it also appears to me that the way to do that under normal circumstances is through the tax structure."

After the show, Strauss was ready for me. He was waiting in the hallway, and when he saw me he covered his face with his hands in anguish and despair—and he wasn't kidding.

He said to me, "I told you not to make any news."

I was surprised and puzzled by his reaction. "Bob," I said, "I didn't make any news. All I said is there might be something that's going to happen."

Then Strauss became specific. "You've got to understand that you're in a different position than you've ever been in before. People are listening to every word you say. You have to understand that whatever you say, and the way you say it, is going to have an impact on things."

The headlines in America's newspapers on Monday said:

LANCE SEES TAX CUT COMING

The stock market shot up forty points.

I GOT TO KNOW Fritz Mondale well during the transition, and I learned that to know him is to love him. He has the same compassion for people, the same keen intellect, and the same high moral code as our mutual friend, Jimmy Carter, and the man Fritz succeeded in the Senate, Hubert Humphrey. Now Fritz was also going to be Vice President, just like his mentor from Minnesota.

I was delighted to discover right away that Fritz also has a refreshing sense of humor, always ready and able to find a chuckle in even the most serious of surroundings.

My discovery came during one of our meetings after the election. Jimmy called us together in Plains at the home of his mother, Miss Lillian. The place was called the Pond House because she had a pond out back where she did her fishing.

It was December, and Jimmy had forty or fifty folks there—Tip O'Neill of Massachusetts as Speaker of the House; Robert Byrd of West Virginia as the Senate majority leader, various congressional committee chairmen, and others who would be part of the leadership beginning in January. Several business leaders were there too, including Irv Shapiro of Du Pont and Tom Clausen, chairman of the Bank of America. Jimmy hadn't announced any of his appointments yet, but he asked me to be there, too.

We had a marathon round-robin session in which we covered the whole waterfront of what we had to do now and in the immediate future to jump on top of things right away. It also was a get-acquainted meeting. Many people in the meeting hadn't met before, and even Jimmy and Fritz were just getting to know each other.

The session seemed to last forever, and one reason was that the ambiance was vintage Carter. We sat on hard metal chairs, like the ones you sit on in a funeral home. Jimmy didn't offer any drinks or anything else. The austerity of that atmosphere was just as surprising as when people walked into his governor's office for lunch expecting to find a comfortable executive setting and a first-class spread of food. The ambiance wasn't anything you'd read about in a travel magazine.

Jimmy, with the noblest of intentions, made it even worse. The man is blessed with what seems like unlimited endurance. He never seems to get tired in a meeting. He never changes his position. He never even has to go to the bathroom. And if you start squirming or looking antsy, he glares at you and tells you to stop distracting him.

At the end of the meeting everybody was exhausted, hungry, and looking for the bathroom. At this moment of unanimous fatigue, except for Carter, Mondale walked over to me and gave one of the all-time great descriptions of Jimmy, one that's never been equaled or published. And he was paying Carter a high compliment.

"Well, Bert," he said, "I learned three things about your friend Carter today."

"What's that, Fritz?"

"First, he has a cast-iron rear end. Second, he has a bladder the size of a football. And third, his idea of a party is a half a glass of Scotch."

DURING THE transition period, another incident occurred involving Jimmy's dislike for dealing with members of the legislative branch. It bore an unfortunate similarity to the episode with Senator Ford Spinks while Jimmy was governor.

I suggested to him that I should arrange to fly Congressman Jack Brooks of Texas down to Georgia for an introductory meeting, and Jimmy readily agreed. Brooks was chairman of the House Government Operations Committee and would have a strong voice over any reorganization proposals that we would send up to Capitol Hill.

Reorganization was of critical importance to Carter. He viewed it as the keystone of his efforts and desires to reshape the federal government so it would once again be responsive to the people. And if reorganization was important to Carter, then Brooks was too.

Brooks was no unknown quantity to either of us. We were well aware of his reputation as a seasoned congressional committee chairman, which was precisely why we went out of our way to invite him to Georgia. Brooks is an intelligent, salty, blunt, cigar-chomping veteran of Capitol Hill, a no-nonsense guy who can be tough to deal with, to say the least. And he has a great ability to make himself clear.

He's the man who raised the first questions about President Nixon's financial affairs and thus is widely credited with being instrumental in Nixon's eventual downfall. He also gave Oliver North some of his most uncomfortable moments during the Iran-Contra hearings in the summer of 1987.

Brooks and I flew down from Washington in early December for a meeting at Jimmy's house. I've always liked Brooks, so we had a pleasant flight down. I've also been well aware of the blunt and colorful style of the gentleman from Texas in his dealings with people and issues, and his personality is one reason I like him. But anybody who challenges folks the way he does is nobody to take for granted, especially as a committee chairman. Even with my awareness of the Brooks candor, nothing could have prepared me for the disaster that awaited Jimmy and the rest of us, right from the start of the meeting. I felt a tête-à-tête between the two would score some points with this influential committee chairman and give our new administration a leg up on our reorganization efforts. It was a terrible mistake.

At their meeting, Carter launched into a didactic explanation of how he was going to reorganize the federal government. Brooks started squirming and moving closer to the edge of his chair. Suddenly he interrupted Jimmy and told him that the government wasn't going to be reorganized the way Carter wanted—it was going to be reorganized the way Brooks and the rest of Congress wanted.

The more the two men talked, the more they disagreed. It was not a promising beginning, the chairman of the key congressional committee and the President-elect disagreeing even before the inauguration on how things were going to be done. It was no way to start an administration.

Finally I felt compelled to try to break the logjam so we could move on to other items on the agenda. "Mr. President," I said, trying to get used to the sound of that title before Jimmy took office, "we might want to strike this conversation and start over at some point in the near future because you two have such vast differences of opinion on this subject."

It produced the desired cease-fire. The two men disengaged, but the odor of fireworks lingered throughout the afternoon.

That meeting was a signal to me, and to anyone else who was paying attention, that the new President was going to deal with the Congress of the United States exactly the same he dealt with the Georgia General Assembly. My concern was compounded by his apparent blindness to fundamental differences in the two legislatures.

We were able to muscle our way to a reorganization victory in the Georgia legislature, but I knew we weren't going to muscle our way through the Congress of the United States. Men like Jack Brooks had seen Presidents come and go. I knew after that confrontation that we had to find a new way of doing things if the Carter administration was going to be successful.

But it didn't turn out that way. Carter didn't get much help on this point after I left Washington eight months into his term. This was ironic, because he had put together a cabinet of Washington insiders that belied his own outsider image and campaign: Cyrus Vance, Joe Califano, Brock Adams, James Schlesinger, Mike Blumenthal, Andy Young, and Zbigniew Brzezinski. All of these men could have helped Jimmy on Capitol Hill. But some of them developed agendas and constituencies of their own. They did not serve Jimmy Carter as well as they should have, especially in his dealings with Congress.

Califano was an example. Was he qualified to be secretary of health, education and welfare? I don't think there's any question about that. But he always seemed interested in advancing himself first. There's nothing necessarily wrong with that, but he didn't really think much of us Georgia folks. He seemed to look at us askance, as if to say, "Where did you all come from? We were here when you came, and we'll be here when you leave."

He was 100 percent right.

People talk about the great mistake Carter made in not dealing with the Washington establishment, and to a certain degree that's true—but he went farther in that direction than most people remember by appointing so many of those insiders to his administration. Those folks could have made Jimmy's acceptance level on Capitol Hill a whole lot higher than it was, but for their own reasons, they didn't. They let him down. And when you're not helping the President get along with Congress, you're doing more than just letting him down—you're letting the country down, too.

Jody Powell, Hamilton Jordan, and Stu Eizenstat—Carter's brain trust if a man of his superior intelligence can be said to have a brain trust—all worked faithfully and hard for Jimmy, but they never applied for membership in what I call the Washington Insiders Club. Stu and Jody stayed in Washington after Carter left office, and here's another irony: Jody was the most confirmed of all us outsiders in 1976 when we went to that town, but now he has become a Washington insider himself. That's fine, and I'm glad he's successful because he is still a good friend of mine, but the possibility in '76 that Jody would become a Washington insider was out of the question. He didn't take a backseat to anybody in his great disdain for that type.

NOT MANY phone calls turn out to be as meaningful and helpful as one I received during the transition. It came from Harold Hughes, a former governor of Iowa, former Senator, and former candidate for President.

While still a Senator, Hughes had started a prayer group in Congress. He told me he thought a similar group in the White House would be a good idea. He mentioned it to Jimmy, who agreed and told him, "Talk to Bert about it."

Harold and I worked together to recruit the first members. The new group met regularly at 7:30 every Monday morning in the White House mess, a half-hour before our Monday morning cabinet meetings. Eventually, the group grew to include Cecil Andrus, the secretary of the interior; Ray Marshall, the secretary of labor; Bob Bergland, the secretary of agriculture; our Georgia friend, Andy Young, the United States ambassador to the United Nations; General David Jones, the Air Force chief of staff; General Louis Wilson, the commandant of the Marine Corps; and Dr. Arthur Burns, the chairman of the Federal Reserve Board. Also attending often were Senator Sam Nunn, another of our Georgia friends; Senator Lawton Chiles of Florida; Patricia Bates Harris, the secretary of housing and urban development; and Joseph Califano, the secretary of health, education and welfare.

CARTER AND MONDALE got to know each other better during interviews of the many candidates for cabinet and subcabinet positions in our administration. On one occasion, they spent the night at our house in Atlanta, violating the Secret Service practice of never having the President and Vice President, incumbent or incoming, spend the night in the same location or fly on the same airplane. If something should happen to one, they don't want the other injured or killed at the same time.

One of those meetings at our house was a classic example of how decisions of great importance are often made in the plainest of surroundings, without any of the crystal chandeliers, high ceilings, and mahogany conference tables that are the standard trappings for affairs of state. Charles Schultze, who became Carter's White House economist, came to the house with Mike Blumenthal one evening so we could put together the economic program for the new administration. None of us could type, so we sat there in the shank of the night writing everything out in longhand on legal pads.

Everything has to be done in haste in those ten weeks between the election and the inauguration. Many of the products have to be turned out literally overnight, and this was one of them, but the three of us couldn't very well submit our economic recommendations for the future of the nation to the President-elect in longhand. So I recruited our son, David, a college student at the time, who not only knew how to type, but was the only one in the house with a typewriter. As the rest of us slept, David set up office in the bathroom so as not to keep us awake and finished his contribution to the future of the country at 6:30 in the morning.

On another occasion during the transition, Jimmy, Fritz, Rosalynn, and I had lunch in Plains. By that time, Mondale was becoming familiar with Jimmy's personal austerity. He was learning how to accept it and work around it.

We were at Jimmy and Rosalynn's house, and we were about to eat lunch in their kitchen. As we sat down, Fritz looked at the table and saw three sandwiches for four people—and I saw him put his hand on one of those sandwiches before Jimmy even finished the blessing.

Later in the afternoon, I told Fritz I saw him make his move on that sandwich. But he wouldn't let me get away with kidding him about it. He shot right back with, "What were you doing with your eyes open during the blessing?"

I told him, "I was counting them, too."

6

The Outsider

DESPITE ALL THE HOOPLA and adulation that greets a new President, Jimmy Carter was alert enough to know that his arrival in Washington was something less than good news to a lot of folks who make their living there. He was an outsider, and that was plenty bad enough. But what made it even worse was that he was a *southern* outsider.

Folks from the South know all too well that they have to overcome a deep-seated prejudice against them when they cross the Mason-Dixon line. Blacks, Jews, and others point out that they have to work twice as hard to succeed because of the bias by which they are judged. It's the same way with southerners.

Racial and religious prejudice in this nation at times seems just as bad as it's ever been, and when Jimmy took office in January of 1977, another form came into evidence—regional prejudice. Jimmy was ridiculed even before taking office for the way he talked and for the speech mannerisms of those of us around him, the way we dressed, the music we liked, and the food we ate.

Jimmy was coming to Washington as a graduate of the United States Naval Academy, a former career Navy officer, a nuclear engineer, a successful businessman, and the former governor of his state. Yet the Washington crowd mocked him for taking his own carry-on luggage when he was boarding an airplane, and for the life of me I still can't figure out what that had to do with his ability to be President.

They snickered about his sweaters, and for wearing his hair just over his ears in the style of the day and using "Jimmy" instead of James. And worst of all, the man wore jeans. When John Kennedy wore khakis and loafers, nobody ridiculed him for it. But they talked as if they expected Jimmy to meet the Queen of England and the Pope in jeans, boots, and a plaid shirt, with a weed stuck between his teeth.

Southerners are not surprised at such reactions. And Jimmy wasn't the first President to be the target of regional prejudice. Lyndon Johnson felt the same stings and barbs, and the treatment he got was even more pronounced because he followed not just a northerner but a New Englander into office. The same folks who used to swoon when Kennedy talked about "vigah" and the island of "Cuber" laughed in scorn when LBJ mentioned "the Yewnited States"—even though Harry Truman used the same pronunciation.

I thought Jimmy himself delivered the best commentary on the subject, and he wasn't just talking about speech mannerisms when he said it. He summarized the whole question of attitudes toward southerners right after his election when he said, "It sure will be nice to have a President who doesn't have an accent."

He knew that prejudice often is in the ears of the beholder.

The staff of the White House mess, which is not a mess but one of Washington's first-class eating places, made another telling point on the subject. Reporters asked one of the cooks if it was going to be a problem to prepare southern-style food for the new First Family, and the cook said, "Oh, no—the servants have been eating it for years."

WHEN JIMMY got out of his limousine and started walking up Pennsylvania Avenue toward the White House hand in hand with Rosalynn and their daughter, Amy, in thirty-degree temperatures during his Inauguration Day parade, he was doing more than just showing the American people that he was one of them. He was symbolizing the difference between government up until then and the kind he intended to provide.

In the ten years from his first run for governor until his election as President, Jimmy objected strongly to the kind of government he saw at both the state and federal levels. In Georgia before his election and in Washington throughout his term, Jimmy became increasingly upset with the aloofness of government, its disregard for the people, and the concern of too many officials for advancing their personal ambitions and riches instead of the public interest.

The problem with government at all levels—and especially in

Washington, except when Jimmy was President—is that everything is so inaccessible to the people. It's what I call "sidewalk government." People need to have access to their government, and to know they do. If you set up government behind a barrier, unavoidably it will become what it is in many cases today: too big, bloated, arrogant, and unresponsive, all the things that politicians have been able to lambaste government for—while they are helping to make it that way.

When people walk along the sidewalks of Washington and in state capitals and county seats, they see the entrances to government buildings protected by security guards in front of metal detectors. They have no direct knowledge of what is going on inside those buildings and no sense that they are a part of any of it or that the work inside those buildings, whatever it might be, is for their benefit. They know only what they see from the sidewalk: government buildings housing things they can't see, activities they don't know about, and people they never meet except on the evening news. The message emanating from those buildings is clear: Stay on the sidewalk. Don't come in here, and don't expect us to tell you what we're doing here.

That may not always be the case, but it is the message. Because of the size and bureaucracy in Washington today, too many Americans feel that they have no way of penetrating those fortresses and the people who run them. Instead, they are expected to stay on the sidewalk and take whatever information the government is willing to dole out—but not to be included in the discussions on which decisions are based.

Ronald Reagan made political hay through two terms as governor of California and two as President by lashing out at government—too big, too distant, and all those other things he always criticized government for. He became the only President in the history of this nation to use the occasion of his inaugural address to call our national government a "problem." On other Inauguration Days, other Presidents appealed to the best in us, but Reagan stood at the United States Capitol and told the world in his first inaugural address:

> In this present crisis, government is not the solution to the problem—government *is* the problem.

That declaration caused some of us to wonder what Washington, Jefferson, and Franklin would have thought about that kind of attitude in one of the holders of the office they created.

But talk is cheap. Regardless of Reagan's constant preachings to the contrary, the government never stopped growing under Reagan, in California or in Washington. "Sidewalk government," which was plenty bad in the Nixon and Ford years, became even worse under Reagan.

After Reagan's eight years in Washington, the federal government had more federal employees than when he took office, the White House staff had more positions, and the federal payroll was higher, not to mention the all-time high budget deficit and trade imbalance. While all this was going on, the "Great Communicator" wasn't communicating anything to the American people except the material that his scriptwriters were putting on three-by-five file cards for him to recite.

Sidewalk government was more of a problem than ever. That's another irony. Ronald Reagan, the man who kept promising to "get the government off your back," allowed that unchecked growth of the government throughout his eight years as President.

Jimmy wanted to put a stop to that before Reagan ever came on the scene, and he wanted to demonstrate his commitment through symbolic acts at the outset, followed by the tough decisions that he and I would be making through the budget process and the reorganization to follow.

That's why Jimmy took that walk up Pennsylvania Avenue with Rosalynn and Amy. It's also why he went six blocks down Pennsylvania Avenue nine days later, met his new attorney general, Griffin Bell, and joined him in actually unbolting the front doors of the Justice Department. They had been locked since the days of the Vietnam demonstrations in the early 1970s during the administration of Richard Nixon.

CARTER TOOK STEPS immediately to limit government growth. He imposed a hiring freeze as soon as he got to Washington, allowing the federal departments to fill only a certain percentage of their vacancies. He moved to reduce the White House staff by one-third, which in reality was a mistake because we were already badly outnumbered by the rest of the executive branch. But we cut out a third of the employees we had, at a time when we needed all we could get, because Jimmy meant what he said and he wanted to keep faith with the American people while also leading by example.

I told President Carter I thought it was a mistake to cut the White House staff. I didn't think we accomplished one thing by doing that. We had only sixteen hundred employees in comparison to two million other federal workers in the rest of the executive branch and on Capitol Hill. We were fighting a losing battle to begin with, and to cut one-third of our staff simply meant we were going to be less able than ever to push our program through the departments, where Jimmy had no surplus of supporters, and on the Hill, where he had even fewer.

The only folks a President can really depend on to advance his agenda for the nation are the ones he controls directly, the members of the White House staff. To reduce that staff by one-third seemed to me merely to reduce his effectiveness by at least that much and maybe a whole lot more.

Ninety-nine percent of the American people have no idea at all of how many people are on the White House staff anyhow, and don't really care, campaign promise or no campaign promise. The staff members themselves usually don't know, because so many of them are on loan from the military and other agencies and departments that there isn't any way to count them, even in this computer age.

We got all hung up on numbers instead of just adopting a position that said, "We've reduced the White House staff by this many positions—here's the number—and that's absolutely all we can cut at this time. We anticipate further reductions through attrition."

That puts you on record as having kept your campaign promise. You've started to do what you promised to do, and you're going to keep on doing it until you reach that one-third goal. You don't have to feel compelled to lop five hundred employees off your own staff five minutes after the last unit of the inaugural parade passes your reviewing stand. Then you go on with the business of getting an administration started, which is what people elected you for in the first place.

Instead, we continued cutting and kept calculating numbers, and the whole project took on a life of its own. The most serious obstacle we encountered was Rosalynn: she didn't want to cut her First Lady's staff. Frankly, I agreed with her. She never did, either. We made the cuts somewhere else within the White House staff just to keep peace and harmony in the First Family.

That's how serious Jimmy Carter is about keeping campaign promises. He'd made this promise because he thought the White House staff had grown too large under Nixon and Ford, and he told the American people he was going to cut that staff by a third, so by damn that's what we are going to do.

But we didn't have to do it all in one swing of a meat ax. And we didn't have to use all those valuable weeks and months at the very start of a new administration to analyze the size and organization of the staff and prepare statistical reports and analyze some more, but that's what happened. We weren't even working on reorganizing the federal government. We were working on numbers.

That episode may have been a mistake, but at least we had a noble goal in mind. It was all part of our determination to get rid of sidewalk government and bring the people back into things so they would know what their government was doing, would understand the reasons, and would support it. When you employ sidewalk government, everybody loses sooner or later. When you get rid of it, everybody wins.

As a practical matter, you cannot invite the public to come in and sit on your shoulder and watch everything you're doing. And in this day of terrorist acts and other threats to the public safety, you need to use a certain amount of prudence in deciding just how open your government can be, especially in the physical sense. Admittedly, there must be a balance between openness and security.

However, if the people become convinced that what they're getting is only sidewalk government and they're being excluded from things they have a right to know about and to help decide, the ultimate victim of that attitude and policy will be the government itself. The people will lose their respect, trust, and confidence in the American institutions of government. They will stop believing that the government really is the servant of the people and not their master. And when enough people feel that way, things will change in a hurry and some of those folks limiting the public to sidewalk government will be out there on the sidewalk themselves.

This is what Jimmy talked about in his campaigns, when he promised to give the people "a government as good as you are." He was saying to the voters that they deserved more access to their government and more responsiveness from it.

It's too bad and too true that the lack of responsiveness on the part of the federal government that Jimmy was talking about affects us every day of our lives. The Reagan administration was full of examples, and the evidence didn't end with his administration. In December 1989, almost a year after Reagan left office, the Social Security Administration reported that more than half of the elderly and disabled poor people whose federal assistance had been cut off by Reagan should not have lost their monthly government checks.

The report said the Reagan administration stopped the checks without giving the people time to prove they were eligible for the income under a government program called SSI—Supplemental Security Income. It provides a minimum income to 4.5 million low-income, aged, blind, or disabled people. It's not much—$386 a month for an individual or $579 for a couple, and it was even less under Reagan. The study found that the number of beneficiaries whose monthly checks were cut off was 80,000 in 1987, and 105,000 in 1988. Such was sidewalk government under Reagan, whose promise to "get the government off your back" apparently included getting the government checks out of your mailbox—if you were poor, disabled, or blind.

Social Security's internal review discovered that in 54 percent of the cases where the monthly income was discontinued, the government was wrong. The recipients were eligible. Social Security's own spokesman said the agency was "extremely concerned about the findings." He said "they do show we're suspending SSI payments which go to some of the most vulnerable people, the elderly and disabled." Then he stated the obvious: "This can cause very serious problems for these people who are living on very limited incomes."

The people on those "very limited incomes" already knew that.

THERE ARE many things that the government does that it should, and many things it doesn't that it should. There are things that only the private sector can do, and things that only the government can do.

The people have to be aware of these distinctions and to feel that they have some kind of role, direct or indirect, in making decisions. But if they see that they are being shut out of the process, that their officials are telling them they have no function and no free expression, then the government becomes its own god, and the public interest suffers serious damage.

This is not to say that the people who run our government are not good, honest, hardworking, highly capable people. They are. I have no greater respect for people anywhere than I do for the people who worked for me in the Georgia Department of Transportation and the U.S. Office of Management and Budget. Likewise, the folks I worked with—my colleagues at the cabinet level in both Atlanta and Washington—were people I would be happy to hire in a minute to work for me.

The problem is one of accountability. The federal government is now too far removed from accountability in too many instances. Reagan's supporters can say that we've deregulated the airlines and the banks and so on, but so what? In fact, deregulation of the airlines was begun during the Carter administration, anyhow.

The truth is that the average American today feels that his life is dictated by the federal government far more than in 1976 or 1980.

This feeling on the part of the voters will continue to be aggravated as the government plays more of a role in our personal lives.

Unfortunately, the federal government hasn't become any less intrusive—it's gotten more so. The abortion issue reflects this.

In addition to the moral questions involved, the problem of government intrusion is also a key part of the abortion debate going on in this country. And to many Americans, the government question is becoming almost as important as the moral one. Whether folks agree or disagree with the right to have an abortion, the role of the state or federal government in that activity is a separate concern. Does the government have the responsibility of ensuring abortion on demand, or does that constitute government interference in our private lives? Many people think it does.

Does the government have the right to say you can't smoke on an airplane, or in a government building? I'm delighted not to have to worry about cigarette smoke on a flight, because smoke bothers me. But is the passenger next to me the victim of government interference because he's told he can't smoke when he wants to? Is that a legitimate function of government?

With these trends, accompanied by the unchecked growth in its size, government will exceed the tolerance level of the American people. It will become such an intruder into our private lives that people will lose their respect for our institutions, and the institutions will crumble and fall apart from lack of public support.

The colossal events of 1989 are an example of the extreme result of sidewalk government. The upheavals in the Soviet Union, China, East Germany, Poland, Czechoslovakia, Romania, Hungary, and South Africa were the ultimate response by people who had concluded that their government leaders were ignoring them and even defying them while providing themselves with lifestyles befitting a Roman emperor and stashing millions away in Swiss bank accounts.

Nobody, including me, is predicting such dire consequences in this nation. Conditions here are far different. But 1989, and what followed in the Soviet Union, including the Baltic states, in 1990 and 1991, should be a sobering reminder to every political leader at every level in every society.

The message of 1989 and later was that when the people conclude that their leaders are ignoring them and excluding them—telling them to stay out on the sidewalk and don't ask any questions—changes will follow. Leaders will be replaced, and maybe their institutions of government will too, with new institutions demanded by the people on the sidewalk.

Unfortunately, we seem to be fast approaching the point in this country when the people will say "enough"—that the federal government is too big, too unresponsive, and too dictatorial. What can we do about it? In terms of laws and regulations, probably nothing yet. The trend has to run its course. And when it has finished its course, the voters will demand that government get out of their lives wherever appropriate.

When that happens, sidewalk government will become a thing of the past, and the federal government will once again become our servant instead of our master.

Jimmy and the rest of us were committed to exactly that goal, and Jimmy put together a team fully capable of achieving it. From the beginning, Jimmy held weekly meetings of his cabinet members. I was pleased about this practice and urged Jimmy to follow it for a basic reason: it was the one sure way to know that his cabinet members were in Washington for direct communication at least once a week.

I'm the last person in the world to advocate holding meetings on a regular basis. I don't tolerate meetings well unless they are productive, which most of them are not. And knowing Jimmy Carter's ability and even enthusiasm for enduring meetings of marathon length, I certainly didn't want to volunteer for one more Carter meeting than necessary. But I thought weekly cabinet meetings *were* necessary so Jimmy could keep some semblance of control over his cabinet members and their travels and could be sure of having them in Washington for consultation at least once every week.

I told Jimmy I thought it was essential for his troops to be in Washington on Monday mornings and not Hawaii or California or New England. I said, "Mr. President, there's just one way to do that. I believed it when I was running the highway department for you. We had a staff meeting every Monday morning, and we required everybody to be there. I don't think your cabinet ought to be any different. If it is, they're going to be off with their own constituents and making speeches and traveling all around the countryside."

There was a distinct advantage to the cabinet members, too, in having those meetings. It gave them the opportunity to speak directly to the President, to make the case for whatever items they had on their agendas and grab a few minutes with him after the cabinet meeting if necessary.

So we had those cabinet meetings every Monday morning the whole time I was in Washington. As soon as I left, they were discontinued.

●   ●   ●

1 I am sworn in by Governor Lester Maddox as Director of the State Highway Department, 1970. From left: Stuart, David, LaBelle, Governor-elect Carter, me, and Maddox.

2 Judy Woodruff interviews me after my campaign for governor, primary election night, 1974.

3 Coming home to Calhoun after leaving Washington, 1977.

4 Sitting on the front porch with La-Belle and our children—Stuart, David, Beverly, Tram's wife, Patti, and Tram—during my 1974 campaign for governor.

5 Meeting with President Carter in the Oval Office. My recommendation to reject the B-1 bomber is sticking out of my coat pocket.

6 From left: our hunter's guide, President Carter, me, Jody Powell, and Lucien Whittle and Bill Harper of Carter's staff. Four turkeys were bagged by five hunters. The one smiling the most is the one who didn't get a turkey.

7 Wishing happy birthday to Robert Strauss (left), one of America's most respected political strategists, 1988.

8 President Carter's Economic Policy Group, from left: Charles Schultze, Chairman of the Council of Economic Advisors, Labor Secretary Ray Marshall, Special Trade Negotiator Robert Strauss, Treasury Secretary Michael Blumenthal, me, Commerce Secretary Juanita Kreps, and Agriculture Secretary Bob Bergland. This was one of many meetings to shape the economic policies of the new administration.

9 One of the meetings in the worst political mistake in President Carter's term in office—the controversial list of water projects that were being eliminated from the budget. The man who bravely volunteered to take the heat, Secretary of the Interior Cecil Andrus, is on Carter's right.

10 A meeting in the Oval Office with President Carter and (from left), Vice President Walter Mondale, National Security Advisor Zbigniew Brzezinski, and Air Force Chief of Staff Harold Brown.

11 Our first grandchild, Trey, gets to meet the President of the United States in the Oval Office.

12 Amy races down the steps ahead of President Carter after a visit to LaBelle and me at our home in Washington.

13 LaBelle and I with President Carter outside our Washington home.

14 Jimmy and Rosalynn share a moment with us at the reception in our honor just before we left Washington.

15 With Jesse Jackson during his 1988 presidential campaign. Jesse called me every day during the campaign, eight or ten times on some days. My main advice to him throughout the campaign was to convince the voters that he is "a mature political leader."

16 LaBelle and I were grade school sweethearts and have been married for forty years.

17 Part of the growing Lance family at Christmas.

As we began operations in Washington I felt more and more that we made a mistake back in the transition period by not appointing a White House chief of staff. President Nixon had Alexander Haig, and President Ford had Dick Cheney, but Jimmy didn't want one and felt he didn't need one. He wanted to be his own chief of staff.

Several of us disagreed. I thought he should retain the position. I also thought he should immediately put Hamilton Jordan, the architect of his victory, to work to plan his campaign for reelection in 1980, and that in addition to my OMB duties I should take on the responsibility of relations with Congress, because I knew Jimmy simply would never bother himself with them.

Jimmy rejected two of those three suggestions. He didn't appoint a chief of staff, at least not until so late in his administration that the damage was already done, and he didn't put Hamilton to work on his 1980 reelection campaign until that was too late, too.

Carter had his own reasons for opposing my suggestion about the chief of staff position. Contrary to the stereotyped, simplistic image that the media tried to hang on Jimmy as a dumb southerner, he is a highly intelligent, even brilliant, person and, like so many people of great intellect, he is also extremely complex. As a matter of preference in that complex makeup, he operates on the basis that those close to him will have partial knowledge—but only partial—of his plans and objectives. Only he and Rosalynn will know the whole picture in any particular situation.

It followed, then, that he wanted to be his own chief of staff. I talked to Jimmy and Charlie Kirbo at great length about the subject, because I felt strongly that not appointing a chief of staff would be a major mistake. Kirbo was Jimmy's chief of staff in Georgia, but that was another case where there was no similarity between our situation in Atlanta and the new one facing us in Washington. Kirbo's position in Georgia involved relations with the general assembly and raising funds. There was no management function. At the White House, however, the position of chief of staff involves exactly what the title implies: managing the White House staff, determining the order of priorities for items to be brought to the President's attention, and serving as his spokesman at the policy level beyond what the press secretary is able to say.

There is another key advantage to having a chief of staff position and the right person in it. If a President selects someone with whom he has a strong personal relationship, he is much better served than he would be without such a right-hand man or woman. He will have something every President needs—someone who is willing to tell him he's crazy when he is on the verge of a full-blown political mistake and who can survive giving such candid advice.

Certainly chiefs of staff who served other Presidents were that blunt. Carter did not give himself this strong and valuable resource until midway through his presidency, when he reestablished the position and appointed Hamilton Jordan and later Jack Watson. Even then, Jimmy didn't get the full value out of the position that he could have. Hamilton, Jack, Jody Powell, and Stu Eizenstat, his ranking staff members, were all outstanding, highly capable professionals, but they were staff people—and their relationship with Carter was more a *staff* relationship than a personal one.

Kirbo had the strong personal relationship that would have benefited Jimmy enormously in the chief of staff slot. So did I. And Bob Strauss would have developed it immediately in that job. But Carter never had the benefit of that kind of a relationship with his White House chief of staff, and when I left Washington after only eight months of his presidency, he didn't have that kind of personal give-and-take with anyone in any job anywhere in his administration. It was a glaring deficiency that undercut his effectiveness every day.

Folks can say what they want to about John Sununu and his penchant for using government cars for personal trips to buy stamps in New York and for using government airplanes and military crews to fly to skiing vacations and to see his dentist, but my guess is that he is no shrinking violet when it comes to giving Bush his candid advice. In that sense, it is entirely possible that he is an effective White House chief of staff who serves his President well, something Carter did not have until it was too late.

That was a distinct resource shortage for Jimmy. He had only two close friends, Charlie Kirbo and me, who could advise him in total candor without fear of being fired, because we didn't care whether we were fired or not. And of the two of us, I was gone from Jimmy's administration after only eight months, and Charlie, who chose not to come to Washington with us, was never a part of it.

JIMMY TOLD ME he wanted a group of equals so there wouldn't be any appearance of one of them outranking the others. That's a noble ideal, but it simply doesn't work in the real world, and certainly not in the White House. There everything is based on perceptions—by the leadership on Capitol Hill, by the members of the President's cabinet, and by members of the news media. Folks view you on the basis of how close they think you are—or aren't—to the President.

With a chief of staff there is no doubt about who is closest to the President. All the other staff members can be considered equal, if that's what the President wants, and go on about their jobs without all those outside the White House wondering who has been invited to the family quarters on the second floor and who is getting the preferred seating on Air Force One.

When we started the new administration, Jimmy appointed Hamilton as counsel to the President, a significant position in which the counsel advises the President and carries out his programs and policies, but without the management responsibility associated with the chief of staff position.

As for me, I preferred the position of secretary of the treasury, but management and budget director suited me fine. I thought I could do more at Treasury to ensure the success of the President's economic policies, but if Jimmy thought I could be of more use to him at OMB, especially in view of his eagerness to reorganize the federal government, then I was ready to go to work, and I told him so.

In appointing me as director of management and budget, Jimmy was naming me to a position that 215 million Americans, including me, knew nothing about. Carter said he needed someone in a powerful position who could speak for him. He felt that with the authority of being OMB director too, I could talk to members of the Senate and House without being harangued. Jimmy knew that decisions from the director of OMB usually gave him the muscle needed to deal with resistance on Capitol Hill.

He also knew my attitude about the unique relationship between people and their money. I once told him, "As a young bank teller, I learned fast there are three things that folks are peculiar about: their family, their religion, and their money—and they're most peculiar about their money. So if you're going to get along with them and deal with them, you'd better understand just how peculiar they feel about protecting their money."

Some time between 1976 and 1980, that subject stopped receiving the attention it should have, and we all know what happened in 1980.

THE NUMEROUS similarities between our experiences in Atlanta and those in Washington came to the fore in what was almost a replay in Washington of the Jim Gillis situation in Atlanta. It was another case of our having our hands full with an official we proposed to replace, or at least bypass, who possessed considerable clout to use against us in fighting for his career and his advancement. Failure to recognize it in that light cost us dearly.

The episode began in a thoroughly commendable fashion, with Carter telling the administrator of the General Services Administration, Jack Eckerd, that we wanted him to remain in that position during the Carter administration. Eckerd had been appointed by President Ford and was an executive with a respected reputation, a Republican who once ran for the Senate from Florida and was a member of the Eckerd drug chain family. He was especially respected for having helped to depoliticize the GSA by replacing political appointees with competent career public servants.

Jimmy and I thought we were doing the right thing, but unknown to us, the White House staff had made a commitment to Tip O'Neill to appoint one of his best friends and neighbors to the top GSA job, a man named Robert Griffin, who was the number-three executive at GSA when we took office. When the Speaker of the House got word that Carter and I were going to keep Eckerd in the top job, he exploded, which is a vast understatement. Our problems were compounded by Eckerd's desire to keep his acting deputy, who, like Jack, was also a Ford appointee. Jimmy and I took the understandable view that a new administration ought to be able to appoint *somebody* to *something* at GSA.

The Speaker of the House got on the phone, although he didn't really need one, and let me know in his best Boston politics that if this new administration wanted any help at all from the Democratic leadership in the House of Representatives, we would find a way to appoint Griffin as head of GSA. O'Neill and I agreed to meet the next morning. In the meantime, Carter got on the phone to Griffin and asked him to come to the Oval Office that night. Griffin tried to decline, saying it really wasn't necessary for the President of the United States to meet with a government worker late at night over a promise about a job.

But Jimmy had a problem and he wanted to solve it. That's the way he is. Besides, he was concerned about promises being made that he couldn't keep.

Jimmy met Griffin in the Oval Office at 11:30 that night. He was especially anxious to clear up the problem before I had to face O'Neill the next morning. Griffin says today that he remains convinced Carter and I knew nothing about the promise to him from Carter's staff and that Jimmy was telling the truth when he told Griffin that night that he was unaware of the promise when he and I asked Eckerd to stay in his job.

What infuriated O'Neill—and that's also putting it mildly—is that a commitment had been made, and in the Tip O'Neill school of politics, folks who make promises are supposed to keep them. Jimmy and I agreed 100 percent, which was why we were as concerned about it as Tip was.

(This latest impression of us on the part of the Speaker was about as favorable as his first. At Carter's first 8 A.M. Tuesday breakfast for congressional leaders, the menu consisted of coffee, orange juice, and a roll. This was no surprise to me. It was consistent with those lunches in Carter's office in Atlanta, only better.

(O'Neill tells the story in his book written with William Novak, *Man of the House*. He didn't say anything on that first Tuesday morning, but when he noticed the same offerings the second week, he told Carter, "Mr. President, if you're going to get me out at eight in the morning, you're getting me out for breakfast. Hell, Nixon served us better than this."

(Tip explained that any meeting before nine included breakfast. After nine, rolls and coffee were acceptable. After that second week, all of us ate a whole lot better—eggs, toast, sausages and bacon, plus grits.)

Now we had this far more serious problem with him. We did what any new administration would do: we went back to Jack Eckerd and told him the facts of life. We needed Griffin in that job. Eckerd said he simply could not agree, so he resigned and Jimmy appointed Jay Solomon, a Chattanooga developer, as the head of GSA—and Robert Griffin as his deputy director. Later on, Griffin himself became director after Solomon resigned.

Eckerd voiced some complaints to the media about Carter trying to play politics with his agency, but the irony is that we were doing what Eckerd won respect for doing—promoting civil servants instead of political appointees. Griffin had been a federal employee for thirty-three years by that time and had worked for GSA since its establishment in 1949.

No new President needs that kind of battle while he's trying to get his administration off to a running start. This was strictly a political decision. Unlike the Jim Gillis situation, we didn't have to stick to our guns on this one. Jimmy hadn't promised the American people every day during his campaign that he was going to fire Robert Griffin. The American people had never even heard of this career bureaucrat.

We didn't need Robert Griffin, but we definitely needed Tip O'Neill. Our best course of action was simply to exercise some fast damage control—tell Griffin he could be GSA's deputy, and then repair our political fence with Tip O'Neill. As the point man in this drama, that's exactly what I did. The only other choice, and it was no choice at all, was to incur the permanent wrath of the Speaker of the House and watch everything we tried to do go up in smoke on the House side of Capitol Hill.

Tip called me and lectured me sternly on the facts of life in Washington. I took my lumps from him for my mistake, because he was right in everything he was saying about the realities involved. Then the two of us began working together to help the new President.

7

Winners and Losers

WITH MY APPOINTMENT, I got something besides the job of heading OMB. Jimmy assured me that as President he would continue to tell folks what he told them as governor: "Talk to Bert about that." That was important to me, because I thought I could help my friend in my additional role as his troubleshooter over the years almost as much as I could as head of OMB.

However, being regarded as the closest adviser to a new President can be a double-edged sword. It's quite flattering for the media to call you the "deputy President," which was what happened in my case. I was always accessible to the media and was always willing to take the time to visit the editorial boards of the *Washington Post*, the *New York Times*, and the *Wall Street Journal*, and I suppose they thought they were doing me a favor by linking me so closely to the President and hanging such nicknames around my neck. *Forbes* magazine called me the "assistant President" in its March 1977 issue, less than two months after Jimmy took office. The next month, *U.S. News & World Report* called me the sixth-most powerful person in the country and the most influential cabinet-level member of the administration.

As complimentary as those descriptions were, they also produced the unwanted effect of focusing the attention of cabinet members on Washington's most popular and unproductive, even destructive, pastime: Winners and Losers.

Washington is essentially a company town where banks, newspapers, consulting firms commonly referred to as "Beltway bandits," and other businesses depend on the dominant "company"—the federal government. In this case, the President is the head of the company, and the cabinet members are its senior executives. At times their performances are of secondary importance compared to their relationship to the head of the company. Winners and losers are chosen on that basis in Washington—and in the corporate world too.

Washington places a premium on being on the winning side. If you're not viewed as being on that side in a clear majority of the issues involving your jurisdiction, others will attach all manner of interpretations to your batting average and say that you're losing favor with the President. Maybe you are and maybe you aren't, but that's what they're going to say.

Even your pursuit of what you consider the common good might have to be put on hold briefly if you face a challenge from someone else in the administration. You may feel you must devote all the time necessary to defeating that challenge and retaining your standing as one of Washington's winners. The most honorable and dedicated public servants sometimes are forced to take time to fight these battles of perception, and the intramural backbiting and debate that result become terribly counterproductive to the achievement of any administration's goals.

Cabinet officers get up every morning wondering whether they are going to win or lose that day. Sometimes it doesn't make any difference what the common good is—it's whether they win or lose.

I was lucky. This was never a problem for me because most of the others in the new Carter administration considered me the closest person to Jimmy except Rosalynn. Perception has a way of becoming reality in Washington, so I didn't have to worry about playing the game of Washington Winners and Losers.

For the most part, the members of Jimmy's cabinet accepted the prevailing view that I was at the top of the administration's pecking order, whether I deserved the position or not. The director of OMB is not a member of the President's cabinet in the statutory sense, but the job is what's called a "cabinet-level" position, bringing the same standing and degree of authority as the cabinet members themselves have in their positions as secretaries of the federal departments. With only two exceptions, the senior executives in our administration—the cabinet, Hamilton, Jody, Zbigniew Brzezinski as head of the National Security Council, Admiral Stansfield Turner at CIA, Andy Young at the U.N., and I—worked together harmoniously and effectively in those first weeks and months.

One of those exceptions proved to be only temporary. The other lasted as long as I did. They involved Brzezinski and Mike Blumenthal.

Brzezinski and I can look back at the beginning of our relationship and laugh about it now. We got off to an uncomfortable start, and it began not in the Oval Office or the Cabinet Room or my office or his, but on the White House tennis courts.

The only thing I ever *really* wanted to do in Washington was play tennis on the White House courts. Jimmy loves the game, and so do I. We took to the courts as often as possible after spring arrived in Washington. We always played doubles—Jimmy and Hamilton against Brzezinski and me.

I used to tell Jimmy that I never really had any burning desire to move to Washington on a full-time basis. I told him, "My goal in life was to be able to come up here and play tennis with you once every ninety days so I could go back home and tell all my friends in Georgia that I had just been up to the White House and played tennis with the President of the United States."

Brzezinski is a fair tennis player, but he was intimidated by the President on the courts. Jimmy would catch him foot-faulting, and then Brzezinski would serve from five feet behind the line. It didn't improve our chances—it's hard to win when your partner is being moved around all the time by one of your opponents and psyched out in the process.

Within the administration, instead of being teammates it seemed as if we were becoming opponents, and that concerned me. That wasn't going to do anybody any good, especially the President. Our problem grew out of the unique closeness between Jimmy and me as best friends and our working relationship as peers.

There was a visible reminder of that relationship every Wednesday. I was one of only three people who had lunch with the President privately on a regular basis. (The others were Rosalynn and Vice President Mondale.) Jimmy and I lunched off TV trays in the Oval Office every Wednesday. For the record, those lunches were much better than those old dried-out sandwiches I was tortured with in Atlanta.

Those Wednesday lunches were an opportunity for me to give the President a rundown on developments involving the Congress, the cabinet, and anything else that was on our list of current concerns, and for Jimmy to give me my marching orders on the items at hand. But I paid a stiff price for the help I got from those lunch sessions: they set me up as an object of jealousy and back-stabbing from within the administration. It was great to be considered the President's right-hand man, but not at the expense of becoming a target from both within and without the administration.

It was my guess that Brzezinski was among those who resented my closeness to Carter and things like those weekly private lunches in the Oval Office. For that reason, I don't think it was a coincidence that we clashed in the early weeks of the administration. The bone of contention was my membership on the National Security Council, the President's policy-advising arm on security affairs, later made famous, or infamous, by Oliver North and John Poindexter.

Brzezinski felt that I didn't belong on the NSC. He said I knew nothing about global strategy, which I readily admitted. But I think his real reason was that he thought I had enough influence with Carter already, and he didn't need me on his Security Council making his life difficult by asking a lot of irritating questions about how much things were going to cost. The director of OMB is not a statutory member of the Security Council anyhow, so he wanted me out of there.

However, I had my own reasons for wanting to stay. It wasn't an accident that Jimmy had appointed me to the NSC, and the reason for my being there in the first place was the same reason that I should remain a member. It went back to something I had told him about the Security Council shortly after his inauguration.

We were discussing the areas where I could help him to control government spending. There's another irony. The press and the public always made Ronald Reagan out to be the champion of fiscal conservatism, the hero wearing a white hat, Superman cape, and knight's shining armor all at the same time, who stood for all that was good and holy about controlling government spending. The *fact* is that Carter was cutting spending four years before Reagan took the oath of office. And another fact is that by the time Reagan left office, government spending was more out of control than ever before in American history. The deficit in the federal budget zoomed higher and higher under Ronald Reagan. He had eight years to do something about it, and the only thing he ever did was keep making it worse, and never mind his campaign promise to us to wipe out the deficit.

On the subject of the National Security Council, I told Jimmy, "I'm not an expert in matters of national security, and I probably won't ever fully understand what is talked about at NSC meetings. But I can tell you that every decision you allow the NSC to make ultimately becomes a budgetary decision, and at last count, according to any conversation I've ever had with the NSC, it's costing us money. There are no money-saving programs in the NSC. It's all costs."

Brzezinski devised a means of keeping me out of the NSC meetings, and it worked. He would call a "principals only" meeting on short notice, on an afternoon when I already had another meeting scheduled. He knew I couldn't send my deputy, Jim McIntyre, because he made it for principals only—no pinch hitters allowed. The national security adviser was achieving his objective: he was blocking the budget director out. As a result, he was also denying the President the participation of someone he wanted there—to be more blunt, he was thwarting the wishes of the President.

I'm not big on turf wars or competing for the boss's favor. But I thought this was one battle I had to fight—and win—for Jimmy, as well as for the usual reason, namely that nobody likes to lose a challenge, including me.

The next time I had occasion to speak to Brzezinski, without making a public confrontation of our disagreement, I told him, "I'm not a master strategist in global implications, as you are. But I've got sense enough to know you're trying to keep me out of the NSC by the way you're scheduling principals-only meetings. From now on, if I can't be there, Jim McIntyre's going to be there in my place, principals or no principals. You're talking about things that have an impact on the budget. And if you don't like it, I suggest you go talk to the President about it and see what he says. I'm telling you this is the way it's going to be."

There were no more conflicts between the NSC's meetings schedule and the budget director's calendar.

MIKE BLUMENTHAL was the other exception to my working in an atmosphere of peace and harmony. At least as far as I was concerned, Mike was a problem who wouldn't go away, for reasons best known to himself.

Mike's is a fascinating story: This is a man who should write a book of his own—a war orphan who fled Nazi Germany and raised himself on the streets of Shanghai, a Ph.D. in economics from Princeton, adviser to Presidents Kennedy and Johnson, chief executive officer of the Bendix Corporation before Carter's election, and later chairman of UNISYS and a partner in the investment banking firm of Lazard

Freres. Anyone with those accomplishments is worthy of our respect, and Mike has mine.

For all of his accomplishments and accolades, Mike was never secure in his relationship with President Carter, and he felt mine was too secure. It was another irony that rather than being a threat to Blumenthal, I tried to make Blumenthal's position in the administration even stronger.

Shortly after the election, I told Jimmy—and I even told Mike himself—that as treasury secretary, Blumenthal should be the chief economic spokesman for the administration. Charlie Schultze, the chief economic adviser, and I ended up fulfilling that role simply because Blumenthal spent so much time criticizing the President that he couldn't be an effective spokesman.

There is an obvious connection between the work of the director of OMB and the secretary of the treasury. Blumenthal was aware of the direct and straightforward dialogue and relationship I had with the President, and he didn't like it. In the game of Washington Winners and Losers, Blumenthal felt he was losing.

That, of course, wasn't my fault, or Carter's, or even Blumenthal's. It was just the way it was going to be, and everybody in Washington knew it, and everybody accepted it—except Mike.

I found out later that a source in his own department was leaking information to the media about financial investigations about me that had been conducted by the Ford administration, completed, and then closed because the Justice Department under Ford concluded that I had done nothing wrong in my work as president of the National Bank of Calhoun.

Different people told me where the leaks were coming from, and why, but when folks resort to leaks, it becomes difficult, if not impossible, to confirm the sources and then confront them. I had a pretty good idea of who one or two of them might be, and various people in positions to know agreed with me, but I was never able to face the sources and challenge them.

Someone leaking information to the press becomes a will-o'-the-wisp, impossible to pin down and identify. And because they can't be nailed, they remain unaccountable. They can just keep on leaking their information and whether it's right or wrong doesn't make any difference. They remain nameless and faceless to the public, so they don't have to worry about accountability—and they know at the same time that they'll always be able to find someone in the media to use their information, or misinformation.

The leaks worked. *Time* magazine published a story in May saying I was in trouble because of loans I had authorized while heading the National Bank of Georgia in Atlanta, a position I moved to after running for governor, which the bank was now calling due. I responded to questions from the media by telling them that they were not my loans at all; they were made before I joined the bank. Then questions surfaced about other loans I made to family and friends while at NBG and at the Calhoun bank before that.

The "Lance affair," to use the media's own term for its own invention, flared up into a full-blown controversy, and it wasn't long before the media corps were calling it "Cartergate." I thought those folks could have come up with something more creative than that.

What followed was as unproductive as it was undeserved. But it was far more than that. From the standpoint of the national interest, the controversy damaged the new President immediately and reduced his effectiveness and when that happens the nation is damaged. And for no legitimate reason in this case.

It wasn't what the American people sent us to Washington to do. Jimmy's whole approach to the voters during his campaign was that he was going to Washington to do good things, to streamline the federal government and make it more responsive to the states and their citizens, to lower the rate of inflation and strengthen our economy—to do all of these things, and more, as an outsider, someone not beholden to the Washington establishment, its ways and its special interests.

Instead, he was being burdened and blindsided by what the folks in the media, with help from inside the government, were trying to manufacture into a "scandal" where none existed. No new President needs that kind of an obstacle thrown into his path as he tries to get a firm grip on the ship of state.

From the personal standpoint, the episode subjected a man, his wife, his four sons, and his mother and father to three years of torment and legal bills amounting to a million and a half dollars—all of which resulted in the conclusion that I was innocent. Of course I was innocent. How can you be guilty when you haven't done anything wrong?

I never ducked anything in my life, including that awful time for us. And I won't duck it here. I'm willing to devote a whole chapter to it in this book, not only to give my side of that miserable story but to do all I can to sound some loud alarms about grave dangers facing the internal security of this nation that were evident in my experience and in the experiences of too many others since.

• • •

IN THE YEARS that have passed, I have wondered if any of that nonsense would have happened if Jimmy had decided to have a chief of staff and named Charlie Kirbo, Bob Strauss, or me to the position. If, in the irony of hindsight that always fascinates me, Jimmy had named me chief of staff, I wouldn't have been a threat to Blumenthal or anyone else. I would have been the fellow who got along with everyone, and Blumenthal and Brzezinski could have saved their energy for the productive part of their jobs instead of worrying about me.

One thing I was aware of at the time was that Hamilton would have been a lot better off serving as Jimmy's master political strategist rather than working on congressional relations. His real talent lies not in liaison but in campaign politics and organization. Hamilton didn't want to deal with Congress any more than he wanted to deal with the Georgia General Assembly.

Compared to state legislatures, the United States Congress is the major leagues. To be effective on Capitol Hill, you need a bedrock willingness to work at it. Members of the Senate and House are tough customers for the uninitiated or the unwilling. Hamilton didn't really have the enthusiasm for that kind of work, but I did. I served Jimmy in that additional capacity in Atlanta as well as in Washington. And if Jimmy had decided to name a chief of staff and put me in that slot, I would have had a whole lot more time to help him on the Hill than I did while serving as director of OMB.

The weakness with Congress hurt Jimmy badly, right from the start and through all four years of his presidency. He never did have good relations on the Hill, and when that happens a President's program sooner or later will become dead in the water.

I wasn't just talking about the congressional leadership. I meant some of the other folks up there too, the ones whose names the public doesn't even know. I reminded Carter that there are 535 members in the Senate and House, and the leaders aren't the only ones who have a vote. The representatives of districts with small populations in parts of Iowa and Oregon—and Georgia—have the same number of votes as the Speaker of the House, the Senate majority leader, and the chairmen of the committees. Everybody has one vote.

One thing I learned in Georgia was to pay attention to the unknown legislators. I kept in touch with the unknowns in Georgia, and I did the same thing in Washington. I always felt strongly that the inconspicuous members of Congress have the potential to play a role in the outcome of a House or Senate vote, and I was afraid that the Carter administration simply didn't pay enough attention to them.

But Carter knew that I was willing to take on congressional relations as an additional duty. And intelligent executive that he always was, he knew that as director of the Office of Management and Budget I would be seen in a different light by the members of the Senate and House than a White House chief of staff or a director of congressional relations would have been. Jimmy was smart enough to know that the folks on the Hill would be aware in our conversations that I had the authority to put things into effect. The director of OMB controls the budget, so he can decide which programs to strengthen and which to cut, which departments to expand and which to reduce, and what the first targets of reorganization should be. With my budgetary authority, people on the Hill would want to get along with me for those very pragmatic, real-world reasons, in the same way that I would want to get along with them.

That was a part of Carter's logic, and he was right. But the truth of the matter is that Jimmy flat-out didn't want to work with Congress, for the same reason that he didn't want to work with the legislature in Georgia.

When we were in Atlanta, Jimmy wanted to be governor and spend his time on the problems and concerns that the governor should be dealing with, leaving somebody else to fool with the general assembly. In Washington, he had the same attitude. He didn't want to deal with the Congress.

It wasn't that Jimmy didn't like the members or the institution or that he thought he was any better than they were. His reasoning was that he was the President, and they were members of Congress, and he had staff people who could deal with them.

After Jimmy left the White House, the prime minister of Japan expressed a desire to meet with him in Plains on his trip to the United States, so the consulate general asked me to host a luncheon at the French restaurant there. (Yes, there used to be a French restaurant in Plains. It's gone now, but it was in an old abandoned chicken house—make of that what you will.) During the luncheon, Carter's assistant at that time, Dan Lee, whispered something into his ear, and Jimmy left the room briefly. When he returned he said to us, "Gillis Long is a fine congressman from Louisiana and the chairman of the House Democratic Caucus. He has just had open heart surgery, and I had placed a call to him to wish him a speedy recovery."

Everyone in the restaurant understood and felt that it was a compassionate thing to do for this congressional leader. But when we were getting ready to leave, I said to Jimmy, "Mr. President, I have just one comment about your call to Gillis Long."

"What's that, Bert?"

"It would have been a damn sight better if you had bothered to call him while you were still President."

As soon as Carter was elected President and I began my work as director of the Office of Management and Budget across the street from the White House, Jimmy told me to schedule seventy-five hours of his time for work on the first supplemental budget of his administration, following the submission to Congress of President Ford's final budget.

The request itself gives you an insight into how precisely organized Jimmy always is. He didn't tell me to set aside just *some* time for that project, or to allow maybe a couple of weeks. He told me exactly what he wanted: seventy-five hours.

During that period of meetings, we would sit there in the Cabinet Room of the White House with members of his cabinet and go over their immediate budget needs. It was clear to all the people in the room at every one of those meetings that Jimmy had studied thoroughly beforehand and, in fact, knew more about what they needed than they did.

We had one such session with Jimmy's secretary of defense, Harold Brown, and the Joint Chiefs of Staff, whose chairman was General George Brown. The two Browns weren't related, but they did have one thing in common: both of them were highly intelligent men and well informed on the matters at hand.

I found General Brown especially impressive. He was extremely knowledgeable and tough besides, one of the toughest fellows I ever ran in to in my life. He wore those four stars with authority, and it was clear that he had earned them the old-fashioned way.

Well, those folks started throwing around a lot of talk about force weapons, strategic weapons, tactical weapons, fire power, submarines, airplanes, and I don't know what else. You never heard such a conversation in all your life. I was sitting there as the President's management and budget director, and I don't mind confessing to you that I didn't have the foggiest idea of what they were talking about.

But I had no reason to know, so I wasn't concerned. I knew I didn't have to be an expert on weaponry and tactical and strategic matters. That's what we had these men for—but Carter was a different story.

The man is a graduate of the Naval Academy, a former officer on a Navy ship, and was a member of Admiral Rickover's staff as a nuclear engineer, so he had some background on these complex subjects. But those experiences alone didn't give him the most knowledge of anybody in that room. He got that by reading everything given to him before that meeting—and I mean *everything*—absorbing it, and learning it cold.

He knew more about what we were talking about that day than either of the Browns, and if it showed, that was all right with him.

After several meetings like that with officials from the various departments of the federal government, with Carter dazzling everyone with his displays of knowledge about the budget of each department, I told him I needed to tell him something that he might not like. He encouraged me to speak up, as he always did, so I said, "You don't have to prove to anybody that you're the smartest man in the room. You're the President of the United States. For what that's worth, it implies that you have some attributes that the rest of us don't have."

His displays of knowledge weren't just unnecessary, they were counterproductive. I told him, "Because you're showing how smart you are, you're losing the input of people who do know what's going on in government and understand. They can help you, but they're intimidated. They won't tell you what they might, because they don't want to be embarrassed by your knowing more about things than they do."

We saw a distinct change in him after that. Before, he was not getting the benefits that he could from the people around him because of that intimidation. After, he was getting the kind of candid comments and suggestions that every executive needs if he is going to perform effectively in his job and make the right decisions.

Give him credit. Too many people can't take that kind of blunt advice and react in a constructive manner, but Jimmy can and did. The change enabled him to be a better executive, and a better President.

8

They Were the Best of Decisions and the Worst of Decisions

JIMMY MADE two key decisions in the first months of his administration that were among his best and worst in his four years as President. One was an enormous help as he led this country through a genuine crisis. The other was absolutely the worst political mistake he made, and its effects lasted the rest of his term and doomed any hopes we ever had of developing a good, effective working relationship with the Congress.

The first decision was his bold action to face the energy crisis and do something about it. The second was his decision to cancel nineteen water construction and improvement projects that were the pets of some of the most important members of Congress.

Americans had already gone through one "energy crisis," in 1973, when the OPEC nations slapped an embargo on the sale of oil to other nations so they could force the price up. But a secret report to the President from the CIA in April of 1977 was alarming to all of us who knew about it. The CIA made it dramatically clear that if we didn't do something—fast—long gas lines were going to be the least of our problems. The report warned that the energy outlook for the United States and the rest of the world was poor. The CIA predicted that unless energy conservation was "greatly increased," the entire world would be caught in a severe energy crisis by 1985.

A second report, released a month later by a group of international experts assembled by the Massachusetts Institute of Technology, took the CIA report a frightening step further. The MIT report predicted international economic havoc and possibly even war as early as 1981 and certainly by the year 2000, unless extraordinary efforts were taken to conserve energy and shift from oil to more plentiful energy supplies. It warned that the efforts should be made "with wartime urgency."

Carter declared a "moral equivalent of war" and quickly established a national energy policy and a new Department of Energy. The media had a lot of fun with Carter's declaration, taking the first letter from each word in "moral equivalent of war" and dubbing it "the MEOW issue," but others, including the energy experts, failed to see the humor. There is no question in my mind today, fourteen years and one Mideast war later, that President Carter averted a worldwide crisis and that we are still receiving the benefits of his actions in that crisis.

That whole energy issue wasn't something that we just dreamed up. When you have folks like the CIA and MIT telling you we might have a real shooting war over a particular problem, you'd better listen and then do something fast.

Jimmy was a real President in that crisis, regardless of how hilarious the media thought it was. We didn't have war over energy in 1981, and we didn't have a severe international crisis by 1985. We have Jimmy Carter and his swift, decisive presidential actions in 1977 to thank for what we missed.

Again, irony is inescapable here. In the last half of his presidency and throughout his 1980 campaign against Ronald Reagan, Jimmy was accused of "incompetence" and "vacillation." We heard the words used against him every day during his last two years in office. Yet there never was anything incompetent or vacillating about Jimmy Carter.

His energy decisions were proof. He understood the energy situation better than the leadership on Capitol Hill, and certainly better than the folks in the media who had such a good time ridiculing him on the subject.

He was creative and decisive in the actions he took and in those he wanted the Congress and the states to take. History shows he knew what he was talking about on the energy crisis. He wasn't the first President to call for bold actions because of a national energy problem, but he was the only one who got laughed at for it. The double standard that hurt Jimmy throughout his years in Washington victimized him on the energy issue just as it did on so many others.

During the 1973 shortage, we were urged to turn off our Christmas lights, and President Nixon left Air Force One in its hangar at

Andrews Air Force Base and flew to California for his Christmas vacation on a regular commercial flight—while the Secret Service got ulcers. Nobody laughed at him, and nobody called him incompetent.

And when we went to war in the Persian Gulf in January of 1991, the cry of "incompetence" was not heard in the land.

There wasn't any incompetence or vacillation involved in having the imagination and decisiveness to create the federal executive service, the new system to attract more top-flight executives to government service by providing more compensation and better opportunities for advancement. Or in deregulating the airlines to create stiffer competition and thus lower air fares for the people of the United States. Or in holding the budget deficit to one-tenth of what Reagan allowed to happen. Yet Reagan left office being called a great leader and Jimmy left being called incompetent and a vacillator.

Item: Eight years after Jimmy Carter was turned out of office because of his alleged incompetence, the Democratic nominee made a call for competence the theme of his campaign. He lost, too.

Item: When Jimmy left the governorship of Georgia, one thing he wasn't called was a vacillator. He was criticized for being just the opposite—too strong-willed, bullheaded, even too decisive. Folks said (and they were right) that once he made up his mind to do something after hearing all sides, he went ahead and did it and stuck to his decision. That's not my definition of a vacillator, and I don't think it's anybody else's either.

The truth is that Jimmy Carter was to a great extent the victim of the Washington image mill. He didn't look as handsome and charismatic on television as Ronald Reagan did, his gag writers weren't as good, and he was never accepted by the Washington establishment. There were other reasons for his defeat in 1980, some of which were his own fault, but his poor TV image, Reagan's clever little one-liners on complicated issues, and Carter's rejection by the homesteaders in Washington contributed as much to his departure from the White House as anything else.

As disturbing as this emphasis on style may be, it is the reality in American presidential politics as we approach the next century. The American people will frequently elect the candidate who looks better on TV, even though good looks don't have a thing to do with ability, and the one who rips off cute little sayings like "Go ahead—make my day" or "Read my lips—no new taxes." That kind of oratory will never be chipped into stone on any shrine of white marble, and maybe the people who say them won't either, but in this day of sound-bite TV and bumper-sticker oratory, it gets you elected President.

THE SHEER SPEED with which the Carter administration moved ahead simultaneously with the many complex programs on energy and other issues in January 1977 was due to Jimmy's acute intellect. He is probably the most intelligent chief executive the country has ever had. Jimmy is a gifted serial, multisubject thinker, able to discuss in minute detail any one of his complex programs and to shift fluidly to another without hesitation.

Most of us in his cabinet couldn't do that. To compensate, we redoubled our efforts—and work hours—just to stay in the wake of his operational speed.

But all the intellect in the world doesn't always prevent us from making big mistakes, and Jimmy came up with a real beaut on the water bill. That blunder occurred in our first days, as we went over the last Ford budget, which recommended the construction of 320 local water improvements around the country.

We were reviewing the budget in January and February, so we could advise the congressional leaders of any changes we might want to make in the list. Jimmy considered most of the recommendations to be just so much pork barrel politics—the time-honored congressional practice of appropriating funds for projects that will win points for members of Congress with their voters back home.

To the President, this was a case of a campaign promise that needed to be kept. To me, it was a case of a campaign promise that could have been kept later—in a second term. Jimmy promised to cut out pork-barrel spending, and he aimed to do it right then.

The Carter transition team identified sixty of the proposals as possibilities for elimination and sent the list to me and to the Council on Environmental Quality. The OMB and CEQ cut that list to thirty-five, and I took the short list across the street to the White House for action by Carter, Cecil Andrus at Interior and Clifford Alexander, the secretary of the Army, since the projects would be carried out by the Army Corps of Engineers. Any revisions to the Ford budget were due on Capitol Hill five days later.

The White House group narrowed the list for the final time to nineteen projects to be eliminated, at a savings to the taxpayers of $5.1 billion. Carter dropped the first shoe with a letter to Congress warning that his administration was going to submit a list the next day of nineteen water projects to be eliminated, which quickly became known on Capitol Hill as the "hit list."

The uproar on the Hill the next day, when our specific list arrived, could be heard all the way down Pennsylvania Avenue to the White House. It meant more than just that we were in real trouble in getting our list reduced to nineteen. The "honeymoon" period marking the willingness of Congress to give a new administration time to get off on the right foot normally lasts at least ninety days, and sometimes a lot longer. The violent reaction on Capitol Hill to the cuts in the list of water projects meant the Carter honeymoon was over. It was only February.

Senator Robert Byrd, the senior Democrat in the Senate as the majority leader, warned, "The road can be smooth or the road can be rough." Russell Long, of Louisiana, chairman of the Senate Finance Committee and also from our own party, told *Time* magazine that Carter was "going to find himself at war with his own best soldiers."

Senator Ed Muskie of Maine, one of the most respected Democrats in the nation, vowed a showdown and a defeat for Jimmy. He said, "No president should have the right to frustrate a policy that has been made a part of a law of this land . . ." Muskie promised to "fight fire with fire . . . I am going to look for anything I can fire back with—anything . . ."

Carter had created a real hornets' nest, and unfortunately for the nation it set the tone for the Carter presidency. It provided official Washington and careful political observers an unvarnished glimpse of this new populist President's let-the-chips-fall-where-they-may approach to the issues he promised voters to resolve.

Out of that crisis emerged at least one act of bravery. Jimmy's secretary of the interior, Cecil Andrus, told us straight up, "I'll take full responsibility for the water projects. This is in my area. I'm the Governor who has been a believer in them out in the western part of the country, and I'll deal with this problem. I'll take the heat."

He did, too. It was an act of genuine courage on Cecil's part, one that no one ever heard about and for which he never received credit. Very few folks would have done it.

At this point in the first weeks of his administration, Jimmy may have been scoring points with the electorate, but he was ruining his chances on Capitol Hill. Pleasing the voters is always commendable and even smart politics, but at that time Jimmy didn't have to go before them for another four years. He had to go before the Congress every day.

•   •   •

IN THE MIDST of that chaotic flurry of activity, as we tried to do so many things at once, we also took on an issue of critical importance to the nation, one that the Ford administration chose to cop out on. That was the question of saving New York City.

New York happens to be the most important city in the United States, whether some folks like that town or not. It is the commercial center of this nation, and in 1976 and early 1977 it faced the real possibility of bankruptcy. To me it was unthinkable that the keystone of our commercial, industrial, and financial structure was in such a situation, with all the frightening implications which it held for the entire nation.

The city's financial crisis was full-blown by the time we came to Washington in January 1977. It had been building since 1960, when the city's expenses began to outstrip its income. In the face of that problem, the same kind facing New York again today, the city's administrations continued to borrow money, masking New York's financial problems through accounting gimmickry. That practice was coupled with a policy of continuing to increase public services, which were already the most extensive and expensive in the nation. The combination further imperiled the city's already dark financial future.

People began moving out of America's cities by the millions in the 1960s, leaving minorities, the aged, and the disadvantaged behind to pay the bills that kept our cities going. But those folks pay lower taxes, or none at all, while also requiring more city services in programs for the poor and the elderly.

New York's financial house of cards collapsed during the 1974–1975 recession, when the city's sales taxes took a pounding. Investor confidence dropped, and the city was left holding its hat in its hand. When its future looked bleakest, the city asked the Ford administration for help, but Ford and his advisers said no. That prompted the New York *Daily News* to tell its readers in one of the classic page one headlines of all time:

FORD TO CITY: DROP DEAD

At that point, with its future dark, and with the threat that such a future posed for the rest of the nation at its worst, New York City got what it needed in Washington just in the nick of time—a change of administrations, accompanied by a change of heart.

Jimmy invited the governor, Hugh Carey, and the mayor, Abraham Beame, to a meeting at Musgrove Plantation the day after Christmas to meet with him, Mondale, Charles Schultze, the chairman of the President's Council of Economic Advisers, and me. We would not take office for almost another month, but we were much more concerned about New York City than the Ford people were, and we didn't want to wait until January 20 to start doing something about it.

We had a lengthy and specific discussion of the reasons for the city's money problems, but they weren't the issue at that point. The issue was what could be done. I expressed the view that it was absurd for us to be working as hard as we were on a program of economic recovery for the entire nation and at the same time ignoring our most important city when it faced bankruptcy. All of us were worried that the collapse of New York City would disrupt the entire national economy, and we simply could not allow that to happen.

Because there was unanimity on that point, our discussion advanced quickly to a decision by Carter to take federal action to save New York City. This was another irony, with the Republicans, always considered the champions of big business, thumbing their noses at New York, the very center and symbol of American business, and the Democrats coming to the city's rescue.

The result of our concern and our hard work was a bill proposed by President Carter and passed by Congress that authorized long-term bond guarantees for New York. It was the first time that such guarantees for an American city were ever authorized by Congress. Thanks to the President's swift and decisive action, New York avoided bankruptcy—another example of Jimmy's ability to size up a situation fast and then exercise the leadership necessary to solve the problem.

Jimmy was even able to get his bill approved over the opposition of the chairman of the all-important Senate Banking Committee, Senator William Proxmire of Wisconsin. Proxmire got a lot of publicity for himself with his cute little "Golden Fleece Awards" that supposedly exposed unnecessary government spending. But when it came to a problem of substance, with severe economic implications for the entire nation, he was found wanting. He could stage his clever publicity stunts before the TV cameras, but he couldn't understand the importance of helping New York City. It was an embarrassing defeat for him, and well deserved.

THE ISSUE of a President's willingness to make decisions, or to change his mind, and his freedom to do so without incurring the public's wrath, flared up in Carter's first week as President. The occasion was Carter's commitment to a tax rebate of fifty dollars for every taxpayer in the country.

Jimmy made that proposal as a part of the economic stimulus package he was preparing for submission to Congress shortly after his inauguration. Through a careful analysis of the state of the economy at that point, we reached the conclusion that things were on the sluggish side as the Ford administration was leaving office, and some priming of the pump was necessary to revitalize the economy. Carter and his economic advisers, including me, put together a range of proposals to accomplish this, including a tax rebate of fifty dollars for every wage earner to stimulate the economy quickly.

After we first told reporters of the idea in general terms in Plains on January 6, I announced the details of the proposal to the news media on January 25. Dr. Arthur Burns, the chairman of the Federal Reserve Board, wasn't a big supporter of the rebate itself because, he said, "I feel the economy is improving on its own." But he praised the overall set of proposals, saying Jimmy had "put together a fiscal package smaller and more prudent than many had urged upon him."

Carter favored the rebate from the previous year's income taxes because a tax cut is the one sure way to stimulate an economy. Give the people a check from the government, and the economy will bounce back strongly. There's no question about that cause-and-effect relationship.

However, as so often happens, the anticipation of a tax rebate was enough to stimulate the economy by itself. It became a self-fulfilling prophecy by the time the proposal was approved by the House. To have pushed through a rebate then would have been downright irresponsible on his part, and a gigantic waste of federal revenues. So we withdrew the proposal from the stimulus package in the Senate, because now it wasn't necessary and would have been even counterproductive.

When reporters asked me about the decision, I explained my philosophy in that kind of situation: "If it ain't broke, don't fix it." It made for a nice quote because the reporters liked it, but the decision to drop plans for a tax rebate still came in for criticism before the issue finally died a natural death.

That episode, occurring so early in Jimmy's term, caused him damage because of two criticisms that were heard about him after that. People began to say he was a vacillator, unable to stick with a decision or even to make one. And they said a President shouldn't change his mind on something he's already decided. That was another irony, because as governor Carter had been criticized for being stubborn and unwilling to change his mind.

On the decision not to recommend a tax rebate to Congress, there was no vacillation at all. On the contrary, Jimmy saw the situation accurately and made a quick, bold decision not to go for it. He was also smart enough to know when he made that decision that he was going to catch a certain amount of criticism for it, but he had the courage to make it anyhow because he knew it was the right one for the nation.

I come from the school of thought that believes it is wrong to criticize a President for changing his mind. As conditions change, so must policies and the decisions governing those policies. It was wrong to criticize Carter for an occasional change of mind, just as it was wrong to criticize Reagan for opening up friendly relations with the Soviet Union after calling it "an evil empire" throughout his political career, for pulling the Marines out of Lebanon after telling the American people that the Marines' presence there was critical, and for dozens of other times when Reagan changed his mind.

In such times, Reagan was painted as a bold decision maker, but in the same circumstances, Carter was harshly and sarcastically accused of "flip-flopping."

I am one American who wants a President who is willing to make a decision on the basis of the present situation, not on the basis of what he promised or predicted six months ago. If the conditions today require him to change his mind, then so be it. It's that kind of a job. Any corporate executive runs his company in exactly the same way, or he won't be a corporate executive very long and his company won't survive and prosper.

Those yo-yos who say "He changed his position" simply do not understand the presidency. It's a job that changes day to day, hour to hour, minute to minute. To criticize a President because he does something that's different from his position two years ago just isn't reality. The truth is that you might have to change your position from only two minutes ago. You just can't make a decision as President and then turn out the lights and tell your staff, "Don't bring that one back to me."

Lyndon Johnson might have given the best description of that lonely job where there's no peer to talk to before making your final decision. He said, "The hardest thing for a president isn't to *do* what is right but to *know* what is right."

THE DECISION TO try to rescue the hostages from Iran by helicopter was another example of this. I had left the administration by that time, but

I know that Jimmy got advice from all sides, some for and some against the idea of staging the rescue operation. It is well known by now that Cyrus Vance, the secretary of state, opposed the idea, and that Zbigniew Brzezinski favored it. Others, the military chiefs of staff and Hamilton Jordan and Carter's other advisers, lined up on both sides of the question.

Carter didn't vacillate on that decision, either. He heard out both sides and then gave the word to go. When he made that decision, the others had to understand, and I'm sure they did, that they knew only their part of the background leading to the decision. They didn't know the whole picture. Only the President ever knows that.

Sometimes you get the feeling that the President isn't listening to your argument or taking your advice. I felt that way from time to time, too, but you won't find me criticizing presidential decisions of state. You can question their wisdom in hindsight, but not the way they are made. When a President tells an adviser, "You don't know all that I know," as Jimmy used to tell us, he's stating a fact.

It's a different ball game when it comes to political decisions. Deciding to cancel all those water projects was a political decision. Decisions like that involve instinct more than knowledge, a feel for how the public or the Congress will react. They aren't based on factual information or data in a computer printout. In cases like that, you might even know more than the President. But when it comes to affairs of state, the President is the only one who has all the information leading to the final decision.

Jimmy never had any problems with being the one who had to make the call. It's ironic that he was considered a vacillator, because the truth is that Jimmy Carter was a lot like one of our most decisive presidents, Harry Truman. He even had a replica on his desk in the Oval Office of the sign that was on Truman's desk, the one that said, "The buck stops here."

That was Jimmy's attitude, too, and he was completely at ease with it. He always encourages discussion before he makes a decision and will hear you out and will listen to every word you tell him. But once he makes his decision, he is entirely comfortable with it, and he doesn't tolerate any further discussion from you.

The resemblance between Carter and Truman extended to the subject of changing decisions, too. Truman said that one of the most important parts of the presidency was your willingness to make decisions. He said that if you made a decision that turned out to be wrong at the time or in the light of later events, then you should make another decision to correct it. As Truman used to say, "It's that simple."

It was that simple with Carter, too. Regardless of the sniping he suffered from his critics or what the media said, Carter was always a swift and firm decision maker like Truman, and like Truman, he was always willing to change his mind if that seemed to be the best course of action.

His reversal on the question of a tax rebate was one example. Another occurred during his campaign to convince Americans to start saving energy.

Just as he did in Georgia, he wanted to set the example, so he ordered all the lights on those beautiful shrines and monuments in Washington turned off to save energy. I thought that was a silly idea which would have only one effect—to deprive Americans of seeing the beauty and meaning of those landmarks at night and experiencing the pride and inspiration that all of us feel at the sight of them.

LaBelle and I used to enjoy walking around the monuments in the evening after a day's work, to enjoy Washington's history and beauty. Along the way, we would talk to the other folks who were doing the same thing. It was a frequent after-dinner treat for us. We'd ride over to the Capitol building and admire the paintings and the ceiling of the Rotunda and all the statues. We'd be alone except for the guards, and they were special moments for us as proud Americans.

On one of the first nights after Jimmy ordered the lights turned off, we were visiting the Jefferson Memorial. It was one of the most depressing sights you can imagine. Here was this beautiful white shrine and the towering statue of the man who wrote the Declaration of Independence—and Americans had trouble seeing it.

The ones who were there that night weren't shy about letting each other know what they thought of Carter's energy-saving measure. They grumbled about the dark and said they'd paid their taxes and they ought to be able to see these shrines—day or night. They were right.

I told LaBelle I was going to talk to the President about it the next morning. We both knew how strongly Jimmy felt about the energy problem, and we admired his leadership, especially in the face of the ridicule he was getting, but this was a bad decision, one that he should reverse. It wasn't really any of my business, except that any time I thought Carter made a wrong political decision, I made it my business. I told LaBelle that night, "I'm going to stick my neck out in the morning and tell Jimmy what I think."

The next morning I brought up the subject. We were in his

private study just off the Oval Office, where he liked to work in solitude before and after the business day.

He always played classical music in the background, only it wasn't background music at all. He played that stuff so loud you had to speak up to be heard and concentrate on your thoughts to avoid being distracted. I'm no devotee of classical music anyhow, so to me it seemed even louder than it was for others.

"Mr. President," I began, "I have a problem to mention to you this morning. We have made a serious mistake in turning the lights off at the monuments. Those shrines are a source of great pride to the American people, and I have to remind you honestly that it was my impression you came to Washington to turn the lights on. But one of your first acts is to turn them off. You ought to turn them back on—now."

Without a moment's hesitation, he gave me his response, and he used only two words: "Do it."

When I got back to my office in the old Executive Office Building on the White House grounds across the driveway from the White House itself, I called the secretary of the interior, Cecil Andrus. I was happy to say to him, "Mr. Secretary, I just had a meeting with the President, and I'm delighted to tell you one thing: Turn on the lights."

His response was just as short as Carter's, only two words: "Thank God."

Carter, to his credit and consistent with his method of management, was willing to face a bad decision and make another one to reverse it. Harry Truman would have liked that.

BESIDES BEING CRITICIZED unfairly as a vacillator, Jimmy came in for more than his share of criticism for his style, especially when the telegenic Ronald Reagan succeeded him and established his personality in front of the voters every night in their living rooms. Instead of the complicated, thorough President who had just left office, Americans were seeing a new one who looked good on TV, dealt with their problems in simple—many would say simplistic—terms, and reduced his oratory to one-liners.

After four years of Carter and eight years of Reagan, many Americans have formed new opinions of both men. Maybe Reagan would beat Carter in an election every time they met, but many folks out there are reevaluating their ratings of the two and coming to the conclusion that the box score shows four years of substance over style in the Carter administration and eight years of style over substance under Reagan.

Jimmy came in for heavy criticism from people who said he allowed himself to get bogged down in detail to such a degree that he was not able to function effectively as an executive, that he had no time left for making the big decisions. The criticism that he spent too much time on detail is valid, but the view that this prevented him from making big decisions and running an efficient administration is not. He had the capacity to do both.

Carter's attention to detail was even more pronounced than his critics knew. He definitely was the type who crossed every *t* and dotted every *i* and made sure you did, too. That is another reflection of the Carter discipline in everything he does. He is always willing to get involved in the nuts-and-bolts work so he can know everything humanly possible about the subject at hand; it's a price he has always been willing to pay for acquiring his immense store of knowledge. But this willingness did not serve him well when he became President.

He intimidated you with his comprehensive knowledge, as much in written reports and documents as in meetings where he made it clear that he knew more than anyone else in the room. If you sent him a memo with spelling or punctuation mistakes, he'd send it back to you with the mistakes marked, just like a schoolteacher correcting a student's homework. That's just the way he does things—as a serious, self-disciplined individual with an unlimited capacity for detail.

I was among the lucky ones. I never got those notations in the margin in the memos I sent to Jimmy. I'm lucky enough to be a good speller—but if I weren't, I'd have made sure to become one in a hurry. I suspect a few of my colleagues took a crash course in the subject.

Jimmy accomplished something positive with that habit. He let you know that when you sent him a memo, he read it. Members of his cabinet knew before their meetings with him that if there were going to be any memos, reports, or other materials on the table, they'd better read them ahead of time—thoroughly—because Carter would have already done so.

As one who burned the midnight oil many a night, I can tell you that those habits of Jimmy's made his cabinet members better informed than they would have been.

THE QUESTION of whether to have a chief of staff and who could best run interference for the Carter programs on Capitol Hill was a point of continuing disagreement between Jimmy and me.

Shortly after he decided he wasn't going to have such a position, I told him again—and Hamilton, too—that he should take Hamilton out of the White House and put him in charge of planning the re-election campaign. I told Jimmy in no uncertain terms that if unemployment, inflation, and interest rates—the "misery index"—remained high in 1980, he could forget about being reelected. I said that anything else he might or might not do as President wouldn't matter to the voters if the misery index was high at the end of his term. Based on the way he governed in Georgia, I knew Jimmy had the ability to affect economic change for better or worse, and that would determine his reelectability.

Even after his inauguration I sounded the same warning, but still to no avail. I told the President that his administration had no economic planning program, that we didn't understand markets, and that his team was generally deficient in broad areas of economic understanding.

There were times when Jimmy simply refused my advice. This, unfortunately, was one of them. He didn't listen to me, and I don't know whether he listened to anybody else on that problem. Four years later, he paid a President's ultimate price for being wrong.

ANOTHER PROBLEM that hit Carter in the first days of his presidency and forced him to play catch-up ball for his entire four years in office was a simple case of taking on too much. We committed ourselves to do more than what was humanly possible, and we paid the price for our overzealousness.

We compounded this mistake by assigning deadlines to everything. It's one thing to commit yourself to doing something about the economy, but it's another to say you're going to do it by next Monday morning at nine o'clock. We managed to paint ourselves into that corner immediately.

Make the development of an economic policy one of your highest priorities, propose a tax bill right away, put together an emergency energy program for submission to Congress in April, make a proposal to Congress on the B-1 bomber, reorganize the federal government, reduce unemployment, accelerate environmental activities, and fill a couple of thousand policy positions—our plate wasn't just full; it was spilling over, and every item came with a deadline attached.

That's the engineer in Carter. He knows precisely what needs to be done, precisely how it needs to be done, and precisely when it needs to be done. So he puts a deadline on everything he does—and on everything you do. He's hidebound on the subject of deadlines, so I never wasted my time or his by trying to talk him out of that practice. What I did try to do was get him to postpone certain issues out of practical time considerations and for political reasons as well.

We didn't need to get into issues like the Panama Canal treaty in the first term. We could have been spending our time on other, more pressing problems, put the Canal question on the back burner for Jimmy's second term, and used the political capital to gain important first-term objectives.

Carter, however, has always been supremely confident of his ability to deal with a multitude of issues at the same time. That's fine, and he's right in feeling that he has that ability. But reality sets in when you remember that the Congress has an agenda, too. Jimmy was working on what was important to him, but he was unwilling to concede that Congress was going to work on what was important to Congress.

When the leadership from the Hill came over for Tuesday morning breakfasts, we'd have the Senate majority leader, Robert Byrd of West Virginia, plus Speaker O'Neill and the Democratic whip, Jim Wright of Texas, and other leaders sipping their coffee and hearing us throw a whole array of things at them. Frankly, I think it just became too much for everybody to absorb—except Carter.

We had so much to do that we didn't have enough time to keep people who were important to us well informed. We couldn't communicate with them the way we should have about what we were doing, what our objectives were and how they might be able to help us. This situation led to the later criticism that the Carter administration had no set agenda. We had a set agenda all right, but we had so many items on it, all of them marked URGENT, that it looked more like a smorgasbord than an agenda.

In his brilliance, Jimmy assumed that the rest of us, including the media, could keep pace with him and absorb everything he had in mind for his national agenda and his plans for making it all come together. In that respect, he did a poor job of communicating his program, and himself, to the American people through the news media.

I don't criticize the media for not being able to keep pace with Carter, for the same reason that I don't criticize the rest of us for it. But I *do* criticize them for not working harder to understand the man and his message.

America's political reporters and commentators spent the entire

1984 and 1988 campaigns complaining that Reagan and Bush never told the nation anything specific about what they had in mind for the next four years. But Carter told them in 1976, and he told them all through the early months of his presidency.

Carter was not "The Great Communicator" spoon-feeding Pablum to the American people and saying "It's morning in America" and "We're standing tall," whatever those things mean. The reporters covering Carter were either unwilling or unable to do what was necessary to learn about the new President and his ways. As a result, they couldn't keep up with his complex personality and intellect. They never knew the real Jimmy Carter, so they made one up. And having done so, they proceeded to destroy their own creation.

9

With Malice Toward One

UNFORTUNATELY, one of my most vivid memories of my days in Washington is also one of the most painful. It was the day I resigned, September 21, 1977.

The furnace of controversy that I had been living in—involving charges of irregular banking practices made against me by a few members of the media, a career bureaucrat, and a convicted felon who was in prison—had burned me up and burned me out. It was time to leave, and so I did. I told Jimmy I was going home to Calhoun.

When I returned that afternoon to the home LaBelle and I rented in the Georgetown section of Washington, I told her it was all over. I had submitted my letter of resignation, a decision she had fiercely opposed, and Jimmy had accepted it.

I went upstairs and flopped across the bed in physical and emotional exhaustion. But LaBelle didn't feel like collapsing at all. She felt just the opposite. She went straight to the nearest telephone and dialed the White House. When she got Jimmy in the Oval Office, she blurted out to the President of the United States, "I want to tell you one thing—you can go with the rest of the jackals, and I hope you're happy."

She wasn't through. She told me she wanted to go out front and say something to all those media folks waiting at the front door, which had become their home away from home for weeks on end. She asked me if I wanted to say something to them too, and I told her no.

LaBelle was persistent. She said, "Let me talk to them. I want to make a statement of faith. I promised some of them I would. I'll ask them to give us some peace now."

That was fine with me, but I told her, "Don't say anything against all this, though—and don't say anything about the President." She promised not to. Then she stepped out the front door.

There were reporters, photographers, TV camera crews all over our sidewalk and front lawn. It was a hot, sunny afternoon, and they had been out there all day, so LaBelle gave them something to write about—and think about. She said, "I didn't have anything to do with the resignation. As far as I'm concerned, I didn't think my husband had to resign . . . He's honest, he's good and I'm proud of him . . ."

Then she added a comment worthy of any statesman. She said, "We're all citizens together, and I want you to know that God's hand is over this country, and I'm proud to be a servant of God . . . My husband shares that faith, and we're still proud to be Americans."

Then those media folks, whose colleagues had left me cut and bleeding for four months, applauded.

THE WHOLE ORDEAL started in the spring, when an old nature lover like me thrills to the beauty of Washington, with its cherry blossoms that have ringed the Tidal Basin since before World War I, and the yellow fields of jonquils that Lady Bird Johnson encouraged the National Park Service and others to plant all over town—one of her enduring legacies to the American people. It's a shame to have anything to worry about in Washington in the spring.

But I did. The seeds of my troubles were planted in the first days of the Carter presidency. Just as the people didn't send Carter to Washington to waste his time on such nonsense, Jimmy didn't appoint me his Director of Management and Budget for such things, either. Almost everything that he wanted to change had profound budgetary and management implications. But no executive can handle all of that and then devote hours every day to defending himself against unspecified charges by unnamed accusers.

Even though the Ford administration had cleared me of any wrongdoing in making loans to the good folks of Georgia as president of the bank in Calhoun and later in Atlanta, someone resurrected the charges. From the beginning, I was told that folks inside Treasury were slipping information to William Safire, the New York Times columnist, in a whispering campaign against me.

In Bill's 1980 book, Safire's Washington, he wrote about what happened and about his certainty that I must be guilty of something—he just didn't know what. He said, "I hung in there . . . encouraging some whistle blowers to do their thing." Safire also wrote that the executive editor of the *Times*, A. M. Rosenthal, asked him after reading several of Safire's columns about me what specific law he thought I had broken.

Safire had a ready answer: "18 U. S. Code 656—misapplication of bank funds." Then his book reports that he told his boss, "Abe, the President's best friend could be going to jail."

He continued to write a series of columns about me, talking about "Lancegate" and trotting out as many descriptions and one-liners as he could think of. To his readers he called me "Broken Lance" and "a walking conflict of interest." The headings on his columns were as clever as his prose: "Boiling the Lance" and "The Lance Cover-Up," and "Mr. Carter's Confession."

Meanwhile, the leaks were becoming something more than a trickle. They even included sensitive information from Treasury Department reports compiled by the Office of the Comptroller of the Currency. The OCC information was getting to the news media. That was the start of the "Lance affair."

It was a chapter in the ways of Washington that still bothers those members of the news media and the Washington establishment who were there when the episode reached its peak in the summer.

Some reporters will tell you that the timing may have been significant. When John Sununu was caught in the furor over his travel habits in the summer of 1991, one reporter wrote in the *Washington Post* that such things have a habit of happening in the summer time, when there just isn't anything going on because most folks have headed for Rehoboth Beach. It's a slow news time, one filled nicely if the media can dig up just one "scandal."

The *Post* reporter said his first memory of such a manufactured event during the summer doldrums was what happened to me. He confessed he doesn't even remember now what it was about. He told his readers it "had something to do with a bank, as I recall."

I SAW the storm clouds before Jimmy did, and more clearly, because I had the background with which to recognize the potentially grave difficulties that were emerging for both of us. I got word that *Time* was preparing to run an article alleging that I had serious financial problems because the bank in Atlanta was going to be charging off various loans, an action that would seriously affect its ability to continue its dividend payment. I alerted Jimmy about the coming story right away.

We were having our usual Wednesday lunch in private, only this time we were eating on the patio outside the Oval Office because it was such a beautiful spring day. Carter's response was quick, decisive and simple.

"I don't pay any attention to stuff like that," the President said, "and don't you either."

But the problem wouldn't go away. I received word shortly afterward that the National Bank of Georgia was about to charge off some of those loans, which would make it extremely difficult for me to keep my promise to the Senate during my confirmation hearing to sell my bank stock. If the bank charged off those loans, the value of my stock would drop right through the floor, which would be a serious blow to my financial situation.

I called Jimmy in the family quarters on the second floor of the White House and told him I needed to see him first thing the next morning. Carter said fine.

Early the following day, I walked across the narrow asphalt lane that separates the big, stately, ornate old Executive Office Building from the White House and headed straight for the Oval Office. Jimmy was sitting at his desk, behind that replica of the Truman sign saying, "The buck stops here." It was just like any of our early-morning meetings during Carter's governorship and presidency, but this time the subject held the gravest implications for both of us. Jimmy didn't know that yet, but I was about to tell him.

"I've got a major problem that relates to my economic viability," I began. "They're going to cut the dividend at the National Bank of Georgia. They're going to charge off a bunch of loans that are going to look bad in the press. It's going to call into question whether I can sell my stock." I told him the article in *Time* was just the beginning of the problem.

"So I think you ought to just let me resign. That way we go ahead and I do it now before there's more controversy, other than the fact that they know I have a financial problem that I have to deal with. I'll go back and straighten the bank out, and then I'll come back if you want me back."

I could see I wasn't convincing Jimmy, so I applied even more emphasis. "I believe this to be that serious and that important. You're going to have to realize that it would be better if I resigned, and I think this is the time to do it."

Jimmy looked me squarely in the eye. Suddenly it wasn't Jimmy and Bert. It was the President of the United States telling one of the members of his administration how it was going to be. And he was presidentially firm when he spoke.

"I'm not about to hear that," he said. "That's foolishness and it doesn't make any sense. We'll get the situation straightened out, and you'll get your stock sold. We'll get the Senate to give you an extension on your deadline for that."

Jimmy kept his promise to me. He got the deadline extended, by a vote of the Senate Governmental Affairs Committee, chaired by Senator Abraham Ribicoff of Connecticut. It was the same committee that had confirmed my appointment six months earlier. But that was not the last time that Ribicoff and I were to cross paths during this episode.

The extension had a harmful side effect: it gave the media more time to keep zinging Jimmy and me. The decibel level continued to increase, as my unique closeness to Jimmy added fuel to the fire. A typical example was a postmortem article in the *Washington Post* after my departure, written by Haynes Johnson and George Lardner, two reporters I respected then and still do today.

The *Post* was in a unique position on this issue. In the competitive environment that unfortunately characterizes the news business today—and it *is* a business—papers and networks attach maximum importance to beating each other to the story. The *New York Times* and Bill Safire were going after me with a vengeance, and one reason was that they were still smarting over the way the *Post* had beaten them consistently in reporting the Watergate scandal beginning five years earlier.

Safire was one of Nixon's speech writers in those years, and nobody had to remind him of the job the *Post* did on that continuing story. The *Times* saw the "Lance affair" as its Watergate, a chance to get out ahead of the *Post* on the big national "scandal" and restore its national prestige, even if the news wasn't always fit to print.

The *Post*, on the other hand, would be perfectly content to help go after a Democratic President and his administration. Maybe Kay Graham and Ben Bradlee weren't suffering from a guilt complex—or maybe they were—but they weren't going to be sorry if a Democratic President got into trouble. So for different reasons, the editors at each paper were licking their chops at the prospect of going after me—and America's new President.

Proof of the *Post*'s willingness to put me on the rack was the feature by Johnson and Lardner. It ran 145 inches long, which reflected another change in Washington: the *Post* was becoming a wealthy paper, with more pages and news columns than ever after buying out its only morning competition, the *Times-Herald*, in 1954. The same paper whose editors used to have to tell their reporters, "Keep it short," could now afford 145 inches on one story.

The piece was headed "The Political Price of Friendship." Johnson and Lardner compared the relationship between Jimmy and me to the other White House teams such as Harry Hopkins and Franklin Roosevelt, and Robert Kennedy and his brother John. "Certainly," they wrote, "Carter and Lance were an extraordinary White House team."

I never denied that for a minute, the whole time I was in Washington. Nor did I think it was anything to apologize for. The examples the *Post* cited were effective working relationships that served the nation well. Besides, it was an "extraordinary" relationship between a President and his principal adviser, and the President thought the relationship helped him to be a better President.

Presumably, President Kennedy had felt the same way about his relationship with a man who wasn't even a part of his administration—the same Ben Bradlee, Kennedy's Harvard pal and neighbor in Georgetown. Bradlee was said to be privy to information for his articles in *Newsweek* magazine that was not always made known to other White House reporters.

If President Kennedy thought his extraordinary closeness to a reporter named Ben Bradlee was in his best interests—and the nation's, too—then why write 145 inches about the same kind of closeness between a later President and one of his own executives?

THE ONLY WAY out of the mess seemed to be to keep fighting back, especially after Carter rejected my suggestion that I resign. I voluntarily testified before the Ribicoff committee on July 22, and the committee found out the same thing that Ford's Justice Department attorneys did: that I had done nothing wrong.

But that still didn't satisfy the media and some politicians. On August 13, Congressman John Anderson of Illinois, the third-ranking Republican in the House of Representatives, who helped to defeat Jimmy in 1980 by running a hopeless campaign as a third party candidate for President, demanded that I resign. He jumped on the bandwagon with nothing new to contribute.

Anderson's timing was unusual. The comptroller of the currency, John Heimann, had reopened his investigation under pressure from the media but had not yet issued his new report. But Anderson was out there anyhow, in front of the TV cameras, demanding my resignation and declaring me guilty of unspecified charges before the investigation was completed, like a jury reaching its verdict while the trial is still going on.

When the comptroller did complete his investigation, he reported that he found no legal grounds for the "prosecution of any individual." This was after thirty-five days of work by a staff of forty members who wrote a report containing three volumes and 394 pages. It weighed seven and a half pounds.

The comptroller's report was a great break in the whole sorry episode. Jimmy was at Camp David again, enjoying it as much as every President does up there in the Catoctin Mountains of Maryland, and celebrating Rosalynn's birthday, but he couldn't resist the temptation. He hopped on his helicopter and flew back to the White House to hold a press conference to break his silence on the issue. He told me to be there with him. He said to the nation, "My faith in the character and competence of Bert Lance has been reconfirmed."

Then he turned to me with that big smile of his and said, "Bert, I'm proud of you."

Still people wouldn't let up. The *Los Angeles Times* ran an editorial headed:

LANCE SHOULD GO

The editorial said, ". . . Lance's record inside government has been commendable. He has handled his difficult job well, and we find no blemishes on that record. But we are worried about him now. He should resign."

The logic of that argument somehow escaped me, but logic had long since been replaced by emotion. *The New Republic* displayed the same kind of reverse logic, and added a touch of geographical prejudice against southerners just for good measure. The magazine published an editorial saying, "Bert Lance has done nothing illegal. That's what we're told, and we've seen nothing to contradict it." But then the magazine took a swipe at decent public servants everywhere in the South by referring to "the LBJ school of southern cronies, shabby but not indictable."

Over the Labor Day weekend, Ribicoff and Senator Charles Percy of Illinois made a big show of going to the White House and telling President Carter—and the network news reporters—that they had important new information that I might have been involved in embezzling funds from my bank. The *Atlanta Journal*'s headline on page one said:

SWINDLER IMPLICATES LANCE

The information came from a convicted felon who was still in prison, and not just any convicted felon: I was the one who put him there, on a charge of embezzlement. I had uncovered irregularities in his work at the bank and reported him to the federal authorities. My testimony had sent him to jail. But Percy and Ribicoff were willing to take this guy's word for it and run to the President, and the media, with their news.

The felon later recanted his story. He admitted he was lying. Percy apologized.

Then I went before Ribicoff's committee again, on September 15, even though Hamilton Jordan thought I was crazy to do it and said everything he could think of to talk me out of it.

I stayed up late the night before with my attorneys, Clark Clifford and Bob Altman, and my assistant at OMB, A. D. Frazier. After we put the final touches on my testimony, I called Hamilton and asked him to come to Clifford's office and review it. He did, and he immediately became upset.

Hamilton thought I was making a serious mistake in taking on the Senate directly, which I did in my statement. He wanted me to tone down the language. He said the statement as we had drafted it would permanently ruin Jimmy's relations with Congress.

I thought he had a valid point, but the stakes were too high for me to tone anything down. Ribicoff and Percy had maligned me and impugned my integrity. They implied I was a crook and an embezzler. I had to take them on, and I couldn't do that while worrying about being diplomatic in my language. I had to expose the members of that Senate committee for what they were throughout the affair—media puppets.

I told Hamilton I was going to deliver the statement as he saw it. The lawyers agreed.

Newsweek predicted I would be stepping into "the gladiator pit." I tended to agree with that, but to me that's like an athlete worrying about losing a big game before it starts. That's no way to win. And I was going after the win, and nobody's gladiator pit was going to keep me from it.

Earlier in the evening, I had called Jimmy in the family quarters and asked to see him early the next morning. We agreed on 6:30—but only after I tried to get a leg up on him in our long-standing rivalry to beat each other to the office in the morning. I told him, "That's sort of late for me, but if you want to start your day off that late, it's fine with me."

By the time we put the final touches on my testimony, it was 3 A.M.

I parked my car at OMB shortly after daybreak. The capital of the free world was only beginning to stir as I made a brief visit to my office, then slipped out of the building and across the path to the White House. I was carrying my family Bible, the same one I held while being sworn in to office eight months earlier.

I walked to the Oval Office, where the Secret Service agent greeted me with a "Good morning" as he opened the door. Jimmy and I greeted each other warmly. We had been friends for eleven years.

I wanted the meeting for only one purpose: to pray for the strength, guidance, and wisdom that I would need over the next few days, beginning in just two and a half hours. I wanted to put the matter in God's hands, and I wanted to do it with my friend Jimmy there with me.

We left the Oval Office and moved into Jimmy's small study next door. I noticed a difference immediately. There wasn't any classical music playing. There was only the early-morning stillness.

We took turns using my Bible and alternated reading scriptures that I selected the night before. Several passages were subjects of Sunday school classes that I taught for twenty-five years in Calhoun. One was verses five and six of the first chapter of Joshua:

> No man shall be able to stand before you all the days of your life; as I was with Moses, so I will be with you. Be strong and of good courage; for you shall cause this people to inherit the land which I swore to their fathers to give them.

Then Jimmy and I read the twelfth and thirteenth verses of the thirteenth chapter of St. Paul's first letter to the Corinthians:

> For now we see in a mirror dimly, but then face to face. Now I know in part; then I shall understand fully, even as I have been fully understood. So faith, hope, love abide, these three; but the greatest of these is love.

Our last reading from my selections of the night before was from Ecclesiastes:

> To everything there is a season, and a time to every purpose under the heavens . . . a time to keep silent, and a time to speak.

•   •   •

I WALKED INTO the Senate Conference Room with LaBelle and two of our sons, Tram and David, plus my lawyers, Clifford and Altman, and friends of our family. I squinted under the glare of the television lights and made my way carefully over the spaghetti of wire and cable that lay all over the floor. There was a capacity crowd of reporters, photographers and the curious.

It was like the old TV quiz show "The $64,000 Question," the one where they used to put you in an isolation booth to answer the questions. It was as if God put me in His own isolation booth that morning, just as soon as I walked into the room and sat down.

I never heard or saw anything but what I was reading. I wasn't distracted by any of the noises or movements of the people in the room around me, or by all of those staff people who have a habit of popping up like so many jack-in-the-boxes at congressional hearings. They were wandering around and handing Percy a bunch of silly questions to ask me, like whether we were talking about Warm Springs, Georgia, or Hot Springs, Arkansas.

I gave the committee information that I had made readily available to the members of their staff, but which had been ignored: During my term as president of Calhoun First National Bank, its assets increased from $11.9 million to $54.1 million. At the National Bank of Georgia, while I was president there, its assets grew from $254 million to $404 million.

Then I got in a few licks in my own defense. I asked the committee, "Is it part of our American system that a man can be drummed out of government by a series of false charges, half-truths and misrepresentations, innuendoes and the like?"

Ribicoff, the man who had said earlier in the year that I was being smeared by the news media "from one end of this country to the other" but later joined in the smearing, said he "regretted" the charge about embezzling brought forth by the convicted felon who was still in prison.

Percy admitted, "It was wrong of me to even raise the possibility" that I had cheated on my income tax. He apologized for any "anguish" he had caused me.

Their apologies, of course, were supposed to make everything okay.

None of that bothered me. I read my whole opening statement—forty-nine pages—and answered all of the questions from the committee members, and nothing bothered me one bit. If I performed well, I have God to thank for it—and for that isolation booth He wrapped around me.

I was on the hot spot for twenty hours of testimony before Ribicoff's committee. The result was what almost everyone called a smash-
ing victory. There was an immediate flood of support from every part
of the country and from the Senate itself. Hubert Humphrey called me
from his Senate office and said, "I just wanted to tell you that you did
a magnificent job. You have a great deal of courage. I was tremendously impressed."

Senator Muskie, the same man who was so furious with the
Carter administration only five months earlier because of the proposal
to eliminate a water project in Maine, also called me and was just as
complimentary as Humphrey.

My fellow Georgian, Senator Sam Nunn, said, "There's a pulse
beat, but we don't have a Lazarus yet." Sam was my strongest defender
in the Senate, and he expressed his concern about the moral and legal
implications of what was going on. He told reporters, "I believe it is time
to lower the curtain on this media festival, which has been conducted
for so long at the expense of one man's honor and reputation. I am of
the opinion that the presumption of innocence, which is part of our
Constitution—the guarantee of due process—is being eroded."

On the subject of due process, Sam knows what he's talking
about. He's a former prosecuting attorney.

Senator John Glenn came to my defense in talking to reporters.
The man with probably the cleanest image of any member of the
Senate at that time told them, "I think we've gone completely ethics
happy around here. We've gone crazy."

The Speaker of the House, Tip O'Neill, and the majority whip,
Jim Wright, made public statements urging Jimmy to keep me in the
job. Congressman James Jones of Oklahoma circulated a petition of
support in the House of Representatives. He approached ninety members of Congress, and sixty-nine of them signed it.

In the Senate, the Republican leader, Howard Baker, agreed with
O'Neill and Wright on the House side. He said he saw no reason for
me not to continue. Senator Tom Eagleton, himself the victim of an
emotional controversy five years before, when George McGovern
chose him as his running mate, told reporters that I was the victim of
the media's habit of mixing rumors and facts and building the pile
higher every day. Eagleton called it "guilt by accumulation."

I have another term for it. It's "the get-aboard syndrome." That
occurs when a controversy like mine flares up, and all the reporters and
bureaucrats are so eager to be able to say they were among the first
accusers that they all jump on the bandwagon.

Clark Clifford told me in his office after my testimony, "I'm so proud of you, Bert." Then this revered public figure, who has been one of Washington's most respected institutions for decades, said he'd like for me to call him by his first name.

I said, "Thank you, Mr. Clifford."

A flood of support poured into the White House in the form of long-distance telephone calls, letters, and telegrams. The actual count in the forty-eight hours from the conclusion of my testimony at noon Thursday until noon Saturday was:

Calls, telegrams, and mailgrams received—2,257
Calls supporting Lance—2,012
Calls against Lance—245

That's a popularity rating of almost 90 percent, and only George Bush, with his 91 percent rating after Desert Storm, could match that. The White House staff responded by writing all those folks back—thanking them for their support of the Panama Canal treaty.

A FEW DAYS LATER, I called the Senate majority leader, Robert Byrd, and asked him to come over to my office at OMB. I wanted his assessment of the situation. In addition to being the leader of the Senate, he was a man respected for his accurate judgment and his ability to remain objective in analyzing things.

He told me, "You made a fine witness. But we're going to have more hearings. There are unanswered questions. The press is going to continue to explore this."

Some folks in high places were coming to my defense, like the president emeritus of Brown University, Henry M. Wriston. He wrote a column in the New York Times making his point in blunt terms:

> The behavior of the Senate Governmental Affairs committee was scandalous. The chairman, Abraham A. Ribicoff, should be censured or dismissed from the committee. . . .
> The senior minority member, Charles H. Percy, committed such a shocking trespass upon the rights of the "defendant" by suggesting that he had back-dated checks to improperly take an income tax deduction that he had to apologize—a gesture wholly inadequate to the damage done . . .
> Both of these men participated in giving currency to the uncorroborated word of a convicted felon . . . They went in the back door of the White House. They should have left by the basement.

Columnist Hal Gulliver of the Atlanta Constitution faced the issue of the media's role head-on. He wrote, "Lance is being harassed by people in some cases with an ax to grind and in some cases who just simply ought to know better."

Then he quoted a conversation he had had with a government official in Washington who reminded him that folks used to be considered innocent until proven guilty. "These days," the official told Gulliver, "it seems different. The press and a lot of people in government start out from the opposite side, that a man is simply guilty if the charges are made, that there must be some sin there. It's different. It's more cynical. It's harsh. It's unjust. It's wrong."

Then Gulliver concluded his column with his own statement:

> Bert Lance has been through the acid of that kind of treatment this summer. He comes through all right because the man is all right; his abilities and his actions, at any level, can bear whatever prolonged examination that Time and Newsweek might want to devote. But that acid leaves a bitter residue. Is this the price of public service? Is this what an honest and competent man or woman must expect as the price of being willing to serve?

On the morning of my resignation, Haynes Johnson raised other serious questions for members of the media to ponder. His feature article in the *Washington Post* was headed:

ON LANCE: WHAT DID THE MEDIA KNOW AND WHEN?

Johnson wrote, "Even some members of the press are speaking of a 'vendetta' atmosphere present among the correspondents and news organizations. The press is either out to 'get' Carter and his Georgians by 'getting' Lance, or is trying to 'get' news rivals who may have triumphed in earlier competitive contests." That was a thinly veiled reference to the eagerness of the *New York Times* to catch up with the *Post's* journalistic victories on Watergate.

Johnson's article was one of the very few instances—maybe the only one—where the media was willing to write or talk about the desire on the part of some elements of the nation's news media to "get Carter and his Georgians."

It is a sad fact, but a fact nevertheless, that even before the "Lance affair" started, there was a deep and intense dislike for the Carters and the people close to them, by the press and the establishment in Washington. If people are honest about that, they'll admit it was true. And Haynes Johnson was saying it in the *Post*.

Even with people like Lester Maddox and groups that come and go, we are a different sort of folk. I think we have a greater feeling toward people. The people of the South have one chapter in their history that folks in other parts of the United States never have. We lost a war.

People don't think about that, but we're the only ones in this country who suffered through the searing experience of a war, something that has its effects on a people for several future generations, not just on those who lived it at the time. Southerners know firsthand what suffering is, because that suffering endured for decades. So we are compassionate folks. The Southern people have a feeling for others.

We've made great economic progress over the years. We've won jobs away from some other parts of the country, so there's a certain resentment about that, too. As a result, our educational systems are described as inferior, and when we show up in places like Washington and talk with an accent, that latent prejudice comes into play. That's what happened in Carter's case.

When we came into office in January, I didn't feel that I was a victim of those attitudes because I got along with everybody, but Jimmy sure was, and so was Billy. Jimmy wasn't any different than any other smalltown man in wearing jeans and speaking with an accent and having a brother who drank beer down at the corner gas station, but people held it against him when they never held it against anybody else.

Jimmy started off his presidency having to overcome an attitude that never confronted new Presidents like Nixon or Ford or Reagan or Bush. So when my problems hit the headlines—and stayed there—that prejudice was working against me, and it was working against Jimmy. The Washington press corps was only too happy to jump all over the first President from the South in 100 years.

THROUGHOUT the whole sorry episode, four points remained true and still do today. It is a matter of record that:

1. I was never accused by anyone of doing—or even appearing to do—anything wrong while in public office, either as an official of the State of Georgia or as a member of the Carter administration. I handled hundreds of millions of dollars in Georgia and even billions—with a capital B—in Washington, but nobody ever said I did anything wrong with one penny of those vast sums of money. There never was any criticism of my performance in public office.

2. I was never convicted of anything. The main charge against

me was conspiracy, which the judge in my trial threw out of court. I was tried instead on twelve lesser charges. I was found not guilty on nine. The government dropped the other three.

3.   In another round of attempts to indict me and convict me of new charges about alleged violations during the same period in the 1980s, the government dropped everything. Those folks suggested an out-of-court settlement, but only after I filed a countersuit against them. They could have saved themselves a whole lot of time and effort—and the taxpayers a whole lot of money—if they had been honest in the first place and admitted to themselves that I hadn't done anything wrong. The story doesn't end here. There's a few more chapters from here.

4.   The charges that were brought against me while I was a member of the Carter administration included nothing that hadn't been examined thoroughly in that investigation by the Justice Department under President Ford. The department had issued a report at the conclusion of the investigation that was released to the media and published in America's papers and broadcast on the air. It said I wasn't guilty of anything.

That first point was largely overlooked—conveniently so—by the media. It is another irony that a columnist writing in the *Washington Post* pointed this out, while also telling his readers that many of the reporters and columnists discussing the controversy about me simply were in over their heads on a subject that they were unqualified to understand. It is still another irony that that columnist, Lawrence B. Smith, was the son of the man who occupied my position under President Roosevelt and President Truman. He came to my defense by writing what no one else did:

> As the press analyzes the Bert Lance denouement, it neglects key aspects of its own character that contributed to the event. Experts on stories about spread-eagled giraffes and complex arms-control talks, journalists have little feel for commercial matters and the corporate board room. Editorial rooms that monitor the national political scene lifted Lance's private affairs out of context, moved them forward in time and place and judged them as current events happening in Washington to a public official.

There was another "knowledge gap" that contributed to my problems, one that I clearly understood as a member of the banking profession for twenty-five years. It was fundamental to the discussions going on about me, but it escaped most people—politicians and journalists alike—because they simply didn't understand. What eluded them, among many other things, was this fact of life about banking: Country banks are different from city banks. Banks in large cities are a reflection of the metropolitan lifestyle. Everything is by-the-book and impersonal, even cold. That's not a criticism of city banks—it's just the way things are. On the other hand, country banks tend to be more personal and community-oriented, again reflecting the community's lifestyle. I reflected that lifestyle in Calhoun, and when I was appointed to the presidency of the bank in Atlanta, I continued to reflect the management philosophy which I had applied all my life.

Generally speaking, country banks are more flexible in their lending policies than their city brethren are. This flexibility is possible because the lending offices in country banks are a part of the community, and they are on familiar terms with their borrowers. They believe, and I do too, that a person's character is worth more than his collateral. That's a philosophy I adhered to as a country banker, and it's supported by this fact of business: Collateral hasn't repaid a loan yet.

But those differences were ignored by the media in my case, partly because they would have undercut the media's campaign against me and partly because too many of those folks didn't know what they were writing about. That was a serious journalistic flaw. To put it bluntly, those reporters and columnists and anchor folks didn't know as much as they should have about the story they were reporting. They were criticizing the way I supposedly had done my job—while failing in the performance of their own jobs.

Each time a new allegation was raised against me and my practices as a country banker, the media didn't go to a country banker as a source. They went to big-city bankers. That's apples and oranges, like asking a football scout to evaluate a baseball prospect. It's just not logical.

When they went to their sources on Wall Street and other big-city locations, those bankers naturally said they did not agree with my practices. I could have told the reporters that myself, and saved their companies the cost of those long-distance telephone calls. But those boys in the big city also agreed that my activities were routine practice among country bankers, something else I could have told the reporters myself.

Big-city banks don't have a personal relationship with the customers who borrow money from them, but country banks do. A woman in Calhoun named Susie Goforth was a typical case. She borrowed money from our bank to buy a new milch cow—and farmers know that's the correct spelling for that kind of a cow—but she ran into problems and got behind in her payments. She showed up at the bank one morning and found me near the note counter. She came over and said, "Mr. Lance, I brung you your cow."

I had no idea what she was talking about, so I said, "Susie, you did what?"

She said, "I brung you your cow. You've got the mortgage on her, and I can't pay it, so I've got the cow tied up outside."

"Well, Susie, this is a serious situation. Let's just think about this for a minute. First of all, you need that cow badly so you'll have milk for your family.

"Second, we don't have a thing in the world to do with that cow. We don't have any place to put it, and I don't know how to milk it. So I'm going to make a suggestion to you: We'll extend your loan until such time as you think you can take care of it. You take that cow back home with you now and look after it so it will continue to provide milk for you and your family."

That taught me a lesson right there, and it's one that you might not have the opportunity to learn as easily in a big-city bank: Collateral in hand is a poor substitute for paying a loan. I never forgot that.

That cow wasn't going to help our bank one bit, but it could help Susie, so I simply made a commonsense decision that seemed to me to be in everyone's best interests. Susie eventually came on better times and repaid her loan in full, with interest, and in the meantime we didn't have to fool around with a cow in our bank.

10
America's New Danger

SEPTEMBER 21 was the first official day of the fall season, and Washington's famous autumn weather was producing a masterpiece of a morning: sunny and mild, the kind of day that makes you feel good—usually.

I left our home in Georgetown at 6 A.M. after performing the same ritual I had followed for the previous seven years, since I started getting up at four o'clock every morning to get to my office in Atlanta. On this morning in Washington, as always, I got up shortly before five, fixed coffee for myself, and then spent a few minutes in prayer and meditation.

Then I followed the rest of my early-morning routine. I fixed a breakfast tray for LaBelle—coffee, cereal, and orange juice. I plucked a rose, tiny and fragrant, from the small garden in front of our house and put it in a vase to decorate the tray. LaBelle would be expecting the rose. Roses are a traditional remembrance from me to her. That flower on her tray seemed to bring a touch of tranquility to what I knew would be a stormy day.

I added a small pot of coffee, ready for her to plug in at her bedside when she woke up. Then I carried the tray up the stairs to our bedroom, put a copy of the *Washington Post* on the bed beside her, and left a note, as always:

My Dearest—
I love you, LaBelle.
Will call later.
                    —Bert

Twelve days before, we had celebrated our twenty-seventh wedding anniversary.

I met LaBelle at the White House later that morning in the hall outside the Oval Office. We were there only a moment when the President opened the door and invited us in. There we were, three old friends from Georgia, for whom life was so different now in so many ways. We walked across the light-colored oval rug past the eggshell-white walls and the gold draperies that framed the three windows behind Jimmy's huge carved desk. The desk was flanked by the American flag on the left and the presidential flag on the right. We moved past the graceful and formal eighteenth-century furniture, the traditional winged chairs by the fireplace and the two striped sofas facing each other across the butler's table.

We didn't stop in the Oval Office. Instead, the President escorted us to his study next door, where he preferred the much more intimate atmosphere, with its decorations and photographs of Jimmy and Rosalynn and their children. LaBelle and I sat together on a sofa against a wall on one side of Jimmy's desk. He sat at the desk and listened as LaBelle stated her case for keeping me in his administration.

Jimmy listened, as he always did, and asked questions and spoke honestly about the problems being caused by this whole business. He told us he had scheduled a news conference for later that afternoon, and he wanted to stress the importance of several of his top-priority items, including his proposed treaty on the Panama Canal. He said he felt the American people needed to hear more about these issues, but realistically he knew that when he threw the floor open to questions from the reporters, eight out of ten would be about me. I thought it might be more like ten of ten.

Jimmy told LaBelle that he knew I understood all of this and that I therefore had decided to resign. That was the truth. Jimmy and I had played a doubles match the afternoon before on the White House tennis court against Hamilton and Jimmy's speechwriter, James Fallows. The match lasted ninety minutes, and after Jordan and Fallows left, Jimmy and I sat down on a bench at courtside and talked for forty-five minutes.

I told the President my mind was made up. I was going to resign. He did not argue with me. He said only that it should be my decision, and he would defend me in whatever I decided.

Jimmy described the situation completely and accurately, but he didn't change LaBelle's mind. She was still strongly opposed to my resignation. All three of us realized that there was nothing more that could be said, or needed to. We rose to leave. LaBelle put her hand on Jimmy's arm and told him, "You know I'll always pray for you."

Then LaBelle and I went to the cabinet room in the White House, down the hall from the Oval Office, to talk privately for a few minutes. I told her I'd like her help in deciding the exact wording for my letter of resignation. But she was still adamant; she told me she just couldn't bring herself to help me.

"I can't," she said. "I'm still against it. It's one thing I can't help you with . . . you'll have to do it alone." We both understood. Then she went home while I drafted my letter.

In my letter to the President, I mentioned my gratitude and sense of satisfaction in having worked with him to try to bring the federal government under control and accomplish all the good things that Jimmy hoped for in behalf of all Americans. Then I added:

> However, I have to ask the question at what price do I remain? My only intention in coming to Washington in the first place was to make a contribution to this country and to you.
>
> I am convinced that I can continue to be an effective Director of the Office of Management and Budget. However, because of the amount of controversy and the continuing nature of it, I have decided to submit my resignation as Director of OMB. I desire to return to my native State of Georgia.
>
> It has been a high privilege and honor to be a part of your administration. Hopefully, I have made a contribution which will be of lasting value.
>
> Respectfully yours,
> Bert Lance

Jody wrote a statement for the President to read at his press conference, but Jimmy declined. He told Jody, "I don't feel right about reading a statement about Bert. I just want to talk." Later in the afternoon, after two delays, he held his press conference. His prediction was right. Almost all of the questions were about me.

The press conference lasted thirty-seven minutes. Jimmy told the reporters, "I accept Bert's resignation with the greatest sense of regret and sorrow. He's a good man . . . I think he's made the right decision, because it would be difficult for him to devote full time to his responsibilities in the future."

Jimmy was kind enough to tell reporters that nothing "has shaken my belief in Bert's ability or his integrity." He went beyond that to say he considered himself partly to blame for my problems, because he wanted me to break my ties with the banking business when I became budget director.

He reminded the reporters that I could have stayed in Georgia and just not come to Washington with the new administration. Jimmy told them, "Had he stayed there in a selfish fashion and enriched himself and his own family financially, I'm sure he would have been spared any allegations of impropriety. But he wanted to come to serve his government because I asked him to, and he did."

Jimmy pulled it off without any serious problems, and for that I think he had LaBelle to thank, at least in part.

After the press conference was over and we turned off the TV set in the bedroom, as I lay there still exhausted, I told LaBelle that if it hadn't been for her phone call to him he might have broken down and cried on national television. I told her, "Your phone call started his adrenaline and gave him the reserve he needed to make it through. It would have been a disaster to see the President of the United States crying on TV. Imagine how much it would have hurt Jimmy politically."

It was another irony: the one who bitterly opposed my resignation and told the President over the phone he was joining "the rest of the jackals" helped him to get through his TV ordeal only a few hours later.

We were supposed to go to the Clark Cliffords' for dinner that evening, but LaBelle called and declined with thanks. We stayed home, and I cooked up one of my special omelettes for our private dinner. Before dinner, we drank a glass of champagne.

BEFORE WE LEFT Washington, one final act remained. LaBelle and I hosted a reception at OMB to say thank-you to our friends, Republicans and Democrats alike. We were curious about it. We weren't sure anyone would show up.

I think what happened shocked everyone, including us. So many people came that the receiving line was hundreds of folks long. People stood in line for up to two hours to shake our hands. Jimmy and Rosalynn came, plus the cabinet officers, leaders from both houses of Congress—on both sides of the aisle—Chief Justice Burger and his wife, even the White House police officers. They took turns filling in for each other so all of them could come over to say good-bye.

When we got back home to Calhoun, there was another turnout

to lift our spirits. Our friends and neighbors held a rally. They carried silhouettes of me, and they waved signs in front of the TV cameras saying, "We're For Bert" and "USA Needs Bert Lance" and "Calhoun Loves Bert." The networks, wire services, newsmagazines, and the major papers were all there to cover something that they obviously considered big news, although I didn't really see how it could be such a big story just because a Georgia boy was coming back to his hometown in the mountains.

Those media folk found out that the good people of north Georgia aren't afraid to speak their piece, either. Beverly Langford was just one example. Beverly was a member of the Georgia senate at that time, representing Calhoun. He told Jeff Prugh of the *Los Angeles Times*, "I don't talk to Yankees, Republicans, or reporters."

As soon as we returned to Calhoun, our four sons—Tram, David, Stuart, and Beverly—received a letter from Senator Eagleton, who knew precisely what I had gone through after being subjected to one of the cruelest, most savage assaults himself when George McGovern selected him as his running mate on the 1972 Democratic ticket. Senator Eagleton wrote to our sons:

> I realize that the past two months have been very difficult for the Lance family. I myself have had a personal experience where reckless and defamatory accusations were made and where the press ran amok. Thus I can empathize with what an ordeal you and your parents have experienced.
>
> I simply want to point out to you that which you already know: Your father is one hell of a fine, honorable, and decent gentleman. When so many others were treating him unfairly, he never lost his own personal sense of fairness. On all occasions he conducted himself with dignity and grace. You bear the good name Lance and about it you can be most proud.

IN THOSE FIRST DAYS out of office, I kept a date to address the Investment Association in New York, eight days after I resigned. I told my audience that my experience reminded me of the woman who went to the meat market, held up a chicken for inspection, and then punched its breast, twisted its legs, and squeezed its wings, all to see how strong and healthy the bird had been. I told those investment folks that the woman put the bird back and told the butcher it wouldn't do, but the butcher said, "Lady, to tell you the truth, I don't think you could pass that kind of a test yourself."

I told them I was in the same position as that chicken. A lot of folks who had been holding me up and punching me around couldn't stand up under that kind of a test themselves.

Then I told the audience about the visitor to the zoo who was amazed to see a lamb lying in the lion's cage right next to the king of the jungle. He ran with great excitement to the zookeeper and told him, "At last! The biblical prophecy has been fulfilled! A lion and a lamb are lying down together!"

Then the zookeeper explained, "You don't understand—we put a new lamb in there every day."

I told the audience, "For the last couple of months I've been looking for a new lamb every day to take my place, but one never did show up."

CHRISTMAS, 1977, produced another irony. In the spirit of the season, I sent a note to William Safire on December 20:

> Dear William:
>   The Bible says "love those who despise you." May you and yours have a Merry Christmas & a Happy New Year.
>   Bert Lance

He answered with cordial greetings of his own, along with another biblical quote: "Ye shall know the truth, and the truth shall set you free." He didn't know it, but that happens to be one of my favorite quotes from the Bible.

After that, we kept in touch. Over the years since, we have become good friends. Three years after I sent him that Christmas message, his book *Safire's Washington* was published, including some of the columns from the "Lance affair." He sent me an autographed copy with a message:

> For Bert Lance, with hopes for a strong comeback.
>   Bill Safire, 1980

I HOPED "the Lance Affair" was over, but in my heart I knew better. A full year later, the *Washington Post* was still after me. The paper ran a story with a Calhoun dateline that said:

> A 15-person team of Justice Department lawyers, FBI agents, bank examiners and support staff have spent nine months combing through bank records, amassing literally miles of documents. This paper chase continues right up to today.

That paper chase went on and on, even after I was indicted on thirteen counts, tried, and cleared. Some folks just don't know when to quit and move on to something productive. The taxpayers subsidized a whole lot of wasted time and travel expenses over a folly that lasted nine years.

Through it all, my family and I were subjected to nothing less than brutalization by the news media, a criminal trial, and an attempt to stage another one—and "stage" is the best word to describe that whole fiasco.

That "paper chase" that the *Washington Post* wrote about—and participated in—had at least one lasting result: it made me the most investigated person in the history of the United States. The files in the Justice Department today contain more than 400,000 pages on me. That's more than they have on Nixon and his whole Watergate crowd.

This was confirmed a few years ago when I called up to Washington and told them I might like to have a copy of that file for my own records. The man I spoke to said, "We'd be happy to Xerox that material and send it to you, Mr. Lance. Just send us your check for $40,000."

In addition to the profound issues raised by the trial that followed, the reporting of the "Lance affair" raised other questions of equal danger for every adult American and for our nation itself. That danger stems from the erosion of individual privacy, one of the keystones of our democracy and our Constitution.

The truth of the matter today is that if you are in the public spotlight—whether you're a public official, an entertainer, an athlete, or anything else that gets your name and picture in the news media—you have no privacy. Civil libertarians raise a great hue and cry about invasion of privacy in talking about everything from abortion on demand to mandatory drug testing, but this new extent to which people's privacy is being invaded by our news media is an even worse threat.

You can be certain that as you read this, in today's litigious society, there are people in every part of this country who are suffering a private agony because they've been put in the same position I was—disruption of their lives, smears against their reputations, embarrassment for the members of the families, and financial ruin in many cases, all caused by some bureaucrat in government or business who doesn't have to account to anybody and can walk away from what he's done and never give it a second thought.

That's what bothers me about my experience. What happened to me was wrong legally—the jury's verdict proved that. But that kind of thing is also wrong morally, and the price to us as individuals and as a nation is just too high. We should be unwilling to pay it.

The threat is compounded by the increased capacity of our news organizations. TV networks can go live on a moment's notice to a breaking story about an earthquake in San Francisco, a human wave of people climbing the Berlin Wall, or protesters being gunned down in Beijing. That capacity spurs competition among the networks, and among the newspapers and newsmagazines as they strive to keep up with TV.

As a result, everybody is competing against everybody else. The day is gone forever when the first word about a big story was from a newsboy on the street hollering, "Extra! Extra! Read all about it!" Today, the unrelenting pressure on reporters, editors, and news directors is to get the story on the air or in the paper first.

That pressure isn't only so you'll be ahead of your competition on the day the news breaks. It's also to give the network or the paper the opportunity to rush a new series of ads onto the air or into print bragging that this news organization was the first to bring you that dramatic story.

All of this pressure feeds on itself, and reporters and their bosses rush into decisions about their information that often don't hold up. The estimate from one of the American wire services about the death toll from the earthquake in Armenia in 1988 was way out of line and was contradicted almost immediately by the facts, but that wire service was the first to report that falsely high figure. Jim Brady was reported to have died when President Reagan was shot. Even as far back as the final days of World War II, there were bulletins about Germany's surrender, followed by denials.

It's not always the fault of the media. In some cases they are given wrong information by their sources in government or business. But that doesn't relieve the reporter and his or her editor from verifying the information before they report it. A guilty journalist may think denials or corrections make everything okay, but when the false information damages a person's reputation, nothing can repair that damage.

When Senators Percy and Ribicoff went to the White House on Labor Day weekend in 1977—they had both served in Washington long enough to know that holidays are always a slow time for news— and blurted out to the media that they had information saying I was guilty of embezzlement, how many reporters bothered to check the source of the senators' information? For that matter, would they have printed the Percy-Ribicoff charges anyhow, even though they came from a convicted felon who was still in prison?

You can bet next month's mortgage payment that there are people in this nation today who still think I embezzled funds from my bank—and that I went to jail.

The truth never catches up with the lie.

THERE IS ANOTHER frightening side to all this at the national level. After allowing more than a year for time to work its magic and heal the wounds, I began to make the transition from the healing process to the questioning process. I began to ask myself why I had been singled out for this experience, where it originated, who was feeding the charges that ignited the controversy, and where the energy was coming from to sustain it.

I took my questions to Bill Safire. I asked him, "Bill, why did this happen? Why was I picked out as one to be put through this business?"

He said, "You really don't know?"

"No. If I knew, I wouldn't be asking you."

His answer was brief and clear: "We didn't want you to become chairman of the Fed."

It began to add up. Early in my time as director of management and budget, I began to warn the banking industry that any idea of raising interest rates was uncalled for because the rate of loans didn't seem to justify it. It was clear to the nation's bankers, my former colleagues, that I was "jawboning" them, pressuring them against taking that course of action.

My statements prompted some members of the economic community to remember that the term of Dr. Arthur Burns as chairman of the Federal Reserve Board was due to expire during 1978. It is a seven-year appointment, and it was becoming fairly obvious that Carter was not going to reappoint him. Out of that feeling grew the fear in some circles that Jimmy would appoint me to the Fed chairmanship. Those folks were afraid they would be stuck with me as Federal Reserve Board chairman for seven years, throughout Carter's first term and for his entire second term, if there was one.

I have never talked to President Carter about this aspect of the "Lance affair," but what Bill told me fits perfectly into the rest of the reality of that experience. Safire's answer shed new light on everything that happened after that. And, of course, an unspoken concern was that with me as Fed chairman, there was a possibility of working harmoniously with Jimmy that never existed between Burns and

Jimmy. That effective working relationship between the two officials most directly responsible for the decisions affecting the nation's economy could even increase the possibility that they dreaded: that Carter could be elected to a second term.

The people who run the Washington establishment have the intelligence and long-range vision to anticipate such developments and to prevent them from happening if that is the desired course of action. In my case it was, especially with my talk against higher interest rates. One surefire way to see that certain folks don't advance any farther is to head them off at the pass by making them unconfirmable for the position you want to deny them.

Carter might think this is a preposterous suggestion, but the truth is that once I started speaking out against higher interest rates, the "Lance affair" suddenly was born. What had been gone over to the satisfaction of everyone in two presidential administrations, including a Republican one, as well as during my confirmation hearings for the OMB position, was resurrected. Safire's answer confirmed both the reason and the timing.

Even if I survived, one thing was certain early in that whole business: I was becoming unconfirmable for the Fed job. I wasn't the first person to fall victim to that strategy, nor was I the last. Early in the Reagan administration it became apparent that Reagan's friend, Ed Meese, was destined for nomination to the Supreme Court after serving in the White House and then as attorney general.

But the attorney general's job was as far as some of the Washington establishment wanted Meese to go. So during the confirmation hearings for that position, enough rumors and insinuations were spread about him through the news media that by the time he was confirmed as attorney general he had become unconfirmable for the Supreme Court.

That's the way things are done in Washington—not always, but when enough folks in the establishment want to block someone from moving into a particular position. At the time the "Lance affair" was created—and that's the right word—there were forces within the nation's financial and political communities who clearly did not want me to become chairman of the Federal Reserve Board. They were all too aware that Carter had considered me for the position of secretary of the treasury before appointing me to the OMB job. They knew I had been his banker, and they knew we were the closest of friends. They also knew Jimmy was from Plains, and they didn't want the other member of the economic team to be from Calhoun.

•   •   •

I WAS invited to speak on the issue of invasion of privacy at a dinner by the National Libel Defense Fund at the Waldorf-Astoria in New York in November 1989. Nina Totenburg was on the program with me. She is the reporter for National Public Radio who broke the story about Judge Douglas Ginsburg smoking pot while teaching law at Harvard, the story that destroyed Reagan's nomination of Ginsburg to become a member of the Supreme Court.

Our audience consisted mostly of attorneys for large news organizations—the men and women who defend the networks, newspapers and other news organizations when someone sues them for libel. I told them in the simplest of terms that any concern about invasion of privacy by the news media is now a waste of time.

My reason: "There is none. And furthermore, there isn't likely to be any for the foreseeable future."

I told those lawyers that people ought to just accept the fact that privacy for public figures is a thing of the past, and move on to other public issues. Nothing about anybody is sacrosanct today. And being a public figure makes no difference. If a paper wants to print something about you, they'll print it.

We have moved 180 degrees from respecting the right to privacy to having no privacy at all. Franklin Roosevelt was President for years before many Americans realized that the man couldn't walk. The White House press corps respected his privacy—maybe more than they should have. You could argue that the American people had a right to know that they were electing a President who was confined to a wheelchair and had to be helped to his feet, had his legs encased in heavy, cumbersome braces, and was a dying man when he was elected to his fourth term.

But the White House correspondents, if they didn't go out of their way to protect that information, certainly never went out of their way to report it. Maybe they should have, and I am one of those who believe they should. But I mention the case here to illustrate how far the pendulum has traveled.

In John Kennedy's years as President, we never got one hint from those covering him that he might have had feminine company other than his wife at times, but some of those same reporters have written such allegations since. When Harry Truman was President, he and Sam Rayburn used to hoist a few glasses of bourbon to "strike a blow for liberty" and play poker on Saturday nights. The White House press corps knew about those habits, but the public didn't. Today those harmless tendencies would be shaped into a full-blown scandal, and Harry would have trouble surviving it.

If you're the one who is being focused upon, you think your privacy is being violated, and in fact it is. But if there is no such thing as privacy to start with, then that's a different story. We have now reached that point. If you are confronted by a reporter today and your answer is, "That's my private business," that will protect your privacy only as long as it takes the reporter to get to the nearest telephone. That reporter will get an answer from somebody, whether it's you or someone else. The answer may be factual or it may not, but he will get an answer.

The erosion of privacy even occurs in biographies, the Kitty Kelley school of journalism. Now we have a biography about her, in which she has lost her privacy, too. This is where I came in.

The issue of privacy has been kicked at and stomped upon and run over, and now it's a thing of the past. Everyone is fair game. Nancy Reagan found that out when we read all about her habit of consulting an astrologer and then asking her not to talk to the media about it. So what does the astrologer do? She talks to the media about it. She tells reporters she was the one who decided when the IMF treaty would be signed and when Reagan should meet with Gorbachev. Is that public business, or should it remain private—a woman who is not a government official talking to an astrologer and attempting to influence the decisions of the President of the United States?

Unfortunately, I seem to have been one of the pioneers in the trend toward celebrities' being stripped of their privacy. I was on the cutting edge, and I was the one being cut. It's not a question of fairness. Fairness doesn't enter into it. Reporters loved to ask me during my experience if I'd been treated fairly. I used to remind them that fairness is in the mind of the reporter.

The trend to strip anyone in public life of any shred of privacy has gone far beyond the reporting on government officials and has caught up with some of the biggest names in business, entertainment, and sports. Baseball's Wade Boggs found that out. So did the most successful televangelist in America, Jimmy Bakker. The corporate executive is vulnerable now, and so is the college president. There is no longer any distinction between groups that are immune from invasions of their privacy by the media and groups that are not. No one is immune.

Evidently the public shares this feeling that the press has gone too far in invading people's privacy. No less an authority than the Times Mirror Company, owner of the *Los Angeles Times*, which had so much to say about my private life, released a poll in November 1989 showing a "significant erosion of public confidence" in the objectivity of the news media. The poll covered members of the general public, journalists, government officials, business executives, and academic leaders. Andrew Kohut, who used to be president of the Gallup organization, said the survey showed that "the public is significantly more critical about the way the press does its job."

There's a message in that statement. But will it produce a stop to the invasion of our privacy by members of the news media, or even slow it down to a morally and professionally justified degree? No.

THERE IS ANOTHER area of equally grave danger where protection of privacy is concerned. That is the deliberation by a jury, a key component of our system of justice that has remained preserved from the time it was instituted in America by our founding fathers until now. But it's going by the boards almost as fast as the protection of personal privacy.

My own experience in our criminal justice system—I didn't volunteer—has given me an insight into that subject that no one can have who hasn't gone through it. I assure you that something is taking place today that is a grave threat to the constitutional guarantee of a fair trial by a jury of your peers.

That threat is the absurd practice of allowing reporters to interview jurors after they have rendered their verdict.

I watched Larry King on the night that Jim Bakker was convicted. I'm a fan of Larry King, and I like his show and watch it often, but he did something that night that worried me then and still does. He had two members of that jury on his program who told the millions of viewers exactly what happened in the jury room during their deliberations. They told us that two jurors were holding out, and the rest of them finally had to overwhelm the two holdouts with their arguments and convince them to vote for a guilty verdict.

In Larry's defense, he's not the first journalist to interview jurors after a verdict. It happened after John Hinckley was found not guilty by reason of insanity for shooting President Reagan. It happened in my case too, and what was even worse, it came several years after the fact.

The *Wall Street Journal* went back to some of the folks who served on the jury for my trial and questioned them about their verdict. The jury heard my case—the trial lasted four months, twice as long as Hinckley's—and then handed down its verdict. That should be the end of it. But not for the *Wall Street Journal*.

That's wrong. What goes on in a jury room should be confidential information, but it's not anymore, and therein lies the danger. Once people who are selected to serve on a jury start making their decisions of guilt or innocence on the basis of what they think some TV reporter is going to ask them, then the fairness of the whole jury system collapses.

Our system of trial by jury is one of the strongest threads in the fabric of our freedom. Once it collapses, the individual freedom of every American citizen might also collapse, and we will no longer be a free country.

People are in trouble already when they fall into the criminal justice system. A lot of them deserve to be—but not all of them. Some folks are innocent. An innocent person in our criminal justice system, however, is an aberration. Judges, prosecutors, and investigators are all biased against the defendant and carry out their duties with the suspicion that you are guilty because if you weren't you wouldn't be there. Add to that bias the practice of a TV or print reporter approaching a juror and asking, "Are you happy with the verdict? What did you discuss in your deliberations?" The combination endangers the rights of the accused more seriously than anything I can imagine—but we're allowing it to happen.

Our system isn't perfect for a simple reason: it was designed and is conducted by human beings. We make mistakes. Sometimes an innocent person is convicted, and sometimes a guilty person is acquitted. But that ought to be the way the system works, and it certainly is what our founding fathers had in mind. But if we continue to allow reporters to intrude into jury deliberations, any defendant is going to have far greater trouble proving his or her innocence. It's much easier for a juror to explain on the evening news why he or she voted to convict the defendant than to explain holding out for acquittal against the rest of the jurors.

The guilty verdict is always the easier course to take, and jurors will be more inclined to find someone guilty rather than defend themselves to the news media—especially in a trial of a well-known person or a trial that has aroused the public's emotions.

No one believes in openness more enthusiastically than I do. That's why I have always vigorously opposed sidewalk government and all the bureaucratic isolation that goes with it. But at some point, someone who is innocent is going to be convicted of something he or she didn't do simply because the jurors decided that the guilty verdict would be more popular and would play better on the evening news and in the morning paper.

I witnessed a clear example of the media's influence on jurors in my own trial. One of the jurors was a nice-looking, soft-spoken black lady, the wife of a tenant farmer. Every day the members of the jury were instructed not to read the papers or watch the news on TV. The coverage of the trial was heavy and constant, and the judge didn't want the jurors to be influenced by anything a reporter wrote or said.

That is always the prudent instruction in a trial of high visibility, but the reality is that those jurors are going to be exposed to some news coverage regardless of how hard they try to avoid it. The media is just too dominant a part of our lives for anyone to be able to avoid it completely. If you don't hear or read something at home, you'll hear it on your car radio, or someone will tell you what they saw or read. It's unavoidable.

The wife of the tenant farmer wore the same outfit every day of my trial—except one. It was a blue denim jacket and skirt. Her outfit was always freshly laundered and pressed. She was spotless in her appearance.

The one day when she wore something else happened to be the day that Daddy King—Martin Luther King, Sr.—testified as a character witness on my behalf. On that day, the lady wore her Sunday go-to-meetin' dress. It was important for her to make a good impression on a man who was one of her heroes.

It proved two things to me: First, jurors are affected by various influences in the courtroom and in the news coverage of the trial. Why did she wear her best dress on that one day and no other? Because she knew the day before that Daddy King was going to be there. How did she know? A story on the air or in the paper is a good guess. Second, there is no way to keep jurors from knowing what the reporters are doing and saying.

Confidentiality concerning jury deliberations should be required at all levels of our criminal justice system. In my trial, I'm sure the jurors said certain things to their families and friends about their deliberations. That's also unavoidable and understandable. But when jurors start going public about what was said in the secrecy of their deliberations, the rights of innocent people are no longer protected.

What is said within the walls of the jury room should be required to stay there, under force of law. Until it is, however, we are putting ourselves in the position of replacing trial by jury with trial by talk show, and the judges have been replaced by Oprah, Phil, and Geraldo.

● ● ●

THE GREAT PAPER CHASE went on. It was an exhaustive ordeal for all of us, and a financial drain as well. I went through a million and a half dollars defending myself against things that were not true. Still, it was an enlightening experience for me. I learned some things. It wasn't my preferred way of acquiring an education, but every experience can be instructive.

Eight different federal agencies conducted investigations against me, trying to dig up anything they possibly could against me. At one time or another, I was under investigation by the Federal Bureau of Investigation, the Office of the Comptroller of the Currency, the Securities Exchange Commission, the Federal Election Commission, the Internal Revenue Service, the Federal Deposit Insurance Corporation, the Federal Reserve Bank, and the United States Senate. I must have been one of their most visible targets. It's hard to miss a man who stands six feet, five inches tall and weighs 245 pounds.

I told LaBelle, "The only agency that's not investigating me is the only one that should—the Bureau of Weights and Measures."

I learned at least two things. One, to my astonishment, was that the University of Georgia football team was capable of playing a game in my absence. The other was that the FBI isn't all it's cracked up to be. I used to have a lot of respect for that outfit until it took those fellas two years to find out that LaBelle's checks to the Big Star were to our little grocery store in Calhoun and not to some Communist organization.

11

The Living Sentence

ON THE FIRST MORNING of my trial, LaBelle and I approached the federal courthouse in Atlanta and immediately ran into the inevitable mob of reporters. I told them there were so many of them that I was worried about their safety. I said, "Don't any of you folks out here in the street get hit by a car. I want all of you to be able to come back here when I'm acquitted."

A reporter asked me if I had any other comment as my trial was about to begin, and I said, "Yes—I count seventeen cameras in this crowd. I expect to see that same number when the jury finds me not guilty."

I never for one minute doubted that I would be found not guilty, because I knew I wasn't guilty of anything. To this day I don't know what crime I'm accused of committing, so I never doubted the outcome of any of those stages I was put through, including my marathon trial that started on January 14 and lasted until April 30.

It would make this part of the book into a real page-turner if I told you that my trial was high drama in the courtroom, a real-life Ben Matlock episode, even set in the same city. The truth is that instead of being like "Matlock," my trial was as exciting as something else you see on TV—the test pattern.

It was boredom of the most burdensome kind. In addition to running up my legal bills to $1.5 million, the government was costing me even more money by keeping me away from my work for four months. The only folks in that courtroom who were making money were the lawyers and the judge. The jurors were in the same position I was. They were losing money too, unless they were getting paid by the hour.

The most notable things about my trial were the fact that the jury showed its courage and common sense in the face of the federal government's onslaught, and the length of the thing. It became the longest trial in the history of Georgia. Two years later, the government took only half as long in trying to convict John Hinckley for shooting the President of the United States.

My trial was noteworthy not for its drama but for the inside view it provided of our judicial system and its virtues and dangers. No one believes in our system of criminal justice more than I do, but from my chair at the defense table, I was an eyewitness not only to the system's greatness but to its potential for harm.

Our system is designed to punish the guilty, which is fine as far as it goes, but it doesn't go far enough. It is not designed to find the innocent in judicial proceedings. There is a built-in bias against the defendant resulting from the pressure on the investigators to "close the case," the prosecutors to win a conviction, and the judge and jury to return a guilty verdict.

In my case, the main charge was conspiracy. That was another irony—and that's being kind to the government. Here the feds were saying on one hand that I was guilty of careless banking practices, while on the other hand they were saying I was guilty of conspiracy. I read a lot of books, including Perry Mason and Agatha Christie, and I've never heard of a case yet where the alleged conspirators were charged with being careless and sloppy. I always thought conspiracy required meticulous planning right down to the smallest detail, but here was the government saying I was carrying out a conspiracy, but in a sloppy way.

The prosecutors seemed to be telling the jury I was sort of a careless conspirator. Obviously the jury never heard of that kind either. The jurors not only found me not guilty, but they cleared all three of the other "codefendants," too.

After all that time and money, the box score read:

Bert Lance—Charged with twelve counts of banking irregularities. Not guilty on nine, the other three dropped.
Tom Mitchell—Charged with four counts of making false financial statements to banks. Not guilty.

Richard Carr—Charged with three counts of misapplication
   of bank funds. Not guilty.
Jack Mullins—Charged with three counts of misapplication
   of bank funds. Not guilty.
Estimated cost of case to taxpayers—$7 million.

There has never been any question in my mind that Mitchell,
Carr, and Mullins were tried only because the federal government
made them victims of what I call "the throwaway theory." That's when
the prosecution—the government—commits the premeditated act of
going after one big fish but, knowing that it does not have a strong case,
decides to try several lesser-known defendants at the same time. The
prosecution's thinking is that maybe the jury, realizing that it can't
convict the others, will then feel compelled to convict the celebrity.

Under that theory, the prosecution is willing to throw away the
others for the sake of getting its real target. That is clearly what happened in my trial. The government's case against me was weak from
the start, and thus its case against the three others was even weaker. No
violation of laws or criminal codes was involved. No crime was committed by anyone. There was no intent—how could there be when
there wasn't any crime? Nobody was said to have lost money or been
injured in any other respect.

But some folks in the federal bureaucracy were so anxious to get
at me—because of my closeness to the President—that they were willing to engage in this massive charade, spend $7 million of the taxpay-
ers' money, and even drag in three other innocent men under the
throwaway theory. Those men never should have been subjected to
anything, but instead they were forced to endure most of that ordeal
with me, incur some of the same expenses, and feel some of the same
public embarrassment—all because of the prosecution's zeal in trying
to humiliate Carter by going through me. There can never be any
justification for what the government did to three innocent men—
Mitchell, Carr, and Mullins.

Mitchell was partially protected because of the insurance on
members of the bank's board of directors. But Mullins and Carr were
not on the board and had no protection. They were financially dev-
astated, and being found not guilty didn't help their financial punishment one bit. That's just not right. The federal government should be
forced to pay the expenses in a case like that.

THE DECISIVE and dramatic point of the trial came when the judge,
Charles Moye, threw out the conspiracy charge, which was the back-

bone of the government's case. There was a sizable irony in that action, too, because this was the same judge who earlier gave each of the jurors a copy of the indictment against me. I told my lawyer in the courtroom, Nickolas Chilivas, that I'd never heard of such a thing. He said he hadn't either. I didn't remember everything in the indictment, but I remembered one thing that wasn't there: a section telling folks what a nice, pleasant man Bert Lance is.

For that reason, when Judge Moye threw out the conspiracy charge, I preferred to think of it as what sports people term a "makeup call." Then the judge topped himself by instructing the ladies and gentlemen of the jury to tear up the first forty-one pages of their copies of the indictment because they dealt with the conspiracy count. The judge seemed to me erratic at best and biased at worst.

He is a Republican, appointed by Nixon, and he made it clear he didn't like Jimmy Carter. Then, my lawyers told me that during my trial, he told the lawyers for both sides that I must be guilty because if I weren't, all I had to do was whisper in the President's ear and those prosecutors would be transferred to some remote outpost. It's bad enough for others in a trial to have an attitude like that, but if the prejudice against the defendant is coming from the presiding judge himself, you begin to wonder about justice for all.

Judge Moye kept coming up with new actions that revealed to me his attitude toward this defendant who was trying to receive a fair trial in his courtroom. Before the jurors reached a verdict, he made a big fuss out of giving each one of them a certificate of appreciation— signed by him—and embossed with a gold seal. The certificate said how proud the government was of that particular juror. The judge made a big presentation to each juror in a ceremony in his courtroom.

I served on a jury as recently as 1989, and the judge didn't give any of us a certificate. But there I was, sitting at the defense table and watching Judge Moye honor the jurors in behalf of the government, with everyone in his courtroom aware that the government presenting those nice awards to the jurors was one of the parties in the case being considered by them.

There is simply no excuse in the world for that kind of judicial conduct. That seemed to me to be a highly prejudicial act. No lawyer would ever do that. Neither would any other judge. And any lawyer or judge who hears that story stands openmouthed in shock when I tell it. But it happened.

There was another interruption near the end of my trial. A new district director for the Internal Revenue Service was sworn in to office, and Moye's courtroom was used because, as the chief judge of that federal judicial district, his is the ceremonial courtroom in the federal courthouse in Atlanta.

My trial was suspended, and the jurors were allowed to attend the swearing-in. An IRS employee talked to one of the jurors about the possibility that the juror might be able to get a job with the IRS. Now we had a member of the jury as a prospective employee of the government, putting the juror in the position of ruling for or against his possible future employer. That's as close to a stacked deck as I ever want to be.

The only interruption to the tedium and the boredom were the actions on the part of Judge Moye and others in his courtroom. They reached the height of absurdity when LaBelle was sitting in the spectators' section reading her small pocket Bible, making far better use of her time than those who sat there listening to the unending humdrum.

A U.S. marshal came over to her and ordered her to stop reading.

I became so resentful about what I considered blatant bias and repeated impugning of my integrity on the part of the judge that I told my lawyers I was about to get up and walk out, and I didn't much care what Moye might do to me. I demanded that they make a motion that the judge "recuse" himself—remove himself from hearing this case. I told them, "If you don't make a motion to recuse this fellow, I'm telling you I'm going to stand up and walk out. They can put me in jail or do whatever they want to, but I'm not going to sit there any longer and put up with this prejudice. We're going to win simply because nobody in this case is guilty of anything, but I'm not going to put up with his prejudice any longer."

As we challenged Moye on a motion to recuse him, we ran into another example of the system's being tilted against the defendant, whether guilty or innocent. When you act to have a judge removed from a case on your motion to recuse him because of his alleged prejudice or incompetence, guess who rules on your motion—the same judge.

Moye listened to our argument—that's when he allegedly said that Carter would have transferred those prosecutors if I weren't guilty—and then he handed down his decision: "Motion denied."

That's all. He didn't have to give any explanation for his ruling, and the defense is not given the opportunity to ask for one. It's just "motion denied," then back to the trial.

•   •   •

THE JURY deliberated for almost a week, but there was no nail-biting, unbearable suspense for any member of the Lance family. All of us were completely at peace. We grew closer, as often happens in an experience like that, and our closeness became even greater when my father, the former president of Young Harris College in Georgia, died the first week of my trial.

I slept just as well every night of the week during jury deliberations as I did every night of the trial. The biggest burden was not suspense. It was just the opposite—more boredom, the same fatiguing feeling that burdened all of us for the entire four months. Not only did the feds fail in the trial, they didn't even put on a good show.

Nothing new was introduced during the trial. There was never any intent on the part of the four defendants, so the prosecutors couldn't prove intent because it never existed, and you can't prove something that doesn't exist.

What saved me from being railroaded was the jury of twelve citizens. The system worked, but only because those ladies and gentlemen of the jury were able and willing to defy the intimidations and prejudices which unfortunately can surface from the human element in our system of criminal justice.

As we walked out onto the courthouse steps and into the Georgia fresh air and sunshine, I noticed one final thing: on the last day of my trial, there weren't as many media folk as there were on the first day.

YOU CAN GET THROUGH a punishment like that if you know the truth, and I knew it. The Bible says, "The truth shall set you free." I've always believed that, and my experience during this so-called Lance affair proved it to me. If you know the truth, you don't have to worry.

I never did. Right in the midst of my darkest times in Washington, I had to have a few spots burned off my shoulder, so I went to my doctor. He took my blood pressure in the midst of all that controversy and said it was exactly the same as it always was—normal.

All of us in the family were able to draw from the same emotional reserve, our religious faith. We had something then, as we do now, that my opponents could not attack, penetrate, or erode: a strong sense of faith and a firm belief in God.

In many ways, my travails with the federal bureaucracy were like the situations in life that face virtually every person, whether it's the death of a loved one, financial reversals, lingering illness, or some other worry. Each of those circumstances causes people to reach down deep inside themselves for the courage and strength to continue.

The way we respond reflects the depth of faith and trust we have in God. It's easy to get caught up in asking, "Why me?" But to do that is to lose sight of the central fact that we determine our reactions to adversity ourselves. As my ordeal dragged on for nine years, I found myself from time to time remembering the words of Disraeli:

> Circumstances may be beyond the control of man, but his conduct is within his own power.

During my time in Washington, I was helped by the small number of men and women in the White House prayer group. While the controversy swirled around me, the members of the prayer group supported me. When I hurt, they hurt. They were truly sensitive, caring people who eased the pain of those long days and nights and shared my firm faith that God would provide the strength and wisdom to get us, LaBelle and me and our family, through the ordeal.

Throughout the "Lance affair" we drew heavily on the reservoir of strength that comes from the belief that God gives you the power to overcome evil and challenges. The only difference between the evil that disrupted my life and that which tests other people's mettle is that my situation was very public.

I never could have made it through that whole, long ordeal by relying only on my own strength. I might have made it to a certain point, but ultimately I would have failed. Even now, and perhaps for the rest of my life, my wounds have not completely healed and those who will can reopen them.

I could not survive without something that is sustaining, and the sustenance comes from the faith and knowledge that God will give you the power to survive and overcome your ordeal. But you can't store it up. You can't put it in a bank and draw on it. You have to have the faith to believe it will be there for you in every occasion of adversity.

The case of someone like John DeLorean, the automobile designer, is a good point. When he was on trial a few years ago, some folks questioned whether his faith was real and whether he was guilty or innocent, but they were missing the point. The point about John DeLorean was that if his faith had not been real, there was no way he could have persevered through two trials. It isn't easy going through that process while you are abandoned by just about everyone.

Oliver North made that point less than a month after the Iran-Contra arms scandal broke. I never agreed with Reagan that North was "a national hero," but I could identify with North on one important point. Early in his troubles he said he was being cast aside already by his former friends and associates. I knew something that he didn't—he was going to be cast aside by a whole lot more people.

I knew as LaBelle and I entered the courtroom on that first morning that even a not-guilty verdict by the jury would not prevent me from serving a sentence. I was just as sure of it when the jury cleared me, even after the *Washington Post* published an editorial saying the verdict "was a careful one, reached after a long examination of the case, and it deserves to be accepted as final."

As commendable as the *Post*'s message was, I knew it wouldn't happen that way. Human nature doesn't permit it. On the contrary, it is the ultimate indignity of folks in such circumstances that you will live under public suspicion and prejudice the rest of your life.

It's the "living sentence," and the public and the news media will see to it that you serve it.

THE MEDIA must be singled out here for special mention. They were a willing—at times apparently gleeful—partner in this entire episode, and as you read this, there are reporters, editors, and news executives around the nation who are still working hard at perpetuating their own creation, the "Lance affair," fourteen years after costing me my job, assailing my honor, punishing my family, and severely damaging a presidency.

In this year of 1991, *Time* magazine and even the *Atlanta Constitution* in my own state have continued to bang away at me with innuendo, outright misstatements, and a boring rehash of my court case of more than a decade ago. And when they go out of their way to mention that I was indicted for what they vaguely call "banking irregularities" or "questionable banking practices," they somehow fail to mention that I was cleared of all charges.

Through it all, of course, the media remain conveniently unaccountable. No one believes more devoutly than I do in the importance of, and the rights of, a free press in our free society. However, I also believe devoutly in the *responsibilities* of that press. When those responsibilities are ignored, or even held in contempt, the threat to our individual freedom—and that's what it is—becomes grave.

Various members of the media—writing or broadcasting about the people involved in government, business, sports, entertainment, medicine, education, the law, or anything else—have gotten away with so many abuses in recent years and even over a period of decades that they have almost built up an immunity around themselves. The courts have held that public figures have not been libeled unless intent can be proved. That has been used by various members of the media as a license to kill, and that's not putting it too strongly. As a result, individuals who find themselves attacked by the media, with its growing malice and disregard for the truth, have no redress—unless you'd like to find a lawyer in the yellow pages, hope you can afford his fee, and then try to outspend and outlast *Time* magazine or *60 Minutes* in a court case.

At some point, somebody is going to have to redefine the issue: What is harmful? What is libel? What is slander? Until that happens, those of us who have been victimized by the media's reckless practices will continue to serve the "living sentence." And it reaches a point where it's not just embarrassing or unfair. It becomes harmful to your own honest efforts to earn a living because it constantly resurrects old information and leaves the impression that the charges against you may not have been resolved.

I've had news *executives* tell me privately that news stories about me in recent years—and you can be sure this applies to all too many other people—are simply the result of laziness, incompetence, or general sloppiness, or all three. The obvious response to that is if a doctor operating on you took out the wrong organ, would you say his laziness, incompetence, or general sloppiness were okay? You'd sue his shingle off for malpractice. And so would those same people in the news media who are guilty themselves of *journalistic* malpractice when they damage people's lives.

My latest, but presumably not last, service as one of the media's punching bags came when *Time* published a four-page spread titled "Masters of Deceit," above a subhead that told its readers: "How the men behind an audacious bank expanded it via global duplicity, touching Jimmy Carter, Arab sheiks, and Manuel Noriega along the way."

The reporters, Jonathan Beaty and S.C. Gwynne, wrote about an investigation into whether Washington's largest bank was owned by the Bank of Credit and Commerce International—B.C.C.I. I haven't done any banking business with anyone in the article in a dozen years, but Beaty and Gwynne made sure to mention a "Lance connection."

They also wrote this for all their readers to see: "Lance had resigned in September as Carter's budget director under charges of impropriety . . ." What they *didn't* write was as harmful to me as what they did—they did not mention that I was cleared of all charges.

The *Washington Post*, by contrast, published a far longer account of the investigation. My name never appeared. Doesn't that say something about the *Time* version?

One Sunday night early in 1991 I had a call from a friend who said, "*Time* is doing a story on you. It's about the B.C.C.I."

I told him I didn't know how *Time* could write such a story linking me with the B.C.C.I., because there isn't any link. Then he read me a promotion piece released by *Time* and sent all across the country over the wires of the Associated Press. It was headed:

BANKING SCANDAL TRACES ROOTS TO GEORGIA

I immediately called the reporter who had come to see me before the article was written, Jonathan Beaty, whom I had talked to for more than two hours in my office. He had come to me for information on the subject, and I had spent that much time walking him through a fairly complicated subject so he would have the story straight.

I told him I was the focus of a story that just went out over the AP's national wire and I wanted to know what in the world was going on.

He said, "There's no way you could be."

I said, "Well, I am."

"Well, whoever called you is kidding you."

"No, it wasn't a kidding sort of call."

Beaty said, "You were in only two paragraphs out of four pages, and that was historical."

I asked him to check into it and give me a call, and he said he would. He tried to call once and missed me. I returned his call several times but missed him, and he never called back.

I called Joelle Attinger, one of the magazine's deputy chiefs of correspondents. Her boss, John Stacks, the chief of correspondents and assistant managing editor, happened to be on vacation. I registered my complaints again, and she said she would look into it.

When Stacks returned from vacation, I was in New York on other business, so I called him and told him I'd like to see him. He graciously agreed. We met in his office and had a detailed discussion of my complaints about the article. It clearly implied that I had done something wrong—since I was the same fellow who was indicted on all those charges years ago—yet failed to mention my acquittal.

He said he'd look into it and call me the next week, which he didn't. On Monday morning of the following week, I started trying to reach him. He was always in meetings, but he finally sent word that I could try him around five o'clock. I couldn't try him then, so I started in again on Tuesday morning.

I reached him shortly after lunch that day, when he made the mistake of answering the phone himself. He said, "Oh, you haven't gotten my letter?"

I told him no. He said, "Well, it went out last week." Ten days later I still hadn't received it. I thought that might say something about the Postal Service—or *Time* magazine.

He said, "I've talked to Jonathan Beaty and to our attorney, and we've gone back over the article and we think the story is essentially correct." Then he added that he thought I was more upset over what I considered inaccuracies in the article because I had taken so much time to be kind to his reporter.

I told Stacks I couldn't believe what he was telling me. I said, "I'm not that naive. I told you why the fellow came to see me, and the only reason why I saw him, and that was to help walk him through a fairly complicated subject. There wouldn't be any other reason to take two or three hours of my time and talk to him. I don't owe *Time* magazine anything, and *Time* doesn't owe me anything, except fair treatment."

Then I reminded him of the purpose for my visit to his office two weeks before. "That wasn't the reason I came to see you. I came to see you to tell you that you had done me harm and that I needed to have it redressed in some way."

I went though my recitation of complaints. As exhibit A, I pointed out that some people wouldn't feel it made much difference whether I met Mr. Abedi in 1976 or 1977. But it makes a whole world of difference. The truth of the matter is that I met him in 1977, after I left government service. *Time's* implication is that after Carter was elected Abedi sought me out and put me on his payroll, which is just a damn lie.

Stacks suggested I write him a letter. I told him, "Look, I've got no interest in writing you a letter to put in the pages of your magazine, requoting everything that you put in that article that was wrong. I'm not going to do that." Instead, we agreed that I would send him my list of everything that was wrong in his article, knowing, of course, that it could never change the harm his magazine had already done to me.

Meanwhile, the CBS television station in Atlanta, station WAGA, channel 5, picked up the story off the AP wire and broadcast it. The station was sure to say I was charged with banking improprieties, but not to get around to saying I was acquitted.

I called the station and ran into a new example of why the media's attitude is both wrong and harmful. I got to talk to the WAGA news director, Mark Hoffman, and asked him to fax me his story so I could review it and respond if appropriate.

Hoffman said, "Oh, that's against our policy. I can give that to you only if you subpoena us."

Here was a television station, operating under a license granted by the U.S. government and broadcasting through the air waves that belong to all of us, telling me that I had to go to the time and expense of hiring an attorney and go into a court to subpoena a transcript of something they said about me that was wrong and harmful to me. Surely that must be the most supreme example of media arrogance I've run in to. If it's not, it will do until a better example comes along.

In fairness, I have to say that other stations and even networks have sent me transcripts on request. Most public affairs programs and documentaries on TV even make sure at the end of the show to tell you where you can write for a transcript and show you the information on the screen.

But then there is always this arrogance, as demonstrated by Hoffman, looming in front of any of us who are, or have been, public figures. I've been out of public office since 1977. But the media still reserves the right to keep going after me for things I was cleared of, or other imaginary connections that exist only in the minds of some frustrated Woodward-Bernstein impersonators.

My problems stemming from the *Time* article weren't finished. A few days later, a reporter for the *Atlanta Constitution*, Beth Kurlow, called and said, "My editor wants me to do a story about you and the B.C.C.I. as a result of the *Time* magazine article."

Beth reported on President Carter in the years since he left the White House. She's called me for information or with questions, and I've always returned her calls and helped her in every way I could, and there's another irony. Even in the worst moments of what I went through in Washington and in my trial, I always cooperated with the members of the news media, returned their calls, answered their questions when I could, referred them elsewhere when I couldn't, and was always the most accessible person I could be. And they'll admit that. Yet some of them—too many—keep roasting me on their open grill.

I told Beth, "I don't think it would be logical, consistent, or smart for me to do an interview with you for something I've just roundly criticized *Time* magazine for carrying." I told her my problem with *Time* was that its article was not newsworthy, topical, or true. I told her I had nothing to say to her except that she should be certain to get her facts straight—especially that there has been no business relationship between the B.C.C.I. and me for the past ten years.

Then she both shocked and infuriated me by asking, "Are you a target of that grand jury investigation?"

I said, "Let me tell you something. I cannot describe to you how offended I am by that question, because I know beyond any doubt whatsoever that there is no information that you could possibly have from *any*body that could give you any rationale at all for asking me that."

The paper ran a big Sunday story on page one about connections between the Carter Center in Atlanta and the B.C.C.I. The article made no mention of the good that the Carter Center has done in wiping out diseases in Third World countries, that farmers in Ghana have become independent, or any other humanitarian deeds performed by the Carter Center.

On the following page, the *Constitution* ran my picture and a story, with the information that I had appeared before the grand jury and repeating some of the allegations from the *Time* piece. It's a common practice in the media to repeat someone else's allegations and to claim, when they are found to be false, that the reporter was only repeating what he or she had picked up from someone else's earlier story. The truth, of course, is that the tale bearer carries the same responsibility as the tale maker, or should. Beth made sure, of course, to say in her story that I denied I was a target of the investigation, knowing that the denial always compounds the problem for the one who is the media's target.

As a result of her story, I immediately lost a client in my business. He called me on Monday morning, the day after her article, to tell me that folks in his organization were getting skittish about doing business with me. They were canceling the retainer they had been paying me. It cost me $25,000 a year.

That's wrong, and it doesn't make any difference who the victim is—Bert Lance, Mother Teresa, or anybody else.

It's ironic that some people in the news media are guilty of the very things that they accuse others of—distortion, withholding information, and other practices that they view with such horror when they allege them in others.

One of journalism's own members, William Cullen Bryant, foresaw this element in the news media and the dangers it poses in something he wrote in the last century:

The press, important as is its office, is but the servant of human intellect, and its ministry is for good or evil, *according to the character of those who direct it*. The press is a mill that grinds all that is put into its hopper. Fill the hopper with poisoned grain and it will grind it to meal, but there is death in the bread.

The *New York Times* even admitted in its own pages that it does not always limit itself to the news that's fit to print, regardless of its motto. David Wise wrote an article in the *Times* Sunday magazine five years later under the title "Why the President's Men Stumble." After five pages of reasons, Wise said in his conclusion:

No doubt, there are other reasons why Presidential appointees continue to get into trouble. Perhaps one is the national appetite for scandal. Both press and public seem to relish the fall from grace of a high official. This is particularly true in the nation's capital: Washington loves a victim.

12

"Malaise": The Beginning of the End

THE HANDWRITING was on the wall for the Carter presidency as early as the summer of 1979, when everybody was using a word that folks don't use often: "malaise." It's a fact that one person who never used that word during the whole period was Carter himself.

It sounded like something you spread on a bacon, lettuce, and tomato sandwich, but it became fashionable for folks go to around talking about "the great malaise" that was gripping Washington and the Carter administration. That's another one of those cases in Washington where appearance has a way of becoming reality.

I don't know whether the administration was wallowing in any great malaise or not. I was half a world away, with my family on an around-the-world business/pleasure trip, and I wasn't letting what might or might not be happening in Washington interfere with the fun LaBelle, our son Beverly, and I were having.

I was catching up with the news from the U.S.A. wherever I could, though, and I spotted a few stories in the overseas editions of the *New York Times* and the *Washington Post*, those two papers which decided I was so worthy of their coverage two years earlier, reporting a growing feeling in Washington that the administration was in danger of becoming moribund.

Near the end of our trip, Jewell Miller, who was my secretary in Calhoun and Washington and still works for me back in Calhoun, caught up with me in San Francisco. She told me that Brock Adams, Jimmy's secretary of transportation, was trying to get hold of me. The date was July 3, 1979.

The tone of urgency in the message from Brock made it clear that I should return his call as quickly as I could. I called him back that night from our hotel room.

Adams was clearly worried. Even over the phone from three thousand miles away, that was obvious. He didn't waste time asking me about the trip, the weather, or my health. He got right to the reason for his call. "Bert, the President is in deep trouble. I don't understand what's going on. He's not talking to any of us who are close to him. And he thinks everything is falling apart for him. You need to call him and find out what's going on. I think he's having real problems."

Brock told me that Jimmy was at Camp David for the Fourth of July holiday. It was too late back east for me to call him that night, so I promised to call him in the morning.

I'm not the kind of person who loses sleep over much of anything. Throughout the whole so-called Lance affair, I never lost a moment's sleep about the controversy swirling all around me. But I lost a lot of sleep that night. I didn't want the President of the United States to be a troubled man. That's not good for the nation. And I didn't want my friend to be troubled either.

I read in my travels overseas that Carter felt many of the problems facing our nation at that time stemmed from an apathy on the part of the American people. He may well have been right, and I remember thinking at the time that Jimmy was probably saying what many people were thinking. What worried me, though, was that Jimmy was worried about the symptom and not the cause.

Jimmy Carter, who should have been well into the planning for his second campaign to run *for* the presidency, was instead running *from* it. That was the problem.

After I tossed and turned most of the night, I reached Jimmy at Camp David the next morning, at six o'clock San Francisco time. Just like Brock the night before, I didn't waste any time with small talk. "Mr. President," I said. "I've been out of the country, and I feel I need to talk to you. What I've been reading and hearing doesn't reflect the Jimmy Carter I know."

There was a long pause on the other end of the line. Finally he said, "In fact, Bert, I came back from my meeting in Tokyo, and it all seemed to be falling down around me in the White House. I don't know what to do about it."

I was sure I could help him in his dilemma, just as I had done in the past, so I didn't hesitate in giving him my response. I told him flat-out: "I can solve that problem for you. Why don't you just be Jimmy Carter for a change? Everybody's trying to mold you and everybody's trying to make you do this, that, and the other. Why don't you be what you are? And that is the person who really is concerned about the human needs in the world.

"You have access to a lot of bright people. I told you that before. Listen to their ideas and what they have to say. But when you make your decisions, let them be your own, as President. Don't let your decisions be forced upon you by somebody else's will. That's what you need to be about."

Jimmy thanked me for my thoughts and advice. I like to think he was grateful that an old friend was showing not only his concern but his loyalty, too. Presidents don't always see a whole lot of loyalty in difficult times. But he had always been loyal to me, and I wanted him to know without any doubt at all on his part that I was still loyal to him, malaise or no malaise.

I didn't need much time back on these shores to see just how much trouble my friend was in. It was a terrible time for the nation and thus a terrible time for him. The public opinion polls showed that his performance rating from the American people had dropped to its lowest point—only slightly above Nixon's low point in the Gallup poll and slightly below it in a Lou Harris survey. A poll in ten southern states by the Darden Research Corporation of Atlanta showed Jimmy trailing Ted Kennedy.

The culprit at the moment was the energy shortage, what we were calling "the gasoline crunch." It was an albatross around his neck, and even though he didn't put it there, it was choking his presidency and his hopes for a second term.

Jimmy had accomplished some great things in three years in the White House—the Camp David Accord between Israel and Egypt, the SALT treaty on strategic arms, civil service reform, low unemployment, and the Panama Canal treaty, to mention a few—and no Americans were being killed in combat anywhere in the world.

But the headlines every day about the gasoline crunch were threatening to inflict mortal wounds on his presidency, if they hadn't done so already. Over one three-day period in the first week of July, these headlines appeared in the *Washington Post*, and Jimmy was reading them every morning:

RAIN, GAS LINES SPOIL HOLIDAY

DOE FIGURES GAS LINES
COULD COST MILLIONS

GASOLINE SHORTAGE HERE
TIED TO DIP IN RESERVES

WORLD RECESSION FORECAST
FOLLOWING OIL PRICE RISE

JULY GAS SUPPLIES UNCERTAIN

One adviser told Martin Schram of the *Washington Post*, "He could have gone on TV and said he was going to call in the oil companies and talk tough with them, but it's just not in Jimmy Carter's nature to do that until he knows all the facts."

That comment was exactly right. That's the methodical, analytical engineer on the job, pulling in all the data before making his decision. It's the enlightened way to proceed if you're Jimmy Carter, but to the voters—and the news media—it was weakness and vacillation, again.

Stu Eizenstat, Carter's adviser on domestic policy, sent him a confidential memo which put the gasoline crunch in stark terms: "In many respects, this would appear to be the worst of times . . . Nothing else has so frustrated, confused, angered the American people—or so targeted their distress at you personally."

Jimmy had gone to Camp David originally to work on an energy speech for a national television address to the nation. He was concerned about it, he was gathering information on which to take action, and he wanted to reassure the nation that he was on top of the crisis and was going to move on it.

But then his concern broadened, going beyond the energy crisis specifically to take in the whole so-called national malaise. And again, he went about things in the classic Jimmy Carter way. He spent ten days at Camp David with Rosalynn, calling his key cabinet members and White House staffers to meet there with him in what John Foster Dulles, when he was secretary of state under Eisenhower during the Cold War, used to call an "agonizing reappraisal" of the state of the nation and his administration. He extended his circle of advisers, calling in prominent figures in business, labor and religious leaders, and eight governors.

He made a short helicopter flight to Carnegie, Pennsylvania, near Pittsburgh, one evening and met with twelve private citizens on the back porch of a machinist named Bill Fisher. The next day he flew to nearby Martinsburg, West Virginia, and spent an hour and a half listening to seventeen other private citizens at the home of Marvin Porterfield, a disabled former Marine pilot and a retired cattle farmer.

Anybody who ever worked for Jimmy Carter could understand the process that was unfolding in such a systematic way. When he returned to Camp David from his second helicopter trip, he briefed eighteen journalists—reporters, editors, columnists, and commentators—and the all-star lineup was proof of how concerned the nation had become with the problems and with Jimmy's response or lack of response to them. The folks in that group included some of the biggest media names in America: Walter Cronkite, Frank Reynolds, David Broder, Hugh Sidey, Meg Greenfield, Jack Germond, Tom Wicker, James J. Kilpatrick, and John Chancellor.

Finally, he was ready to act. He spoke on television on Sunday evening, July 15, at ten o'clock, from his desk in the Oval Office. He expressed his concern about the "crisis of confidence" in America. He told the nation that "the gap between our citizens and our government has never been so wide."

That had to bother Jimmy greatly. He was talking about sidewalk government, and he was admitting that after three years, he had been unable to close the gap that always worried him. He promised that he would act in the next few days to deal with this larger problem facing the nation.

And he did. He shook up his administration, firing Joe Califano and Mike Blumenthal. He made proposals to the Congress to deal with the energy problem on both a short-term and long-term basis, and he tried to activate our citizens to shake off what had become an overnight cliché—"the national malaise."

Three weeks later, Jimmy held a news conference, and I thought his performance was exceptional. I did something I never do—I wrote him a long letter complimenting him on what I told him was "a superb performance last night."

Then I made another suggestion to him:

> Despite what the press, mainly the Washington press has been saying over the last few weeks, I believe that once you are able to get back on the high road of discussion of problems and solutions, then things will begin to show a marked upturn. As one who now exists in the real world, I do not detect any great interest or concern about who the cabinet officers may be or who is on the White House staff, except for the fact that the people want a leader as President and one who in some way can listen and hear their concerns and frustrations.

I went on to remind Jimmy that he was "truly a Proposition 13 candidate long before that became vogue after California voters approved a proposition limiting spending. The things that you talked about from 1974 through 1976 related to what obviously has now become the national malaise . . . I truly believe the American people saw in you a very simple ingredient called hope and expressed what they saw by electing you as President."

I suggested that he establish a "Goals for America" program patterned after the one he had conducted so successfully in Georgia. And I told him he should consider "moving the capital once a month . . . to some other section of the country." I thought he should avoid sliding accidentally into sidewalk government and take his cabinet officers with him to other cities for town meetings, another technique he had employed with success in Georgia. He would be showing the people that the national administration was neither content nor willing to govern from the island of isolation which Washington had become for too many other Presidents.

Near the end of my letter, I wrote:

> As I told you long ago, the Washington press is never going to be happy with the fact that you are the President, and they are going to do all that they can to insure that you don't stay there a minute longer than absolutely required. I am delighted we now are to the point where most people recognize this fact and that there can be give-and-take based on that sort of relationship.
>
> None of us can battle the press just on the basis of fighting all the time, and certainly you have not done that, but as long as we know where everybody stands, then I think we ultimately will be much better off.

I ended my letter with a personal reminder: "You once said that you always hoped I would stay close to you, and I accepted that as a compliment and I hope that would be the case, but I also urge that you always likewise stay close to the American people."

The President responded by thanking me for my letter—but I don't think he ever took my advice to heart.

Malaise, like other things, is in the mind of the beholder. What might be called stability, security, or even prosperity in other times was called "malaise" in 1979, and it stuck. The next year Jimmy paid the political leader's ultimate price, the fifth consecutive President unable to serve two consecutive terms.

•   •   •

IN ANY DISCUSSION of the many reasons for Jimmy Carter's defeat in 1980, special mention is due Teddy Kennedy. He went out of his way to get Jimmy out of the White House so he could move in. He ran against him hard right up to 1980, until Jimmy told the world, "I'm going to whip his ass," and then he did.

Kennedy helped to whip himself, as a matter of fact, when he fumbled around and couldn't come up with an answer to Roger Mudd's question on TV about why he thought the American people should elect him President.

I don't have any problem with Kennedy's decision to run against Jimmy. I think anybody has the right to run for President, and the fact that the person in the White House happens to be a member of your party doesn't deprive you of the right to run yourself.

But what Teddy did to the head of his own party and to the party itself was as disloyal as anything any politician ever did. It was his party's first term in the White House after the Nixon-Ford years, and yet Kennedy violated the interests of his own party and helped ensure the election of the opposition.

The extreme to which Teddy went to make sure he embarrassed Carter on national TV at the 1980 convention is a textbook lesson in disloyalty. There was Carter, having just delivered his acceptance speech, nominated by his—and Kennedy's—party as its standard-bearer for the second straight time, and still President of the United States, holder of the same office Kennedy's brother held, standing on stage waiting for Teddy to show up. And he waited and waited and waited.

I was watching that humiliating spectacle on TV back in Georgia after just winning my court battle against the federal government, and I was appalled at what this Democratic senator was willing to do against his leader and his own party.

I found myself wishing Jimmy would walk up to the microphone and say, "Listen, my fellow Democrats. I promised to whip this guy's ass, and I did, and by damn I'm still the President of the United States, so I don't have to kowtow to this guy or his constituency of Massachusetts liberals who aren't going to vote for me anyhow, so I'm going home. If he shows up, tell him I said to go fly a kite."

I think Jimmy's failure to say something like that, maybe in more presidential terms or maybe not, and walk out of the convention center with his head held high merely added to the public's impression that he was weak and a vacillator. Standing there grinning self-consciously and waiting for the senator from Massachusetts was completely out of character. Jimmy would never react that way in the same kind of situation elsewhere. He's as strong, as forceful, and as decisive as they come, and he can curl your hair when he wants to chew you out and he'll flash those eyes at you so brightly you'll need sunglasses.

But he wanted all the support he could get, which is understandable for any President. In this case, however, I think he would have been far better off taking the initiative and embarrassing Kennedy instead of having it work out the other way around.

By 1979 AND 1980, when the reelection effort got under way, the misery index was stalking Carter. He was beginning to pay the price for not doing what several of us had suggested in early 1977: he never took our advice and strengthened his economic team to establish a solid economic planning program for his administration. When the 1980 election approached, it was too late to expect any help from Congress. Those folks had been neglected from the start.

Ronald Reagan's candidacy may have had something to do with Carter's reelectability, but unemployment, inflation, and interest rates were the real culprits. And since they are cyclical and part of the political decision-making process, the proper approach to correct them was never taken by President Carter. He needed to establish a Federal Reserve policy that would encourage lower interest rates and economic expansion. Instead, he stuck to his tight money policy.

There are many who believe the American hostage situation in Iran cost Carter the presidency. They're wrong. The hostage situation certainly didn't help, but neither did it cost Jimmy the presidency.

Had Operation Desert One, the attempt to rescue the hostages by airlift, been successful, Jimmy might have been able to parlay that success into reelection. But that was the only factor that could have changed the course of the election. Conversely, had the misery index been significantly reduced by 1980—even with the hostage situation unresolved—Jimmy Carter would have been reelected.

President Reagan understood the importance of the misery index and took some of the same measures I had suggested to President Carter to deal with them. When Reagan took office, we were in the midst of the worst economic climate in this country since the Great Depression. He took his lumps during the first three years in office, but he understood that *the economic circumstances* existing in 1984 would determine his reelectability.

Carter was wrong and served one term. Reagan was right and served two.

13

The Rest of the Reasons

FOLKS CAN SPECULATE all they want about which factors contributed to Jimmy's defeat—the misery index, the hostages, his TV image, the gasoline crunch, all that business about incompetence and vacillation, and Teddy Kennedy's unique contribution to the 1980 campaign. But other factors that usually go unmentioned also figured in the Carter downfall.

Jimmy said and did some other things that also damaged him. They totaled up to this: in four years, President Carter made very few popular decisions.

Many of them were right, but too many of them were unpopular. His energy program, his economic policies, the hostages, concern over what the media insisted on calling the national "malaise," the B-1 bomber—any major decision you can name was greeted with criticism, ridicule, or controversy, or all of the above.

Other decisions and statements of less profound magnitude also contributed to the public's overall negative impression of Carter. One was his silly fight against what he called "the three-martini lunch." I don't drink martinis, because I'm afraid their potency will make my hair fall out, but I don't have any problem with folks who do. As for having three of them at lunch, I thought that was an exaggeration in most cases. I know folks who have two, but I'm not sure how many of them have three on a daily basis.

We had a meeting about tax reform in Washington on a Saturday early in the administration. We began discussing the practice of using private clubs for business purposes and deducting lunches as expenses because they are a part of the cost of doing business. The argument against allowing those deductions was that people in certain positions got to deduct the cost of their lunches but the folks who carried a brown bag to work couldn't. I knew going into the meeting that we were in for a bad day.

At one point Carter said to me, "I saw you at the Commerce Club a few months ago having lunch. What do you do at the Commerce Club?"

Instead of answering the question, I turned to him and said, "Mr. President, I saw you there in July of last year, and I know what you were doing. You were getting a campaign contribution. The Commerce Club is a legitimate place for people to get together and talk business."

Jimmy said, "Well, I want to cut it out." He said three martinis shouldn't be allowed as a tax deduction.

I threw up my hands and said, "Mr. President, ain't any sense in you and me engaging in this argument because we simply don't agree about this. I don't drink martinis, and I never have done any business with a fellow who drinks three of them because he's completely incapable of carrying on any business afterward."

Then Carter started going out around the country making all those speeches about three-martini lunches, which didn't seem to me to be the most critical issue in the land. His behavior was typical of him. He'd made his decision after hearing what we had to say, and he was sticking with it. There wasn't any vacillation at all.

But his decisiveness on that issue did not sit well with a lot of folks in the business community, whether they drank martinis or Shirley Temples. Jimmy had trouble throughout his political career winning over the business community, and that three-martini nonsense was another setback for him.

IF WE ASSIGN some of the blame to Carter for his own defeat, we must also give him full credit for his present standing as America's greatest living former President. He has achieved his new popularity and strong standing among the people of this nation and the world because of his great affinity for people and their problems.

That virtue was obvious through all his years in public office, and remains so today. Other Presidents pick up handsome fees for serving on corporate boards after leaving the White House, and there's nothing wrong with that. In Reagan's first year out of the Oval Office, he and Nancy Reagan went to Japan and made two million dollars in two weeks for a twenty-minute speech and other personal appearances. Later Reagan got $60,000 for speaking to franchise owners of Hardee's fast food restaurants. That's their business.

But it tells you something about Jimmy Carter that he has spent his ten years since leaving the White House teaching the Bible in Sunday school in Plains and working for his two favorite causes, the Carter Center in Atlanta and Habitat for Humanity.

At the Center, which he founded himself, he analyzes ways to resolve international disputes peacefully, a service which has involved him in helping to resolve disagreements between nations in Africa and Central America and even in supervising the conduct of elections. At Habitat for Humanity, he travels to cities around the country, puts on jeans and a T-shirt, picks up a hammer and saw, and helps to build better housing for poor people.

Jimmy Carter's concern for people came across clearly in his political campaigns. He was a unique candidate. When he got a chance to talk to voters one-on-one and he shook hands with them, he would win 80 percent of those votes. He has a remarkable ability to win people over in personal contact because he comes across as a sincere person, which he is, and a man concerned about people's problems, which he also is.

In that respect, he's as good a candidate on the campaign trail as there's ever been. He simply has no peer in his ability to reach folks when he's in a small group, whether it's young people, old people, minorities, or any other kind of a group. His eye contact, his body language, his informality, and his natural friendliness—everything about him combines to form the impressions of credibility that voters look for in a candidate.

An article by Paul R. Wieck in *The New Republic* early in the 1976 presidential campaign pointed out this quality in Carter. "He's one of the finest one-to-one campaigners around," Wieck wrote, "and has built a huge personal following in his two Georgia races by meeting personally hundreds of thousands of people. He's ready to repeat it on a national scale." Wieck quoted one official as saying, "He'll shake hands with three-fourths of the voters in New Hampshire."

But Carter ran into a problem as a presidential campaigner. When you run for President, as a challenger and even more so as the incumbent, your campaign takes on an aloofness, a falseness, and a sense of distance from the people. You're removed from them, especially if you're the President. The Secret Service and other security forces build a wall between you and the voters. That's nobody's fault, and it's unfortunate that in this age it's necessary. I'm a big fan of the Secret Service and the job its agents and officials do. We need the Secret Service now more than ever, so I don't want to call the agency and its people impediments, but from a campaigning standpoint that's what they are.

They are also helpful. They make special arrangements for you and carry out details that you don't want to have to spend your time on, but they also take away from a Jimmy Carter kind of a candidate.

For a candidate with Carter's personal attributes, those security precautions represent a serious handicap. You can't reach the people personally, face-to-face and hand-to-hand. You're at a significant disadvantage because the pluses that got you where you are suddenly are taken away from you.

That was not as much of a problem for Carter in 1976 as it was in 1980 when he was the incumbent. In '76, he won early, while he was still getting close to the people. He was not a late bloomer—in fact, he was a late loser. He still managed to defeat President Ford, but his lead in the polls, built on that personal contact in '75 and the first three quarters of '76, slipped badly during October after he lost that closeness to the people.

To overcome the distance that sets in because of the security measures, campaign staffs schedule media events for their candidate. That was a double whammy for Jimmy. Not only did he lose much of his personal contact with people, he also had to rely on television to win votes, and the blunt truth is that Jimmy Carter does not come across well on television, especially against Ronald Reagan, who made his living in front of a camera.

This is not to say that Jimmy would have been reelected in 1980 if he had been able to conduct a more personal campaign with more contact with the American people. The hostage issue and double-digit inflation were hurdles enough, and having to bet on the media event of the day didn't help.

SOMETHING ELSE worked against Carter in 1980, too—the so-called Rose Garden strategy, when a President's advisers convince him that his best bet during a campaign for reelection is to remain at the White House, act presidential, take advantage of the media coverage any

President gets, and avoid exposing himself to controversy out on the campaign trail.

That was the advice Jimmy got, and followed, in 1980. That's another irony, because it was the very thing he needled Gerry Ford about in '76. And it's not Jimmy Carter's nature to play defense. He's an offensive star, so why put him on defense with the Rose Garden strategy? He had no experience in that kind of political strategy, and certainly no taste for it.

It's like the Chicago Bulls taking the ball out of Michael Jordan's hands and telling him to concentrate on defense. That just doesn't make any sense at all. The same was true about Jimmy Carter. His advisers should have encouraged him to get back on the campaign trail, where he always performed with so much sincerity and conviction—and success.

The whole thing even looked contrived, like those TV clips on the evening news the weekend before the election showing his national security adviser, Zbigniew Brzezinski, and Vice President Mondale rushing to greet his helicopter on the White House lawn to discuss exciting new developments in the hostage crisis. They went immediately into the Oval Office, presumably to prepare the announcement that the freeing of the hostages was imminent. But the whole thing looked staged, coming only three days before Election Day. And folks with only an average memory were able to recall that Brzezinski and Mondale had never rushed out to the helicopter before, so how come they were doing it this time? Maybe it was staged and maybe it wasn't, but obviously it didn't work.

That just wasn't Carter's style. The Rose Garden strategy didn't help him any more in 1980 than it helped the man he criticized for following it four years before. In fact, it hurt Jimmy, and in 1980 he had enough things hurting his chances already.

I'M CONFIDENT THAT , in retrospect, many Americans respect Jimmy Carter as a sincere, friendly, moral, and compassionate human being, and there are now statistics to prove it, which yield yet another irony.

Tom Brokaw reported on the NBC Nightly News on March 15, 1990, that a survey by NBC News and the Wall Street Journal earlier that month, in the tenth year after America's voters turned Jimmy out of office, showed that Carter now has a higher approval rating than Reagan. On the same newscast, John Chancellor explained this change in his commentary. He pointed out that Reagan left office with the highest approval rating of any President "since the Second World War," and that Carter's rating "was low." Then he said:

> But today, in our new poll, Carter's standing is better than Reagan's—not by a lot, but better. Why? One reason would seem to lie in different lifestyle. Carter disappeared into the wilds of Georgia nine years ago. Later we saw him, hammer in hand, helping to build housing for the poor. Then he got involved in international negotiations and he did good work in the recent elections in Nicaragua. Today he's in the Middle East on a peace mission. Carter's career after the White House has been characterized by good works.
>
> Then, ask most Americans what they remember about Ronald Reagan's recent activities and they will tell you about the couple of million dollars he picked up for a quick trip to Japan. Mrs. Reagan got two million in advance money for her book last year. The Reagans' career after the White House has been characterized by big bucks.
>
> Appearances matter and the country's mood has changed. The 1980s were noted for greed and avarice. But now we're in the 1990s and the waiter has arrived with the check. Things have changed and Carter is more popular than Reagan.

JIMMY'S CONCERN for his fellow human beings, which led to the results of that NBC/Wall Street Journal poll, was most dramatically evident in his fatiguing work to free the hostages in Iran. The history books show that Jimmy Carter was the one who got the hostages out of there.

It's ironic that no political or emotional issue in the Carter administration or in Jimmy's 1980 campaign came close to equaling the hostages crisis in the eyes of the American people—yet the man who accomplished what Americans yearned for was rejected by them.

Another man might have given up after being defeated on Election Day 1980, out of bitterness, frustration, or simple physical exhaustion. But it is a measure of the man Jimmy Carter is that he didn't do that. If anything, he worked harder than ever in November and December 1980 and January 1981 to gain freedom for those fifty-two Americans.

Then the Ayatollah provided the ultimate insult and hurt. He made damn sure Jimmy wasn't President anymore before he allowed the hostages to clear Iranian air space—thirty minutes after Jimmy's term expired.

And we don't know yet if there is more to this story, whether William Casey, who became Reagan's C.I.A. director, and others in the Reagan campaign made a deal to sell arms to Iran through a third country for the release of the hostages—but only after Election Day—all to head off an "October surprise" by Carter. We know the Reagan campaign lived in fear of such a surprise in that campaign. What we still don't know is whether the Casey deal was actually made, with the result that the hostages were held two or three months longer than they might have been, and whether persons outside the government were negotiating with a foreign power. It's a story that's ten years old and won't go away.

I've been proud of many things about Jimmy over the years, but to me he is a genuine hero for putting his own pain aside and working like Hercules for more than two months after his defeat to save those Americans—all of them.

THERE WERE striking similarities between Governor Jimmy Carter and President Jimmy Carter. Whether running the government in Atlanta or the one in Washington, one of Jimmy's chief characteristics was his consistency, his predictability. As governor and President, he took the high road in making his decisions, a great characteristic if you want to become a statesman but a heavy burden if you want to get reelected.

Jimmy never worried about the political consequences of his decisions, and that's commendable. It is proper for a governor or a President to base his decisions solely on the merits of the case and what's right for the people. Unfortunately, in our political structure, it is not always a realistic attitude.

But with Jimmy Carter, what you see is what you get. Georgia's longtime secretary of state, the late Ben Fortson, compared him to the South Georgia turtle in the way he approaches issues: "When a South Georgia turtle comes to an obstruction in his path, he just keeps on going in a straight line, right over the obstacle." Jimmy used the same approach in Atlanta and Washington, and it cost him dearly in terms of his expenditure of political capital and, ultimately, his reelectability in both offices.

President Carter was committed to carrying out his campaign promises. Once in office, he was faced with decisions that all Presidents grapple with. He had to choose whether to do what was right, based solely on the problem's merits without regard for political considerations, or to reverse his priorities and do what was politically expedient regardless of whether it was the right action or the right time.

In each decision a chief executive makes, whether as mayor, governor, or President, those two factors coexist and must be considered in a delicate balance. Ultimately the questions are these: What political harm or liability can stem from tackling this issue? And how much political capital should be spent—capital that could be valuable in a future situation—in taking a stand on this issue now?

President Carter thought through each decision he made on the basis of what he thought was right. What may have been politically expedient at that moment was never a factor in his decision-making process. And it never ceased to surprise him that he wasn't applauded for relegating his political future to second place in order to wade into an issue meriting his attention, regardless of the political consequences.

The Panama Canal treaty was a classic example. Whether you agreed or disagreed with him about that issue, the political reality is that it should have been a second-term decision. There was no valid reason for Jimmy to get into that controversy in his first term, when he needed to save all the political capital he could to help his chances for reelection.

But to Jimmy that wasn't the question. He was convinced that the time had come for that issue to be discussed and resolved, and if he used up political capital in his first term to do it, then so be it.

That was the way Jimmy Carter governed. The tough issues he tackled had a cumulative effect on his reelectability. But he tackled them because he felt he had to. When the accolades he expected didn't follow those decisions, he was left parrying the sword's other edge—an obvious lack of appreciation among constituents on the other side of the issue.

Many of the issues President Carter tackled, such as the treaty on the canal, his decision to halt production of the B-1 bomber, the reorganization of the federal bureaucracy, and his decision to cancel nineteen water projects that were the personal pets of various members of Congress, were second-term issues. When it came to a reserve of political capital for his reelection as President, Carter was broke. But as distressed as he was about that and later about his defeat, what mattered most to him was that on all of those decisions, he did the right thing—and at the right time.

He still feels that way.

14

The Ashes of San Francisco

By 1982, TWO YEARS after my victory in court, many folks in the Democratic party in Georgia were asking me to run for governor again. I said no thanks for one basic reason: I was sure I would win.

I had been through three gubernatorial campaigns already, two of Carter's and one of my own. A fourth gubernatorial campaign simply didn't hold any appeal. Besides, I wasn't prepared to draw up a vision for the future of Georgia and then make it happen, which I think governors and gubernatorial candidates should do.

Instead, I decided to become active again in the national arena, not as a candidate—all the money in the world couldn't get me to do that—but by serving the party and the country in a variety of ways. I helped my friend, Joe Frank Harris, to get elected governor, even though he was running fifth in the public opinion polls at one point.

After his victory, Governor Harris asked me to become chairman of the Democratic party in Georgia. I was happy to accept this appointment because of my deep feeling that the South was going to be all-important in national politics for the foreseeable future. My strong opinion on that subject, and my acceptance of the Georgia chairmanship, set me on a course destined to lead me into some memorable experiences—not all of them pleasant, but all memorable—with an old associate, Fritz Mondale, and a new one, Jesse Jackson.

When I told Governor Harris I was willing to serve as state chairman, I said, "Joe Frank, I'm not interested in the statewide aspects of the Georgia Democratic party. You have good folks who take care of that. I've been to all the places in Georgia. I don't want to go to all the dinners for Democratic candidates. I've done all that before. I'm interested in the national scene. That's where I'd like to build the image of Georgia and the South. You get somebody else to deal with the Georgia side, and I'll deal with the national side."

Joe Frank agreed. I was excited at this new opportunity, because I believed then—and I believe now—that the South has great political leadership that can guide the nation, and I also believed I had sufficient credibility in predicting political trends and events to represent the South within the party.

In the wake of the Carter presidency, the South had become the laughingstock of the nation rather than the spawning ground of Presidents. Washington, Jefferson, and Madison were from the South, but the activists in the party viewed the South only as the region that had given them Jimmy Carter, and they simply did not like him. They were Kennedyites, not Carterites, and in that attitude they were disenfranchising the South from a role in national politics. I thought that had to be changed.

After helping to raise funds for Democratic candidates across the South through the party—something that had never been done in Georgia—I made my first move to help restore the South to its rightful and historic position as a key member of the Democratic family.

I formed a cohesive, goal-oriented group with my fellow state chairmen throughout the South, through a series of telephone conference calls among the thirteen of us in the closing months of 1982. We agreed unanimously that the South's role in national politics could no longer remain peripheral, but had to become central. We decided to act on that theme—together—when the right opportunity presented itself. That happened early in 1983, not in the South but up north in Chicago.

Mayor Jane Byrne was running for reelection there. Her opponent in the primary, Congressman Harold Washington, had won the nomination of the Illinois Democratic Party, but Mayor Byrne had made it clear she wasn't going to take that lying down. She was threatening a write-in candidacy.

This wasn't going to do the party any good as we headed into another presidential election. It looked like exactly the opportunity the southern chairmen had been talking about. It was an appropriate situation for us to send a signal to the national party apparatus, proving our strength, solidarity, and influence.

On March 15, the thirteen of us got together in another conference call. I said I believed Mayor Byrne's write-in plans were a serious threat to the party at the national level, and the rest of the chairmen agreed. Within thirty-six hours, we mobilized to make our views known in Chicago. We flew there from our various points on the map of Dixie and held a news conference immediately, telling the media what our fears were and what we proposed to do about them.

Clearly united on an issue of serious concern to each of us, we showed not only our concern but the unity and strength of southern Democrats in our national party. Shortly thereafter, Mayor Byrne dropped her write-in plans. Our party was spared a divisive and damaging public fight.

Our actions sent a great signal to the national party and the nation: thirteen white party chairmen were campaigning for the black man, Harold Washington, who eventually won the election. It was a triumphant moment for the southern wing of the Democratic party. Rarely had our wing made its presence known in national political affairs, and even more rarely had it influenced a race in so positive a manner. To me it marked the end of the adolescent role forced on the South for too long. Our rite of passage to the center stage of American politics had now occurred.

If Fritz Mondale and Mike Dukakis had understood this emerging fact of life, their election returns would have been a whole lot better—especially in the case of Dukakis. His campaign in 1988 was a winnable one, but he turned his back on the South after winning the party's nomination and in so doing managed to snatch defeat from the jaws of victory.

Another strong signal was sent out from that press conference in Chicago, one with personal significance for me. The reporters were more interested in my trial—of three years before. As those questions continued to pop up during the press conference, I saw that my slate had not been wiped clean after all. Even when you've been acquitted by a jury, you can still be guilty of something in the eyes of too many people, even though they can't tell you what it is.

I knew I would face these slings and arrows for the rest of my life. The truth still had not caught up with the lie—and I knew then that it never would.

As STATE CHAIRMAN, I wanted to become acquainted with each Democratic presidential candidate as 1983 unfolded, so I stepped up my communications and contacts with each of them. Aside from Mondale, the one I identified with the most and became most closely associated with was Jesse Jackson.

Tyrone Brooks, a member of the Georgia legislature, told me in 1983 that Jesse wanted to meet with me. We set the day before Thanksgiving as the time and my party chairman's office in Atlanta as the place.

Jesse came down with his usual retinue of thirty-four advisers, and almost immediately we got into an argument. The subject was what Jesse considered the inherent unfairness to minority candidates in runoff primaries.

We argued tooth-and-nail. Jackson is an extremely persuasive and forceful person, and I'm always willing to employ whatever powers of persuasion I have, too, so we went at each other toe-to-toe. I was honest with him in my defense of the system, and he was honest with me in his opposition to it, and neither of us blinked. That's important to Jesse in his assessment of you. He has an almost combative sense for instantly detecting fear in another person. And when he does, he is swift and sure in exploiting it.

He didn't sense any inclination to back down on my part. Besides, I'm bigger than he is. I told him flat-out, "Reverend, I understand what you're saying, but I have to tell you that there is nothing racial in the requirement for a majority vote for a candidate to be elected governor of Georgia. It would be just as wrong for a plurality to be sufficient for victory, because then the black vote would be weighted. I like you, and I respect you, but we'll never agree on this subject."

So on the question of runoff primaries, we agreed to disagree. Then we moved on to those issues and concerns where we agreed, remembering the old political truism that there are more things that unite us than divide us.

One of those issues was the question of our party rules for selecting delegates for caucuses, primaries, and the whole nominating process. I agreed with Jesse that the rules were unfair and ought to be changed. Specifically, the requirement that a candidate had to win 20 percent of the votes in a caucus or a primary before winning any of the delegates from that state was blatantly unfair. I promised him I would try to help get that rule changed.

The state chairmen met at a Democratic party conference at the Washington Sheraton Hotel in February 1984, to take up the rules question. Jackson knew I supported Mondale for our party's nomination, and Mondale knew I supported Jackson's effort to change the rules concerning delegate selection.

The South was going to be a key to our chances in '84. Hamilton Jordan and I visited most of the southern governors in 1983 and 1984 and talked to them about that. Jesse's rise to prominence within our party didn't have to complicate the role of the South in the party. On the contrary, Jesse could help to lead us back to the victorious days of "the solid South," if we would just let him.

One of the most poignant moments in my association with Jackson occurred on that trip, at a morning meeting of Jesse with his advisers before the party conference began. Jesse invited me to the meeting, and as I sat there and looked around the room, I was struck profoundly by the realization that I was the only one there who had not been put in jail for what I believe in.

Here we were, preparing to hold a meeting about unfair rules in the Democratic party, and everyone in the room had been put down by unfair rules all his life. These folks and their families and neighbors had been imprisoned for trying to go to the same school as white folks, or for drinking out of a "Whites Only" water fountain, or for using a "Whites Only" rest room or sitting in the "Whites Only" section of the city bus or trying to get waited on at the "Whites Only" section of a drugstore soda fountain. When it came to the subject of unfair rules, these folks wrote the book. Everyone in that room was a better authority on the subject than I was because every one of them had been the victim of unfair rules and had been willing to stand up against them and go to jail when they felt it was necessary. It was a moment and a lesson that I have never forgotten. I knew then that I had to look at the Jesse Jackson phenomenon through their eyes.

The Democratic conference that followed Jesse's meeting was what many folks would call a "no-holds-barred meeting." Jesse likes to describe that kind of a session as "no bull jive."

It was a breakfast meeting, and he arrived late, as usual. All the people in the room—state party chairmen and vice chairmen—were moaning and groaning about his lateness and saying they had more important things to do than stand around and wait for him. Then we received word that he was on his way, having just been interviewed for a cable TV news program.

When he arrived, he shook hands all around, and then went straight to the rules issue. The big question among the national and state party officials was whether Jesse was going to walk out of the conference. He played offense right from the start.

"Let me tell you about the Pharisees," he said. "Some folks wanted Jesus to restore the sight of the blind man, so he did. But it was the Sabbath. Some of them said Jesus broke the rule that says the Sabbath is a day of rest. The Pharisees knew that was the rule. The only one who wasn't complaining was the one who got his eyesight back."

Then Jesse made his point. "That's where we are. The rules aren't fair. If we can restore the vision of this party, we can win an election. We ought to be able to do it."

I could see him winning over his white brothers and sisters from the South. Obviously Jesse Jackson wasn't going to walk out of that party conference, or out of the party either. He was in to stay.

AFTER JESSE'S TRIP to Atlanta in 1983, we got to know each other better in a hurry because of some fortunate political scheduling. Two groups of Democrats made three-city, one-day national tours to raise money for Democratic candidates for the 1984 campaign and present the image of a party united.

Our group, the southern team, was composed of John Glenn, Gary Hart, Jesse, and me. Our itinerary called for breakfast in Atlanta, lunch in Houston, and dinner in Albuquerque. The other group—Fritz Mondale, Senator Fritz Hollings of South Carolina, and Governor Ruben Askew of Florida—was to tour three northern cities and meet us in Albuquerque.

Jesse and I sat together on each of the flights. There we were, the black minister from Chicago and the white chairman from Georgia, on our way to becoming the odd couple of American politics. The chemistry between us was quickly evident, and in Houston I became a true Jesse Jackson believer.

All three candidates spoke to a large audience of Texas Democrats, and Jesse brought the house down. He got the only standing ovation. He simply blew Hart and Glenn out of the water. You could see then Jesse's great gift for going directly to the heart of complex problems, reducing them to simple terms that people can understand, and then providing solutions.

From that experience in Houston, and from seeing him in action in so many other places in 1984 and over the next four years, culminating at the 1988 convention in Atlanta, I know this: if Jackson had been a white candidate in 1984, he would have been the Democratic nominee for President.

As 1984 APPROACHED, I felt an obligation to Walter Mondale because of my fondness for him and his loyalty to me during the "Lance affair."

I also felt he was eminently qualified to be President. I still feel that way, even after the Reagan landslide in '84 and despite that fact that Fritz could have shown more courage in the flap over me that arose at the convention in San Francisco.

My enthusiasm for Mondale's qualifications for the White House is based on my observations of him in the Carter administration and after. The man understands government, the way it works and the way policies are put into effect. He and I differ in that he believes government is the solution to all problems, large and small. I didn't believe that then, and I certainly don't believe it now. On the human side, though, Fritz and I both believe that the government had an obligation to help those who are unable to help themselves.

We disagreed, however, on at least one other point—Lane Kirkland, the president of the AFL-CIO. That became clear early in 1983, when we had lunch in Washington one day with Jim Johnson, soon to be chairman of the Mondale presidential campaign.

I found myself disagreeing with the conventional wisdom of the moment that said Mondale had the nomination in the bag. I told Fritz he had to make a strong showing in the South to fend off any challenge that might materialize during the nomination process. My view was substantiated a year later when Gary Hart shocked a lot of folks by clobbering Fritz in the New Hampshire primary. When that happened, Mondale had an urgent need to win some primaries in the South as a way of slowing down Hart's sudden momentum.

In 1983, of course, no one dreamed that such a turn of events might take place in New Hampshire. Still, I didn't agree with all those experts who kept appearing on talk shows and saying that Mondale was a shoo-in for his party's nomination. Two things bothered me in that connection. One was my unshakable belief that the Democratic party had to begin appealing again to voters in the South. The other was Lane Kirkland.

My concern about Kirkland was that he did Mondale more harm than good. Fritz needed the support of labor people across the country, but it seemed to me that the Kirkland connection did not represent the broader base that a presidential candidate needs. What good would it do to have Kirkland and the AFL-CIO executive council embracing Fritz, if the members of their unions voted for Reagan?

I told Fritz at lunch that day that special interest groups would hurt him in 1984 if he didn't get away from them, for the same reasons that I had told Carter in 1976 to stop using Ralph Nader as his softball umpire in front of the TV cameras. I said, "Fritz, you ought to walk across the street and tell Lane Kirkland that you don't need his support."

He considered the suggestion for a moment. Then he leaned over the table and said, "You know I can't do that."

"Well, if you can't, you probably can't be President of the United States."

Fritz's priority treatment toward special interest groups and his uncertainty about how to deal with Jesse Jackson surfaced together in one experience I had with him shortly before the 1984 convention. I was relaxing at Sea Island, Georgia, when Mondale called and said he was scheduled to meet in Kansas City with Jesse, who was going to be there for the convention of the NAACP. Fritz asked if I could fly out and join them.

The night before their meeting, Mondale asked for my suggestions on how to talk to Jesse. "I need your guidance," he said. "What should I talk to him about?"

I told him that was one thing he didn't have to worry about.

"What do you mean?"

"You're not going to have to worry about what to say, because you're not going to do the talking anyhow. You're just going to listen. Jesse will show up with a list of fifteen or twenty items and there won't be any dialogue about it. It will be a monologue."

Mondale asked, "What can I expect?"

I told him, "Grapes and raisins."

"What?"

"Grapes and raisins."

"What on earth are you talking about?"

"Fritz, you asked me what you can expect, and I'm telling you. You can expect to hear about grapes and raisins."

"Okay, go ahead."

"Jesse will tell you that once you squeeze the juice out of a grape, it becomes a raisin, and you can never turn it back into a grape again because it changes its form. Then he'll tell you that's what's happening in your campaign, that you're paying too much attention to a few special interest groups and in so doing you're squeezing the juice out of the party and our chances."

Fritz said, "I don't know how to respond to that."

I suggested to him, "Just be fair with him. Listen to him."

After their meeting alone, the two were to meet with the party chairmen. On our way to that meeting, I asked Fritz how his meeting with Jesse had gone.

He said, "Ask me about grapes and raisins."

• • •

IT BECAME obvious to me and others that Mondale was not going to vary from those traditional sources of Democratic support to accommodate what I considered a changing electorate, a necessity that Ronald Reagan apparently saw, too. I kept repeating my reminder that the South was rising again in American politics, and that it was "imperative" that Mondale choose a southern running mate.

Fritz didn't reject the idea, but he didn't endorse it either. He told me he "understood" my point. But I don't think he ever did.

There was at least one piece of evidence that he didn't understand. Our thirteen southern party chairmen conducted another series of conference calls and personal visits with Fritz, making it clear that the one thing we would not back down on was our conviction that he needed a southern running mate to balance his ticket. We made the point emphatically and repeatedly, right up to the convention in San Francisco in July. Mondale, for his part, used the final weeks before the convention to screen a long list of potential running mates at his home in North Oaks, Minnesota. He did it with the best of intentions, but he made the same mistakes Jimmy made in 1976 when he entertained the press and all those special interest groups in Plains before kicking off his fall campaign.

Both men sent the wrong messages to the media and the electorate. The message was that a small band of special interest groups owned and operated the candidate.

That parade of potential running mates streaming to North Oaks, along with the ever-present special interest groups, turned Mondale's noble idea of having a woman running mate into a charade and a mockery. It was simply bad politics.

But that was what he chose to do, and he couldn't be dissuaded. So our southern party chairmen made a pilgrimage to St. Paul to restate our belief that he must choose a southerner to run on the ticket with him. The consensus candidate among us, and one I heartily agreed on, was Senator Lloyd Bentsen of Texas. He had all the necessary credentials: a respected member of the Senate, a man with a track record of winning elections, a moderate, and a southerner. And not to be overlooked were those twenty-nine electoral votes from Texas, which always play a significant role in presidential elections—in 1976, Texas was the state that put Carter over the top.

Fritz's response was unenthusiastic, as it was every time we mentioned a southern running mate. As always, he claimed to understand the South, but he didn't. Senator Bentsen was given only cursory consideration before being rejected as "the token white male."

I knew Bentsen never really had much of a chance from a meeting with Jim Johnson at the Atlanta Airport earlier in the campaign. Mondale had sent Johnson down to talk to me about the party chairmanship and the question of a running mate. Johnson told me Fritz was thinking about picking a woman as his running mate if he won the nomination. I told him I agreed with those who were saying the two national parties should be willing at that point in our nation's history to put a woman on their presidential tickets. I thought it would be a stroke of genius for us to beat the Republicans to the punch.

With Johnson's next statement, I knew we had a problem. He said Fritz was considering either Mayor Dianne Feinstein of San Francisco or Geraldine Ferraro, one of the members of Congress from New York. He asked me what I thought of the two. I told him, "That depends on whether you want to lose the election by twenty points or thirty. If you pick Feinstein, you'll lose by thirty. If you pick Ferraro, you'll lose by twenty." My prediction didn't have anything to do with the women but with the geographical and political imbalance of the ticket. And Mondale-Ferraro lost by twenty points.

The problem was that with either of those choices, the ticket would be thrown way out of balance. Both are liberals and both would be considered northerners. The party needed a southerner on the ticket, and a moderate one at that. Both of those women are fine, upstanding Democrats, but with a northern liberal at the head of the ticket, neither of them would pick up a single additional vote for Mondale.

ANOTHER SIGNIFICANT DEVELOPMENT, at least to me, happened before the convention—the "living sentence" was imposed again.

It all began when Mondale wanted to appoint me chairman of the Democratic National Committee so I could be of more help to him when his campaign started. That meeting at the Atlanta airport with Jim Johnson was Mondale's first step in that direction.

Johnson and I talked for an hour and a half one afternoon in Eastern Airline's Ionosphere Lounge at the airport. I told him early in the discussion, "Jim, I haven't given any thought at all to that idea, but on a scale of one to ten, my enthusiasm for it is about a six."

Johnson said he was surprised. "I expected something more like nine and a half."

I wanted to help the party and Fritz, but the idea was against my political instinct. I had a strong suspicion that the past might be repeated. If those reporters at the news conference in Chicago where our southern chairmen expressed their support for Harold Washington could spend so much time asking me about my trial from two years before, that sort of thing could happened again at the '84 convention, and at any time during the campaign. I had no stomach at all for fighting that nonsense again.

I agreed to accept the party chairmanship because Fritz wanted me to and because I thought I could help. But the resentment, bitterness, and distortions reappeared even before Mondale made the announcement.

Fritz and I agreed to keep a tight lid on his plans to appoint me to replace Chuck Manatt, but the word leaked out. By Friday night the wire services were running stories saying Mondale had decided to fire Chuck Manatt as chairman of the Democratic party and replace him with Bert Lance. By early Saturday morning, two days before the start of the convention, national attention had shifted from Mondale's historic announcement of a woman running mate to a fight over the party chairmanship. Who the chairman was wouldn't decide the 1984 presidential election, but there we were—proving again that Democrats are capable of fighting about almost anything.

Bob Beckel, one of Mondale's senior advisers, became alarmed at the growing resistance to Mondale's plan to appoint me. Twice during Friday night he called Johnson, who was staying with Mondale in Lake Tahoe until the convention began on Monday.

In their first conversation, Johnson told Beckel he expected the whole thing to "blow over." In the second phone call, Beckel sounded the alarm loud enough that Mondale got on the phone and told him, "That doesn't bother me. I'm willing to make that fight."

Maybe it didn't bother Mondale, but it bothered me. I had warned those folks for a week that this could happen, so when Beckel asked me for advice on how to put out the brushfire that had erupted into a five-alarm fire, I let him have it with both barrels: "Well, what do you want me to do about it? You put me in this position. I tried to tell you it was a bad idea and it wouldn't work. What am I supposed to do now?"

Beckel said he didn't know.

Fritz canceled the news conference he had scheduled for Saturday to announce my appointment and called me at my hotel in San Francisco. He asked me to travel to Lake Tahoe, 250 miles northeast, to talk about this crisis. He said, "You need to come to Tahoe, and we need to talk about it."

He was right about that much. We met on Saturday afternoon.

LaBelle and our son Beverly went with me, along with John White, a former Democratic chairman, and another irony grew out of that. In that group of middle-aged men, all of us with lengthy experience in Democratic politics, the one who was thirty years younger than everyone else spoke out first—and he laid it right on the line to his elders.

We were sitting on the deck of the condominium that Mondale had rented. With the refreshing frankness and objectivity of the young, Beverly laid things right out in the open for Fritz. "Look, I want you to understand one thing: If there is any problem at the convention about my father's appointment, you'd better stand up for him. You owe him that."

So spoke the twenty-two-year-old to the former Vice President of the United States.

But Mondale didn't stand up for me. When the crisis reached the critical stage, Beckel, who has always been a stand-up guy, was the only member of that whole Mondale group who stuck by me in San Francisco. I know that the man who is about to become his party's nominee for President can hardly afford to get caught in a storm before his campaign even begins, but none of this was my idea.

I thought Mondale, Johnson, and others could have shown something closer to what John Kennedy called "Profiles in Courage." When it came to sticking up for me, there seemed to be a distinct shortage of that human virtue.

I've never gone through life afraid of anyone at all, and I've never been handicapped by thin skin. I've always agreed with Johnny Mercer that you have to accentuate the positive and eliminate the negative. But any human being would have felt hurt by the treatment I received in San Francisco. Those folks who were so anxious for me to become the national chairman of their party that they flew Johnson to Atlanta to talk to me about it were all too willing to leave LaBelle, my family, and me twisting in the wind when my predictions came to pass.

The firestorm erupted immediately, and even our session at Tahoe couldn't put it out. By Saturday night the next course of action was clear and inescapable: the decision would have to be rescinded, someone else would have to serve as party chairman, a meaningful role would have to be found for Manatt, and I would be appointed as Mondale's campaign manager.

My becoming Fritz's campaign manager was his suggestion. When he asked me, during our Saturday meeting at Tahoe, I told him, "Fritz, let's not play any games. If I'm to be your chairman, I'm going to want to play a significant role and have the authority and responsibilities to help you. I don't want to be left out of things and not be able to contribute some help to your campaign."

Mondale said he agreed with that. He said he had been through one experience like that in one of his campaigns for Hubert Humphrey, in which he had been nominally an important policy official but really more window dressing than anything else. He assured me that this wouldn't happen to me.

Late Saturday afternoon, we announced my appointment as Mondale's campaign chairman and told the press we would have something to say about the party chairmanship at a later time. Our hope was to put out that brushfire that had spread into a five-alarm fire. Now if I could just get lucky and avoid a reimposition of the "living sentence". . .

MONDALE WANTED ME to head a selection committee to come up with a recommendation for a new party chairman in time for him to make the announcement the morning after he delivered his acceptance speech, the traditional time for announcing any change in party chairmanship.

My response was, "Well, Fritz, if you want me to do that, I'll do it in the proper professional way. That means you're going to have to get the word to the special interest folks that I have some authority and some say in the selection process."

He said he would, and he did make it clear to Lane Kirkland of the AFL-CIO and others during the rest of Saturday and Sunday that I had his support in the search for a new party chairman.

We began meeting Sunday morning at the Fairmont Hotel in San Francisco—Jim Johnson, John White, Mike Berman, and I. Our talks lasted all day, and we were held hostage in that room the entire time because the Mondale staff was so afraid of a news leak about this embarrassing controversy before the convention even began.

I argued, with eventual success, that Chuck Manatt should be allowed to keep his chairmanship, that he didn't deserve to be humiliated at his own convention in his own state. I thought that should be the beginning and the end of the selection process. By the end of the day, we agreed to face the reporters and tell them of our recommendation to keep Manatt in the party chairmanship.

We called a press conference for late Sunday afternoon and made the announcement. Jim Johnson made the statement and answered all the questions, and that was a portent of things to come right there. I thought the man who was going to be named Mondale's campaign manager might be asked to say one or two words or allowed to answer a question at least once during the session with the press, but Johnson handled everything with a "just-leave-everything-to-me-boys" attitude. The rest of us sat on our chairs and tried to look pretty in front of the still photographers and the TV cameras.

AT THE CONVENTION, the "living sentence" flared up right away and never stopped. Bob Beckel and a few others, plus a whole lot of reporters, will tell you that I was subjected to some of the cruelest and most humiliating treatment anybody ever received at any political convention, and I didn't deserve it.

At the opening session, my family and I were booed as we walked onto the convention floor, and we were booed every time after that. Why? I hadn't held a gun at Mondale's head and ordered him to name me campaign chairman. And I didn't apply for the job. And whether those folks doing the booing liked it or not, I had as much right to be there as any of them did—and a whole lot more than most of them. After all, I was the chairman of the Democratic party in my state. No other state chairman was booed.

I wasn't resisting the convention's desire to nominate Fritz. On the contrary, I knew a whole lot more about Mondale's qualifications than the rest of those folks in that convention hall, and I had done a whole lot more than most of them to help him get there.

And *booing*? This wasn't a ball game. I hadn't just dropped a fly ball to lose the World Series, or fumbled in the Super Bowl. I was there for the same reason the folks doing the booing were—to help my party, which I had worked for almost twenty years, to win the presidency. And the only thing I had done wrong was agree to work as Mondale's chairman if he wanted me.

The delegates on that floor knew all of these things, too. They knew how to read and watch the evening news on television, and the West Coast news media reported the story to the hilt over the entire weekend. It was clear in all of the coverage that the move to get rid of Manatt and replace him with me was the idea of the Mondale camp. But I was the target of the abuse.

As much as all of this hurt my family and me, what hurt even worse was the way the Mondale people were so willing to abandon us. When the whole thing blew up in their faces, they were perfectly willing to let me be the only one who got burned.

Throughout the convention, while I was enduring all this free abuse, I was trying to give the appearance that I had something to do with the Mondale campaign. That was a difficult trick to pull off, because the people around Fritz were leaving me alone and hoping that eventually I would just go away.

In one of my attempts to make it look as if the Mondale organization was conducting itself in a proper professional manner and really knew what it was doing, I went over to Geraldine Ferraro's hotel to accompany her to a meeting of the southern party chairmen. While I was waiting at her hotel, I had my first conversation with her husband, John Zaccaro. I asked him, "How are you adapting to the publicity that comes with being the spouse of the Vice Presidential nominee?"

He said, "Oh, fine. This press attention is something that will eventually move away from me anyhow, so I don't have any problems with it."

I felt obliged to say in response, "Well be my guest, John, because I don't believe you're going to see the press attention move away from you or any member of your family anytime soon." That conversation turned out to be another irony in view of the publicity that hounded the Ferraro family over the next couple of years.

The absurdity of the whole San Francisco fiasco was captured in a column by Herb Caen, the noted columnist for the *San Francisco Chronicle*. He wrote about a couple, real or imagined, whom he overheard in the lobby of the Fairmont Hotel.

The husband asked, "Did you hear that Bert Lance is going to be the chairman of the Democratic party?"

To which Caen said the wife responded, "Oh, I didn't know he was out of prison."

I could have avoided the whole mess by simply walking away, but I'm not the type to walk away when I think folks might be getting ready to commit a serious wrong against me—or against someone close to me. It had occurred to me after our meeting at Mondale's condo in Lake Tahoe that my family and I could just hop on the next airplane and go home to Calhoun.

That was a tempting option. I knew what I was walking into, even if Mondale didn't. But if I had done that, Mondale might not have won the nomination. I knew he didn't have any chance of beating Reagan, especially since I also knew he was not going to balance the ticket by choosing a southerner as his running mate. But I wanted Fritz to get the nomination. If he hadn't, Gary Hart might have, and I didn't think that was in anybody's best interest because I considered Hart unelectable.

All the events which were so humiliating and denigrating were so accurately forecast by my great and good friend, John Jay Hooker, of Nashville, who had come to San Francisco to specifically tell me of his concerns and fears that I would be sorely mistreated. How right he was.

The more determined I became, the more heated the treatment grew. My family and I didn't deserve that. I did everything I could to help Mondale, but he did nothing to intervene in my behalf when the chips were down, an all-too-common deficiency among American political leaders today.

After the convention, LaBelle and I went down to the Monterey Peninsula to play golf for a week. Nothing was going to happen during that time. Mondale had announced that he was going back to Minnesota to get in some fishing before beginning his campaign, so we took advantage of the opportunity to hit some golf balls and enjoy the spectacular beauty of the California coastline.

After several weeks, the furor over my involvement in the campaign had not subsided at all. It was reopening a lot of old wounds and bringing the hurt back into the lives of the whole Lance family, and we didn't deserve that. And it was doing about as much good for the Democrats as it was for the Lances.

Besides, my involvement in the campaign was really a sham from the start. Johnson and the rest of the crowd around Mondale had taken over. Those folks were going to run things their own way, and there's nothing wrong with that—but don't ask me to agree to serve as your campaign manager, put me through all that embarrassment, and then leave me with nothing to do while everybody else runs the campaign.

It didn't take long for me to decide this arrangement just wasn't going to work. I flew to New York in August and met with Bob Beckel and reviewed the situation for him. I told him the idea hadn't been handled well from the beginning, and it wasn't being productive now that the campaign was about to swing into high gear with the traditional kickoff over the Labor Day weekend.

The Mondale people were just too insecure about any Carterites, and about Jimmy and me specifically. What started as something that might have been worth trying—I say *might*—was clearly doomed. Mondale was going to be done a disservice, and I already had been. I told Bob I was going to resign. He agreed without argument, so I did.

•   •   •

I WASN'T the only one the Mondale people tried to do a number on at that convention. No less than our former President was also a target.

The relationship between Mondale and Carter was a subject of continuing concern to Fritz's people throughout 1984 because of the view on the part of many Americans that Carter's had been a failed presidency. Today, the times seem to be showing us that such was not necessarily the case. In fact, it is my belief that as the years go by and emotions and prejudices subside, objective political observers and historians will write that the policies, actions, and moral leadership of President Carter were more substantive and productive over the long run that those of the President who succeeded him.

But such was hardly the case in 1984, and the realities of politics dictated to Mondale and the people around him that he should put some distance between Carter and himself whenever possible. This was no problem during the primaries because he was running against other Democrats anyhow, so it didn't make any difference how much folks associated him with Carter.

Once the convention was over, however, Fritz was running against Reagan, and he could hardly expect to defeat a highly popular President by aligning himself closely with an unpopular one. No one in or out of the Mondale organization suggested that Fritz remind the voters at every opportunity that he was closely associated with Carter because he had been his Vice President and pose with him every day for the evening news.

On the other hand, common sense also told anyone who gave the subject a second thought that Mondale shouldn't waste his time worrying about the voters and the conservatives who didn't like Carter, because they weren't going to vote Democratic anyhow. I told him he should do what I did when I ran for governor of Georgia to succeed Jimmy and was faced with the same problem of a close association with Jimmy. That's when you have to follow the advice in the Johnny Mercer song and accentuate the positive.

There were folks who still liked Carter in 1984 and who also remembered that Carter was the one who picked Mondale to be his Vice President and put Fritz in the position where it was possible for him to become the presidential nominee of their party. They knew Mondale owed Jimmy something better than the treatment he was getting. And they were winnable votes for Mondale.

The issue came to a temporary climax at the convention, when it was clear to everyone connected with Mondale or Carter that the former President was not going to be allowed to address his party's convention during what was prime time on television on the East Coast. That's the maximum exposure for anything or anyone on television, whether you're talking about Presidents, former Presidents, Bill Cosby, or the World Series.

The Mondale people were preparing to schedule Carter's speech for a time in San Francisco when it would be past 11 P.M. on the East Coast. It was a deliberate tactic, designed to make sure that millions of voters would be in bed back east before Carter appeared on television. They were trying to hide him, and they were smacking him in the face with their attempt.

Carter was smart enough to know they were playing games with the schedule. Finally be became fed up and said to me over the telephone, "Look, I want to know what the schedule is."

I went over to the convention center and found Elliott Cutler, who had worked for me at OMB—when Carter was our boss—and I ran into the same games that Jimmy did. Elliott was directing the scheduling for the convention. I told him, "Elliott, you understand—and if you don't I'll have to have Carter tell Mondale—that if Jimmy doesn't appear in prime time, then he's not going to appear at all, because it's demeaning to him as a former President of the United States, the only one the Democrats have, not to appear at that time.

"We don't like the way he's being jerked around, and I'm here to tell you it's going to stop or else he's going to go home, and I don't know who else might go with him."

Elliott said, "I have to do what I'm told." I told him I understood that, so I went to see Mondale and told him, "Fritz, this doesn't make any sense at all. You have to be concentrating on the positives and just forget these negatives about not associating with Carter and all that other nonsense, because you can't do anything about them anyhow." I reminded him that the folks who didn't like Carter weren't going to vote for Fritz anyhow, but the folks who did like Jimmy might.

To his credit, Mondale agreed. Carter spoke on TV in evening prime time.

Those episodes in San Francisco came back to haunt Fritz during the campaign. The people in Georgia didn't want him to visit their state after the way Jimmy and I were treated at the convention. Eventually we were able to work things out to the degree that Mondale was invited to make one trip to Atlanta.

To show solidarity, I went with him for his speech. I don't remember much else about that unfortunate campaign. But I do remember this: Mondale did not carry one southern state. He didn't carry a whole lot of northern ones, either, for that matter, but in the South he was shut out.

To anyone over the age of fifty, that's another irony. The term "solid South" took on a new meaning. The South, always solidly Democratic in presidential elections, was now solidly Republican.

But a new leader rose out of the ashes of San Francisco.

15

Happy Days Are Here Again

JESSE JACKSON probably traveled more in 1984 than Mondale and Ferraro combined. He worked hard at being a presidential candidate right up to the convention. Throughout that time, he and I met occasionally and talked frequently, usually every day, a practice we still follow. We trust each other's judgment and guidance. In '84, Bob Strauss, John White, a few of my Georgia friends, and LaBelle were about the only ones besides Jesse that I was willing to confide in after that treatment at the convention.

I'm not sure that Jesse Jackson ever really decided to run for President in 1988. I think it was more of a case of deciding not to stop running. After making a strong showing at the convention in '84 that surprised almost everyone, there never was any doubt in anyone's mind that he was going to be a candidate again. It was a natural progression.

We continued to grow closer as concerned Democrats and as friends, too. I knew we had become good friends when I looked out the window of our home one day and there was Jesse, heading up our driveway unannounced on a chartered bus with about thirty of his close friends—just in time for supper.

There was ample precedent for a member of the Lance family to affiliate himself with a black man. Other Lances have willingly associated themselves with black people in a just cause—most notably, my father's cousin, Bill Lance, who was always so kind to me that I called him "Uncle Bill" even though he wasn't really my uncle. He was so willing to work with blacks and help their cause that he became the central figure in an act of history and courage that was unmatched in his time and maybe in any time.

In 1946, with racial tensions and the demand for civil rights at the boiling point throughout the South, the administration of Governor Eugene Talmadge was denying one thousand "Negroes" in Gainesville and other parts of Georgia's Hall County the right to vote. Uncle Bill was a lawyer, and he was willing to represent them in court, and to take the risks to his business and personal safety that such stand-up-and-be-counted bravery frequently entailed in those years. He was showing the kind of moral leadership and just plain guts that they make movies about, starring Gregory Peck.

Eight hundred and ninety of those black citizens obtained their right to vote thanks to my Uncle Bill. He was the champion of one thousand people, even the ones who lost. How many of us can say that? His opening argument in their trial is a classic yet uncelebrated expression of moral leadership and historic vision, articulated to a degree worthy of a marble monument in Washington, right next to the Lincoln Memorial.

This son of Georgia and lifelong southerner opened his case by telling the court that the South's cause in the Civil War was doomed before it began because we were on the wrong side of the overriding question. In making the point that the Talmadge administration was on the wrong side of the same question as it was being posed in 1946, Uncle Bill said:

> The issue was determined by the irresistible destiny of mankind . . . The South was being defeated long before a gun was fired at Sumter. The South had a "lost cause" exactly 246 years before Appomattox [referring to the landing of the Pilgrims at Plymouth Rock].
>
> Our sires placed states' rights above human rights. They forgot that there is even a higher law than the Constitution. A woman attempted to sweep back the sea by means of a broom. She had an easier job than the Talmadges, Bilbos, Longs and other fire-eaters are going to have in attempting to sweep back the oncoming tidal wave of universal suffrage.

With that kind of example in my family history, identifying with a black political leader in American politics came naturally to me.

Things began cranking up again in 1986, as the usual bumper crop of Democratic candidates began preparing for the 1988 campaign. Jesse and I were meeting more often now, and talking on the phone four and five times a day. I wanted to help him, and I wanted to help the party. Where winning the White House was concerned, the party could use all the help it could get, a situation which unfortunately continues to this day.

Jesse was still essentially a protestor in those days. He had a great power to disrupt, and he still does. I thought it was critical for Jesse and the party for someone to be willing to tell him to do this or not to do that. I have enough of a background in that department that I thought I could be of some help. Jesse, with his great ability to be either positive or negative, could have harmed the party—maybe not as much as Dukakis did, but the potential for harm was there.

Jesse asked me to be his manager for the 1988 campaign, but I said no thanks. After that business in San Francisco, I had no desire to hold any public position in anybody's campaign. He kept offering me other roles, and I kept declining. You need only so much foolishness of any type before it occurs to you not to subject yourself to it any more.

Presidential campaigns teach you that if you have a personal relationship with the candidate, you're going to spend most of your time fighting off the piranhas. There's a tough, mean-spirited element that finds its way into political campaigns, especially presidential ones. And if I had to endure all that abuse in San Francisco in 1984, imagine how much more I'd have to take as a white man working as Jesse's campaign manager. I would have spent the whole campaign defending myself against a bunch of nothing. I wasn't going to subject myself to that, and I wasn't going to subject my family or Jesse to it, either.

I told him, "Jesse, I care about you and about what happens to you. I'll be delighted to spend my time on the issues that you think people need to hear about, and I'll give you my advice and tell you what I think, just as I will with any other candidate. But I don't want to get involved in any formal way."

I told the other candidates the same thing. I let them know up front that it was important to me to support Jesse. I took their phone calls and responded to their questions and made what suggestions I could, but they knew where I stood because I told them.

As 1988 began, it looked as if Jesse might win 700 to 800 delegates to the convention in Atlanta, with 2,100 needed for nomination. In a multicandidate field, one candidate has to enjoy a dominant position. Nobody did as the year started, including Dukakis.

We had seven candidates, and Gary Hart would have been the leader if he had stayed out of trouble, although I still feel he would have had trouble winning the nomination. If he hadn't become embroiled in all that flap about extracurricular activities, I think we would have had a brokered convention. We would have had some candidates with 200 or 300 votes and others with from 800 to 1,200, but no candidate would have had 2,100 delegates going into the convention.

But Hart withdrew amid all the fury about him, Congressman Dick Gephardt of Missouri was never successful after Iowa, Senator Paul Simon of Illinois struggled to win delegates even in his own Midwest, Senator Albert Gore of Tennessee did well on Super Tuesday but could not build on that and ran into a disaster in New York. All of which meant that if Hart had stayed in the race, Jackson would have held the balance of power.

Jesse was never going to be the presidential nominee of the Democratic party, but he could say who would be. I warned him never to get into a conversation saying the nominee should be someone who has gone through the primaries, which he had. I told him, "We want to pick someone who can win, and the trouble with the Democratic party is that for too long now the fellow who has been nominated was not electable, and the one who was electable was not nominated."

My one recurring piece of advice to Jesse all through 1988 and the years leading up to it was that he had to convince the voters that he was now a mature political leader. I kept using the same term over and over again. He couldn't let them think he was a Bible-pounding southern preacher from South Carolina or a black activist from Chicago. He had to convince everyone—the power structure of the Democratic party, the folks who were going to be delegates to the '88 convention, and the people who would vote in the primaries—that he was *a mature political leader*.

During the New Hampshire primary, just before a debate there among all seven Democratic candidates, Jesse called me. It was snowing hard up there, but in the midst of the snow we saw some sunshine for Jesse.

I told him, "You've run for President before, and some of those people up there with you on that stage haven't. Unless I miss my guess, before that debate is over there will be some sort of brouhaha involving two or three of the others. When that happens, you'll have a perfect opportunity to step up and assume the role of peacemaker, and the Bible tells us, 'Blessed are the peacemakers.' "

Jesse saw the opportunity without any trouble. So when Dukakis and Gephardt got into a sharp argument, Jesse stepped in and in so many words said, "Now, boys. Let's behave like gentlemen." It was another irony, the protestor turning peacemaker. The debate was carried nationally on TV, and people all over the country saw Jackson in that surprising role. It definitely had an impact, one that helped Jesse in later primaries and caucuses as people remembered the favorable impression he had made in that TV debate in New Hampshire.

On Super Tuesday, with primary elections in twelve states, Jesse called me eighteen times, by actual count. He wanted to know what I was hearing about trends in each of the states. Jesse has certain of the same characteristics as Jimmy Carter. He's the same kind of outstanding one-on-one campaigner, and he is just as analytical and objective in assessing his chances.

He never fooled himself about how he was doing, on Super Tuesday or any other day. Even if I asked him, he would only say something like, "I sense that I'm doing pretty well . . ." He was always conservative in estimating where he stood in a particular campaign.

The Wisconsin primary provided a revealing experience for all of us. Jesse had done extremely well in Michigan a few days earlier, and when he marched into Wisconsin in an atmosphere of optimism, it became evident that there was still a serious racial problem in this nation. The "fear factor" set in. People became afraid that this black man might actually win the Democratic nomination.

Jesse was getting 95 percent of the black vote everywhere he went, and the white vote for him was running between 8 and 20 percent. Those white percentages weren't sensational, but they were higher than what they had been in 1984.

As far as the issues were concerned, Jesse ran a textbook campaign in 1988. He made only one mistake, and it cost him in Wisconsin and in the primaries that followed. The mistake was sending a letter to Noriega offering to meet with him to resolve our problems with Panama.

The letter had only one result: it resurrected the old concern that Jesse was a loose cannon, that you could never tell what he was going to do and that he had a habit of involving himself in things that were none of his business. When you combine that concern with the fear factor about a black man heading the Democratic presidential ticket, Jesse was getting himself into some trouble, part of it his fault for sending the letter to Noriega and part of it simply because he was running so well that the news folks were saying in their stories that the man might just win the nomination.

It was another irony. Because he was doing so well, he faced the prospect of not doing so well. Folks were going to start voting against him just to make sure that this black man who had shocked everyone by being so successful in the 1988 campaign wasn't going to be *too* successful.

The truth is that if Jesse had done well in Wisconsin, overcoming the Noriega letter and the fear factor, he might have won the New York primary. And if he had won New York, there's no telling what might have happened. He did very well in California anyhow. With a New York victory under his belt, who knows? He might have won California too. Then the question would have been: How do you keep a candidate off the ticket when he's won the New York and California primaries and done so well in so many others?

I was with Jesse in New York on primary day there. He made an appearance at the Apollo Theater in Harlem, and his ability to work magic with his audiences, even when they don't agree with what he's saying, was clear all over again. There must have been five thousand people in the audience. Maybe the crowd wasn't actually that large, but it seemed like it. All the folks were black, and they stomped their feet and whistled and clapped their hands at everything Jesse said. One other thing was also obvious: A good many of the people in that audience were on drugs.

Jesse shocked them by saying, "I'll tell you this: Y'all better hope I don't get elected President, because if I do I'm going to lock you up. You're breaking the law. You're using illegal drugs."

And they stomped their feet and whistled and clapped some more.

As the convention neared, people started asking Jesse why he didn't quit the race, supposedly for the good of the party. He gave the perfect answer: "You didn't ask anybody else to quit. Why ask me?" When someone would say his candidacy might split the party, he had the perfect answer for that too: "Nobody told Teddy Kennedy to quit in 1980."

By the time the New York primary arrived, the race was down to three men: Gore, Dukakis, and Jackson. If Gore had won New York, Jackson still might have been an even more significant power at the convention than he was. But the mayor up there, Ed Koch, fanned the flames of racism and the fear factor by saying that Jews would have to be crazy to vote for Jesse Jackson because of Jesse's blunder earlier in calling the city "Hymietown."

Dukakis walked away with the win, and Gore did not do well because he was allied with Koch. Jesse needed for Gore to get a significant percentage of the vote to stave off Dukakis, but it didn't happen. Effectively, the Democratic nominating process was over.

I WENT with Jesse to California for his campaign there. I was with him in Bakersfield when he spoke to farm workers who had contracted cancer from working with pesticides in the fields. I saw him reach those folks. He was showing again that he had the most human and most caring message and candidacy of all the Democratic candidates that year.

Jackson made a strong showing in California despite the results in New York. The enthusiasm at his headquarters on the night of the primary would have made you think he'd won. That enthusiasm had meaning too, because most of the people in the crowd were white.

On the heels of New York and California, the talk turned to the question of whether Jesse should accept the vice presidential nomination if Dukakis offered it to him at the convention. He wanted to be sure he handled that one the right way, making the right decision and saying the right things, so he called a meeting of his advisers in Chicago for a few days later and asked me to attend.

Back home in Calhoun before leaving for Chicago, I was getting worried. All this talk about the vice presidential spot for Jesse could set him off, put him out of control. He had performed with such great substance and discipline—more than any of the other candidates—and had been so innovative in determining the issues himself for all of the other candidates to respond to, that it would be a shame for him to spoil all of that by going off the deep end now on this vice presidential business.

It's pretty heady stuff when one of the big stories in America is whether you should accept the vice presidential nomination of your party, and when you're a black man, the effect must be considerably headier. That was what we had to look out for, and Jesse wasn't the only one susceptible to that virus. His key advisers seemed to be coming down with the same bug.

There are two sides to Jesse Jackson: the dream side and the reality, and at the moment his dream side seemed to be winning. That side of his personality was saying to him, "Wouldn't it be wonderful if a black man could become Vice President of the United States!"

There's not a thing wrong with that. I tried to look at it through

Jesse's eyes and those of his advisers, just as I did at the party conference in Washington when we talked about delegate rules. All of these
people had been dumped on during their days in the civil rights movement and had fire hoses aimed at them and police dogs turned loose
against them. They were kicked by police horses, beaten with billy
sticks, and put in jail, and now one of their own had a chance at one
of the most glorified positions in America.

At his meeting in Chicago, Jesse heard all those advisers tell him
that he should accept the nomination and why. Then he turned to me
and said, "What do you have to say, Doctor?"

I said, "Do you want me to tell them the truth?"

And Jesse said, "The truth shall set you free."

So I said to the group, "First, all the talk about the vice presidency
is foolish for several reasons. The first reason is that Dukakis is not
going to do it. He is neither creative nor bold. He is not going to give
the vice presidential spot to somebody who is going to upstage him. So
if any of you think Dukakis is going to offer the vice presidency to Jesse,
you're just plain wrong. It's not going to happen."

Then I mentioned the second reason. "Even if I were wrong
about that, it would be the end of Jesse's political career if he accepted
it. The reason I say that is that if Jesse is Vice President on the ticket,
then when Dukakis barely manages ten states, Jesse will be blamed for
the defeat. Then he will be written off and finished."

And if Dukakis won? "Dukakis is not going to win. He doesn't
know how to win. He doesn't know how to run a national campaign."

Then I got my usual ribbing from Jesse about being a white
honkie who doesn't know what he's talking about. But those folks in
the room, starting with Jesse, always accorded me full respect, wherever we were meeting and regardless of the subject. I always considered
that a high tribute both from them and to them, because I didn't have
their background, yet they listened to me and told me they respected
me for saying what I did. I thought that was as much of a compliment
to them as it was to me.

Jesse's advisers were still in the process of making a journey that
he had already made in his transition from civil rights leader to political leader. In an article U.S News & World Report asked me to write
after the convention, I wrote:

> The decision to walk across the bridge in Selma was a diffi-
> cult decision. They [the protesters] knew that they were going to be
> beaten and have dogs loosed upon them. But they also knew that

what awaited them on the other side of the bridge was equal to or superior to what they were leaving on the back side. Now, that's the civil rights bridge.

The political bridge is different. When you start walking across that bridge, you don't know what's going to happen. They now have to walk across that political bridge, and that's an act of faith—that if they support and elect Michael Dukakis, Michael Dukakis is then going to consider them an integral part of his constituency. They've got to cross that bridge. Jesse, in my judgment, has made that transition.

JESSE AND HIS WIFE, Jackie, went to Boston to have dinner with Dukakis and his wife on July 4. After dinner, they went down to the Boston Common to the annual Boston Pops concert and the fireworks display.

Jesse said Dukakis made it clear he didn't want to talk about anything of interest to Jesse that night. Both Jesse and Jackie came away from the evening feeling they had been put down by Michael and Kitty Dukakis. They felt that clearly there was no relationship at all between the two couples, that Dukakis was merely going through the motions of doing something he thought he should do to keep the black voters happy. They said it was tokenism of the worst kind.

The thing that people in that position fail to realize is that a national campaign is completely different from one at the state level. You run fifty limited campaigns, and then all of a sudden you're running one that's theoretically fifty times bigger in every way than anything you've run before. You have to make a quick switch up to the vastly higher level of magnitude and volume, and you've never operated at that level before. The Dukakis people didn't know how to graduate to that higher level.

We were trying to be helpful. We wanted the Democratic party to win the presidency in November, but that Dukakis crowd didn't want to have anything to do with any Carterite.

I knew Dukakis had been educated at Swarthmore, one of the hotbeds of academic liberalism, and I thought liberals had more tolerance for people than the rest of us folks. But Dukakis and his people were showing themselves to be what Harry Truman called "hothouse liberals"—take them out of their protected environment and their liberalism wilts and dies.

John Dukakis, the candidate's son, came down to Calhoun and we visited for a while. He impressed me as a nice young man who made it a point to learn something about the Jackson candidacy and also about southern politics.

I told John that his father's campaign needed to show a presence in the South. He and his coworkers had to establish relationships, and his father should talk to local elected officials so they wouldn't run from him if he won the nomination.

The Dukakis people didn't do any of those things. They had a great opportunity to win it all, especially with Lloyd Bentsen on the ticket. Mondale and Ferraro had a severe problem in '84 because no local officials running for election wanted to be tied to them. Dukakis had an opportunity in '88 to build a bridge to the local officials all around the country and regain their votes and their campaign support, but he simply never did it.

The truth is that Dukakis wouldn't have had the opportunity to run against George Bush at all if it hadn't been for our part of the country. The South saved the Dukakis candidacy. If Florida and Texas hadn't voted themselves into the Dukakis column on Super Tuesday, he would have been finished.

As THE TIME for the convention drew near, Jesse's stature as a mature political leader grew larger all the time. One of his reasons for his success in the 1988 primaries was his willingness—and ability—to hammer hard at drugs as *the* issue in America that year. People related to that when they voted.

Many politicians have a tendency to move away from the drug issue, or to deal with it in slogans that make better bumper stickers than solutions. But Jesse faced up to it squarely and said it's our number-one issue because it's the one problem in America that had the inherent capability to destroy us as a society. People agreed with him on that, and they admired him for saying it.

Jesse's political growth took a quantum leap after 1984, when he moved outside his black constituency and began appealing to white voters as well. He did that on the drug issue and on others. If you have a drug problem yourself, or someone in your family does, race becomes unimportant. It's a nonfactor. People couldn't understand where Jesse's new acceptance among whites was coming from, but that was a big part of it.

If someone is saying he wants to help you and he happens to be black and you're white, you don't care where the help comes from, or what color it comes in. You just want help. If your house is on fire, you don't ask what color the fire fighters are before you let them turn the hose on. It's the same way with drugs, and from the practical political standpoint, Jesse was brilliant to focus so much on that issue.

In reaching a new level of political maturity and outgrowing the other candidates in the process, Jesse made a genuine contribution to our political process, because he blurred the traditional liberal-conservative lines. He aimed at the issues that hit home.

Day care is an example. When both the young father and his wife have to work, those two folks are going to consider day care a more important issue than the Strategic Defense Initiative. Five years ago, day care was a liberal cause. Now it's just a pragmatic concern, and Jesse, because he is pragmatic himself, has appealed to voters because of his strong support for day-care programs.

You can bet that some of the people who voted for him in 1988 because of his stand on day care were conservatives, but when they went into the voting booth in the primaries, they didn't vote for a conservative candidate for President—they voted for the day-care candidate, and that candidate was Jesse.

Jesse had something else going for him in 1988. While he grew as a mature political leader, the problems were changing from 1984. That prompted the voters to view him differently. It's true of all candidates. Dukakis was just as liberal in '88 as Mondale was in '84, but he was viewed differently because the problems had changed. But he hadn't, so he was viewed as out of touch with the real world—which, of course, he was.

The Jesse Jackson story in 1988 also advanced the practice of "coalition politics" because of his appeal to groups on issues as well as to voters on an individual basis. He brought different groups together more than the other candidates. He understands and practices coalition politics—a true sharing of power—better than any other leader in either party today.

That's one of the main reasons why what he accomplished for his party in 1988 will have an effect on American politics that will last the rest of this century and into the next. He introduced the age of reciprocity, with special impact in the South.

The white power structure will have to support black candidates now, not just the other way around. The 1990s will see this reciprocity becoming a fact of political life, and the effect has already appeared. It happened in Virginia on election night in 1989, when Douglas Wilder became the first black man ever elected governor of any state. It is another irony—a towering one—that the first black man ever elected a governor, the grandson of a slave, was elected not in the North but in the South, and not in just any southern state but in the one whose capital city once was the capital of the Confederacy.

On that same election night, the voters in America's largest city also elected a black chief executive—David Dinkins. A look around the country shows how far we've come on the question of allowing people of every kind to be a part of our political system. Thanks to Jackson's '88 campaign, one of the heroes of Operation Desert Storm, General Colin Powell, can now be mentioned as a credible possibility for a spot on one of the national presidential tickets.

The lineup of black mayors over recent years is all the proof that anyone should need that our system must—and does—have room enough for all of us: Sharon Pratt Dixon in Washington, Tom Bradley in Los Angeles, the late Harold Washington in Chicago, Kenneth Gibson in Newark, Andrew Young and Maynard Jackson in Atlanta, Coleman Young in Detroit, and Kurt Schmoke in Baltimore.

In the 1990s, we'll have more black governors, and black senators too, and maybe a black on one of the national presidential tickets. Jesse Jackson didn't start this. Many of the mayors mentioned above were elected before Jesse became a national political force, but blacks will be elected in far greater numbers, especially in the South, because of his success.

Not everyone agrees with that statement—not even blacks and successful black politicians. Governor Wilder is one who disagrees. The *Richmond Times-Dispatch* has quoted Wilder as saying that Jackson did not help him "directly or indirectly that I know of."

Some folks in the party are trying to argue that the victories by Wilder, Dinkins, and others show that Jesse in fact should change his style and oratory. Those people are looking through the wrong end of the microscope. The truth of the matter is that Wilder and Dinkins won in 1989 partly because Jackson ran interference for them in 1988. And the victors all through the 1990s will win in part for the same reason.

In New York, for example, Ed Koch was considered invincible. But Jesse took him on in the primary there in '88 by opposing his positions and his endorsements, and Jesse carried the city in that primary. The next year, Koch lost to Dinkins in the primary, and Dinkins won the general election.

Despite what Governor Wilder says in Virginia, Jackson had something to do with that victory, too. Certainly Wilder is entitled to all the credit for the campaign he conducted against Marshall Coleman. It was a masterful performance from beginning to end, as he took the high road and let Coleman defeat himself in a long exhibition of negative campaigning. But Jesse helped Wilder, and all the other victorious blacks who will follow Wilder in Virginia, by carrying the state in the Democratic primaries in '84 and '88. He registered voters there, and his people got them to the polls. When Jackson says he "certainly helped create the climate for that breakthrough," he has considerable evidence to support his claim.

As a result of the Jackson candidacy and the skill with which he handled himself in 1988, pragmatism will be of far greater concern to candidates than before, with party affiliation and party loyalty becoming of correspondingly less concern to the voters. Ideology is not a major factor in American voting habits anymore. The new generation of voters is the pragmatic generation, and the young people will be increasing in numbers.

The polls show that the young are beginning to reject the liberal-versus-conservative mentality. They're going to be as pragmatic in the voting booth as they are at the supermarket, and in 1988 they saw Jesse as more pragmatic than any other candidate.

THE TRAVEL PLANS Jesse made for attending the 1988 convention in Atlanta were another stroke of genius. He decided to travel by bus—in a caravan. All the other candidates flew in, which was the thing you'd expect them to do. Only Jesse was coming by bus—with the camera crews from the network evening newscasts taping his arrival at every stop along the way from Chicago.

His itinerary called for him to swing by Calhoun and pick me up at the house, but the Secret Service intercepted a death threat against both of us, so he changed his route and picked me up at Interstate 75 right next to the Calhoun Holiday Inn.

Neither Jesse nor I was worried about having Jesse come to the house. We'd had death threats before and never gave them a second thought, but somebody said they were going to kill both of us, so the Secret Service took every precaution and made sure we did the same. I wasn't disturbed about the threat itself, but I was disappointed over what it represented—another rising of the fear factor, one of the prices of Jesse's continued success.

Meanwhile, Dan Rather called me and asked if he could meet me in Calhoun and ride to Atlanta on Jesse's bus. I told him, "Sure. Come on out to the house and have some coffee. You and I both know Jesse's going to be late anyhow."

We drank coffee while we waited for the call to come that Jesse's bus had arrived at I-75. While we were talking, Rather said, "You know, Bert, it would be great if Jesse accepted the vice presidential spot on the ticket with Dukakis."

I laughed and said, "It might be great for CBS, but it would be a disaster for the Democratic party."

All the reporters were asking what Jesse was going to do about the number-two spot. My stock answer to all of them was, "Jesse Jackson is the Michael Jordan of politics. He has more moves than anybody else, and as long as he knows he has the ball, he'll be the one deciding what happens, not somebody else."

As Jesse's bus made its way south along that same seventy-six mile stretch of I-75 that I had driven at 4:30 every morning for my meetings with Governor Carter fifteen years before, I put my arm around Jesse and spoke in a sports metaphor, something we're both comfortable with because we were both athletes in school and we have a lifelong interest in sports.

I told him that the shot clock was running down and he'd have to make a slam-dunk the next day or so or not at all. Jesse had to decide whether to allow his name to be put into nomination for the vice presidential spot on the ticket, even though Dukakis had already announced that Senator Bentsen was his choice.

Jackson reminded me, as he had before, of his method of operation—the five A's:

First get their *attention*.

Then get their *attendance*.

Then create the *atmosphere*.

Then affect their *attitude*.

And then you *achieve*.

We talked some more on the bus to Atlanta. Jesse was insisting on "a partnership—equity and shared responsibility"—in the Dukakis campaign and in the Democratic National Committee.

I told Jackson later that morning that challenging Bentsen for the vice presidential nomination would be a serious mistake. It would make Jesse look like a spoiler and would erase the gains he had scored with white voters throughout 1988.

He agreed. Jesse's reality side won out over his dream side.

I grinned and patted him on the back and told him, "You're using mature political judgment."

16

Victory and Debacle

ONLY ONE MAN had it in his power to unite the 1988 Democratic convention—Jesse Jackson—and I told him so. He had done a superb job of controlling himself in the four years after San Francisco, and by the time his bus caravan rolled into Atlanta, he was in such a position of strength that he could unite the convention.

It's a good thing too, because nobody else could. Dukakis couldn't do it. Kennedy couldn't, either. Neither could Carter. Only Jesse could, and he did. Then the reporters managed to get the story completely backward. They wrote afterward that Dukakis really handled Jackson. *Dukakis* didn't handle Jackson at all. *Jackson* handled Dukakis.

Jesse started right away. Shortly after we reached Atlanta, he met with 150 "whips," the men and women who would be whipping up enthusiasm for him on the convention floor and making sure all of his delegates remained committed to him. He said to his whips, "Remember—we are right where our parents prayed we would be some day. And right here in the heart of Dixie."

Then he met with Dukakis on Monday morning. Jesse pressed hard for what he thought he deserved. They were in the Dukakis suite in the Hyatt Hotel. Only two other people were in the room—Ron Brown, Jackson's campaign manager, who is now chairman of the Democratic National Committee, and Paul Brountas of the Dukakis camp.

Jesse went right at Dukakis, just like the former college baseball pitcher he is. He was insistent about what he wanted, and Dukakis was equally insistent about his own preferences.

This wasn't like the 1984 meetings between Jackson and Mondale, when Mondale seemed to be afraid of the man across the table from him. Instead, it was more like Jesse's first meeting with me. Neither man was blinking, and out of the confrontation came positive results.

Dukakis and Jackson reached an understanding. They worked out a plan to give Jackson a significant role in the campaign and to give his supporters more access to the Democratic National Committee, the Dukakis campaign, the transition team if they won on November 8, and the Dukakis administration, if there was one.

The word went out to the delegates: The meeting was a success. The party was united.

THERE WAS another meeting at that convention that the world still doesn't know about, and if Jesse decides to run for President again, it will do him a world of good.

He needed to strengthen his ties with Jewish Democrats. I was worried about his problems with our party's Jewish wing. Those problems weren't news to Jesse. He was fully aware of them—and that it is impossible to overstate the importance of the Jewish constituency for any Democratic politician.

It's like the black segment of the party. Both segments are important to us. You can't offend the Jewish people and expect to win elections any more than you can offend blacks—not if you're a Democrat. The Jews are a major help to our party. They are heavy contributors. They provide a valuable viewpoint on issues. And they have been a loyal and valuable segment of our party for generations. We need them, and we want them.

I was convinced that Jesse needed to communicate better with Jews and understand them better, so I took the liberty of trying to help, and I started at the top. I called the Israeli ambassador to the United States, Moshe Arad, whom I had never met, and asked if I could meet with him.

On Thursday morning, the last day of the convention, LaBelle and I had breakfast with the ambassador at the home of a mutual friend, Ed Elson, in Atlanta. We talked for two hours. When we finished, the ambassador agreed to talk to Jackson so Jesse would be more familiar with the interests and concerns of the Jewish community.

I went straight from the breakfast to Jackson's hotel room and told him I had just opened a line of communication for him with Jewish leaders. Jesse had a positive reaction to my move, and he and Ambassador Arad had several conversations over the telephone as a follow-up.

Not long after the convention, Jesse flew to Washington for what the State Department would call "frank discussions" with the ambassador before the start of the Dukakis campaign. The next result was a highly publicized meeting in New York involving Jesse, Mayor Ed Koch, and Governor Mario Cuomo.

Things continued to improve, and Jackson's relations with the Jewish wing of the party are now far stronger than ever—with all that such fence-mending implies for the future.

JACKSON WAS UNDER intense pressure from his supporters through the first days of the convention. Many of them still wanted him to allow his name to be placed in nomination for Vice President. Jesse, still acting like the mature political leader he has become, resorted to one of his sports expressions again and told them, "Long as I got the ball, can't anybody else shoot."

He was controlling the situation himself by not revealing what he was going to do. The Dukakis people would have to react to Jesse, not the other way around.

While he worked with his speech writers, Frank Watkins and Robert Borosage, on the address he would deliver to the convention, Jesse was facing facts. He knew he wouldn't be Dukakis's running mate, and he didn't want it. But those two sides of Jesse—The Dreamer and The Realist—were coming into conflict again.

Jesse the Realist doesn't overanticipate or overguess what's going to happen. He had realized for some time that Dukakis wasn't going to name him to the number-two spot, and he knew the convention surely wasn't going to nominate him.

But Jesse the Dreamer is an equally important side of the man, and that side was reminding him that he was a black man, born in a government housing project, a man who had three different names while he was growing up, and here he was occupying center stage in the biggest political drama in the country for years. It was what Jesse the Dreamer had longed for and worked for. He could go for it and then tell his grandchildren that it really can happen in America.

But Jesse the Realist won out again.

Jackson worked on his speech as late as five o'clock in the afternoon for delivery that evening. He knew what he wanted to say: that he had run a well-executed and dignified campaign, that he never stooped to demagoguery, that he was committed to public service, that people in the convention were of different backgrounds "but the genius of America is that out of the many we become one."

When Jesse starts talking like that, he almost does his writers' work for them. That's how articulate he can be, because of his deep belief in what he is saying.

As I LISTENED to Jesse at the Omni Convention Center that night, I heard him inspire the convention, his political party, and the entire nation. He got rave reviews from the leaders of the party and from the news media. He had united his party and sent it into battle against the opposition in a way that no one else did in Atlanta in those four days, not even the party nominee—*especially* the party nominee.

Dukakis, for reasons best known to himself, decided to excite the nation by calling for "competence." The response on November 8 was about what you'd expect after a rallying cry like that.

Listening to Jesse speak filled me with that special glow that comes with knowing that a long and intense struggle has produced a great victory. And I felt another emotion that night, too.

Hundreds of us had been locked out of the Omni at one point due to the fire marshal's valiant efforts at crowd control, with conditions much like those on Jimmy's election night in 1976. When I told Jesse about it, I added a philosophical note: "I guess it's better to be locked out in Atlanta than booted out in San Francisco."

That was never a problem for me at the '88 convention, for which I was grateful. The "living sentence" never surfaced. Any mentions of me in the local or national news media referred to me as Carter's former budget director or as a political strategist and former chairman of the party in Georgia.

I was never so naive as to think it was all over now, that the "living sentence" was a thing of the past. But for that week, when I was living in a goldfish bowl again, it was nice to know I could be treated like any other public figure.

WHAT THE NATION SAW on television in that convention of the Democratic party was one of the most remarkable achievements in the history of American politics. I felt, as I did about what Jimmy Carter accomplished in his election, privileged to be a part of the story.

But what happens now? What does the future hold for Jesse Jackson in particular and the Democratic party in general? One thing is certain at this writing: Jesse is now a leader of the Democratic party. He occupies center stage as a dominant figure and perhaps as one of those men who can also dominate the entire Democratic scene.

The Dukakis debacle actually helped Jackson because of one key difference from the Mondale defeat four years before: this one was the nominee's own fault. The 1984 loss wasn't really something you could blame on Mondale. Reagan was going to win that election, and it didn't make any difference who the Democratic nominee was or what he said or did. But this one was Dukakis's fault. He blew a seventeen-point lead in the polls by letting Bush simply take it away from him.

Marshall Frady wrote a political essay for the *New Yorker* magazine after the 1988 election, in which he called Jackson the predominant political figure in *either* party. At least until Desert Storm, that rating was justified because Jesse is more attuned to the issues and how the American people feel about them.

Jackson has more insight, he's more articulate, and he can think through issues and alternatives better than anyone else. Before he's finished, his political successes may be the political story of the century, more so than FDR's or Reagan's or anyone else's. The basic reason is that his career and his success symbolize the changes in our society since the start of the 1960s more than anyone else's.

Today's political issues are not right-left, conservative-liberal questions. They are "values issues." That's why Jesse will continue to grow in respect and prominence. More and more voters and folks in the media will come to realize that Jackson is a *values* liberal and not a *program* liberal. They'll see he's closer than anyone else to the issues like drugs, day care, jobs, health care, and the rest.

When Voltaire said that one of the things man learns from history is that man doesn't learn from history, he must have been talking about the Democrats. The party still manages to nominate the man who can't win in November, then follows its usual rite of fall by saying, "Yes, but we still control the House and Senate."

That's fine, but when it comes to controlling the national agenda and setting national priorities, the place where that is done is the White House. The President *pro*poses, and the Congress *dis*poses. That isn't news to the rest of the country, but too many Democrats don't seem to have heard it yet.

When all of us were considerably younger, the Democrats, with the help of the "solid South," put together a string of twenty straight years in the White House—four election victories by Franklin Roosevelt followed by Harry Truman's. Those of us who were babies when FDR was elected the first time and barely in our twenties when Truman left office grew up thinking the Republicans were almost incapable of electing anyone to the White House.

But with the exception of Jimmy Carter's election, the Republicans have topped that Democratic winning streak. With the completion of President Bush's first term in 1992, they will have controlled the White House for twenty-four years out of twenty-eight, and now it's the Democrats who seem incapable of electing anyone to the presidency.

The elections of 1984 and 1988 show that Americans are unwilling to elect a Democrat who is honest and nice, thinks he has a progressive program—and believes he is competent. And they are not going to be fooled by a Democratic nominee who tries to out-Republican the Republicans by pulling silly little stunts like riding in an Army tank wearing a helmet and fatigues—with his white shirt and necktie showing. Such antics merely insult the intelligence of the voters.

The Democrats have to stop worrying about *who* their nominee is going to be and worry first about *what* their nominee will be. On that question, they can learn from what the 1988 nominee was not. One of the central failings of the Dukakis campaign is that it never had a clear, consistent Democratic message. Two themes came out of the Atlanta convention in 1988. One was the Bush-bashing reflected in the political oratory by Ann Richards, who said George Bush "was born with a silver foot in his mouth," and Ted Kennedy, who kept asking, "Where was George?" The other was the underwhelming claim by Dukakis that the campaign was about competence.

I had an answer for Kennedy's question about Bush's whereabouts. I was in Washington right after the election, and I went over to see my friend Milton Pitts at his barbershop. Milton was the White House barber during the Nixon and Ford years. When Carter became President, Hamilton Jordan and Jody Powell decided they wanted unisex barbers in the White House, so Milton moved his shop back to the Sheraton-Carlton Hotel at 16th and K streets, two blocks north of the White House.

Griffin Bell, Jimmy's attorney general, and I continued to go to Milton for our haircuts, and I still do whenever I'm in Washington. In the meantime, Milton made a White House comeback and has been giving presidential haircuts throughout the Reagan and Bush administrations. Every week or so he walks two blocks south and cuts President Bush's hair.

When you walk into his shop at the hotel, it's like going to a Republican cabinet meeting. I walked in there one day during the Reagan administration and Cap Weinberger, Richard Allen, William Rogers, and Brent Scowcroft were all in there. I told them, "This is about the same ratio of Republicans to Democrats that I found out in the country during the campaign."

After all that talk in 1988 about where George was, I told Milton when I was in his barbershop, "The next time you cut the hair of the President-elect, you tell him that this Democrat knew exactly where George was—he was in Boston Harbor eating Dukakis's lunch."

I have every reason to believe Milton relayed my message.

I DON'T KNOW what poll Dukakis was reading when he seized on competence as the burning issue across the land, but nobody else had heard of it as a cause for concern among the American people. With all the things that he could have campaigned for or against, competence seemed to be one of the things the Republicans could claim for themselves.

Whether Democrats liked it or not, or knew it or not, the American people considered Reagan a competent executive. As Tip O'Neill said, "Reagan may go down in history as one of our worst Presidents of all time—but he would have made a great king." The competence of the Republican party in running the White House for the previous eight years was a nonissue in 1988, but Dukakis, in his wisdom, made it *the* issue in his acceptance speech.

The truth of the matter is that Dukakis lost the election by letting Bush capture control of the agenda—which is the exact opposite of what Jesse Jackson does as a campaigner. Jackson seizes control of the agenda, decides what issues will be discussed, and forces his opponent to respond to him, not the other way around. Dukakis didn't learn a thing from Jesse's successes all through 1988.

The Republicans must have rubbed their hands in glee when they heard Dukakis talk from Atlanta about competence. Lee Atwater, Roger Ailes, and company knew that if they allowed Dukakis to set the agenda for the campaign, highlighting the shortcomings of their record and their unwillingness to talk about our nation's problems, they would lose.

So when Dukakis sounded the alarm about "competence" and the nation yawned, the Republicans knew they were home free.

The Democrats have to avoid repeating that mistake if they are to have any chance at all to win in 1992. They must establish control of the campaign agenda. If they do, they have a chance, depending on what happens between now and then. If they don't, they have no chance, regardless of what happens.

Imagine, for example, what might have been—if only Dukakis had firmly tied George Bush to Ronald Reagan's record in 1988 and handcuffed Bush with his own politician's oratory. Bush would have been placed on the defensive, answering complaints and allegations about our national debt, his description in 1980 of Reagan's proposals as "voodoo economics," corruption, the Iran-Contra scandal, our trade debt, racism, drugs, health costs, and who knows what else.

Instead, Dukakis allowed Bush to control the agenda—with such diversions as Willie Horton, Boston Harbor, the American Civil Liberties Union, and the Pledge of Allegiance. What worked for Bush, and against Dukakis, in 1988 weren't issues—they were emotions. Things like America in the morning, standing tall, loyalty, being tough on crime and gun controls.

The mayoralty campaign in New York the next year provided the same kind of insight into Republican campaign strategy, and the inability—even the refusal—of some Democratic candidates to do anything about it. Rudolph Giuliani was running as the Republican candidate against David Dinkins, and Ailes, the mastermind of negative campaigning, was directing the Giuliani effort. The day after the primary, Ailes was asked what positions Giuliani would be taking in the general campaign. Ailes answered, "We're putting together a poll and trying to determine the message." That's a strange way to express your convictions. A week later, Giuliani said the results of the poll were in, he had decided what his principles were, and he was moving to the right.

David Dinkins lost control of the agenda, and almost lost the election. In a city where registered Democrats outnumber Republicans five to one, Dinkins managed to fritter away a twenty-point lead and won by only the narrowest of margins.

For the Democrats, the question is how to regain control of the agenda for their campaigns and how to overcome the negative campaigning that the Republicans surely will throw at them again in 1992. One technique is suggested by Dr. Steven Jonas, a political analyst who has developed a theory called "the new Americanism" as an instrument for Democratic victory in the White House race in 1992.

Dr. Jonas and I have discussed his theory by phone, in correspondence, and during a visit by him to Calhoun. He points out that in virtually every component of a Republican negative campaign, there lies a fundamental internal or external contradiction, and the Democrats must learn to play on these contradictions and give them full public exposure.

For example, the theme of patriotism runs strong through any Republican campaign in recent years, and will again in '92. Against Dukakis in '88, Bush managed to make considerable political hay out of a veto by Dukakis, as the governor of Massachusetts, of a bill which would have required teachers to lead their students in reciting the Pledge of Allegiance in class at the beginning of each schoolday.

I grew up doing that. So did most other middle-aged Americans. Dukakis had a legitimate point in saying that he didn't think Americans should be *forced* to recite the Pledge. During the campaign, Bush jumped all over that one as evidence that Dukakis somehow wasn't as patriotic as he was and didn't love America as much as he should.

Any thinking person knows that's nonsense. But Dukakis let Bush get away with it. He could have defused that nonissue by pointing to the last words of the Pledge itself, the ones that call for "liberty and justice for all," and saying, "There can be neither liberty nor justice if students are *forced* to say it. That kind of forced patriotism was found in the classrooms of Russia, and in the classrooms of Germany in the 1930s, but there should be no room for it in the classrooms of this free country."

Likewise, on the issue of crime there is another Republican contradiction. What a difference it would have made if Dukakis had said, "Crime? The Reagan-Bush administration is saying it can do something about crime? It had eight years and the only thing that happened is that crime got worse."

Drugs? While Nancy was telling people, "Just say no," her own husband was cutting the budget of the Drug Enforcement Administration. Dukakis could have charged that she was giving us a bumpersticker solution to a complicated socioeconomic problem, and doing more harm than good by telling us what a simple solution she had for a problem that can't be simplified.

When Bush tried to picture himself as more opposed to crime than his opponent, Dukakis could have said, "What about crime within the Reagan-Bush administration itself? The administration that gave the American people Oliver North and Mike Deaver at the White House and a cast of thousands at HUD is the last source in the country to brag about its credentials for solving America's crime problem."

Being tough on criminals was another issue where Dukakis allowed Bush to capture control of the agenda, instead of seizing the initiative himself by saying, "Tougher prison sentences and more jails? Reagan and Bush had eight years to do something about those subjects too, so what happened? We now slap people into jail at more than double the rate when Reagan took office, but nobody seems to be dancing in the streets and shouting that we've solved the crime problem."

We were reminded every night in the Bush commercials that the Republican nominee served in the Navy in World War II. Every voter saw that Republican TV commercial over and over. How many of those same people knew that Dukakis served in the Army in Korea? Dukakis let Bush win that one, too.

On the most famous single issues of the entire campaign, Dukakis could have been the winner instead of Bush. As soon as Atwater, Ailes, and company began running that commercial about Willie Horton, including its none-too-subtle appeal to racism, Dukakis could have counterpunched them into defeat by saying, "You want to talk about furlough programs for prisoners? Mr. Bush and his partner for eight years, Mr. Reagan, both know something about that subject."

He could have continued, "Reagan put the same kind of program into effect when he was governor of California, and two prisoners on furlough shot and killed innocent victims in California while Reagan was the state's chief executive. One of the victims was a police officer and the other a schoolteacher. Thirty other states also have the same program. And the federal government operated exactly the same kind of program at its federal prisons during the Reagan-Bush administration."

All of these contradictions in the Republican campaign oratory could have been turned around by Dukakis and used against Bush. But Dukakis never did any of these things. He never took the initiative, and on the rare occasions when he counterpunched, it was too weak, too late, and too bad. Instead of asking where George was, by the end of the campaign some of us were asking, "Where was Mike?"

THE 1988 PRESIDENTIAL CAMPAIGN seemed to be a football game in reverse. The Republicans gave Bush the ball, but the Democrats gave him the opening. When he saw it, he ran through it to the presidency. He hasn't stopped running since.

The Dukakis campaign not only helped to elect George Bush, it also gave him the chance to prove he could be a popular President, so popular that the Democrats are faced with competing in 1992 against a President who had a 90 percent popularity rating among the voters in the spring of 1991. By that time, the Democrats were already in the position of having to play catch-up to win an election a year and a half away.

At this writing, the harsh reality facing the Democrats is that Michael Dukakis might have lost the 1992 election for them, too. However, he might also have shown them accidentally what they have to do to win in '96 if Bush proves unbeatable in '92.

The Democrats have created their own failure in trying to win the White House because they continue to violate one of my own basic laws of presidential politics: The sum of the parts cannot exceed the whole. The Democrats have insisted on accommodating all of the concerns and agendas of every one of their parts—those advocacy groups for Social Security, health care, blacks, women's rights, the environment, abortion, homosexuals, organized labor, you name it. As a result, these parts now far exceed the whole. The Democrats can't elect a President now because in trying to please every one of their parts, they are alienating too many of their other parts. In politics, you cannot be all things to all people on the grand scale that the Democratic party has thought possible.

On a smaller level, it's possible. You can elect a mayor, governor, or legislature by courting many diverse groups. But at the national level, there just ain't room enough for every cause and every organization, because their interests are going to start competing against each other and the party begins to self-destruct. That's exactly the pattern that the Democratic party has insisted on following in every election since Lyndon Johnson told us in 1968 that he wouldn't run again.

This has come about because Franklin Roosevelt back in the 1930s put together a true political coalition. That coalition kept expanding through the 1940s and '50s. By the time the mid-1960s came along, the groups within the coalition had expanded exponentially while the party had grown arithmetically. The result was a great imbalance within the party, with too many large forces competing against each other to get the party's nominee to support their cause, even if it hurt him with other forces whose support within the party was also necessary for his election.

You simply cannot put the sum of all of these parts on the head of the Democratic nominee for President and expect him or her to win. No Democratic nominee can bear such a load and win. That's why I told Mondale not to accept labor's endorsement in 1984. Organized labor has always been an important part of the Democratic party, as it should be, but if you take that group and add all these others, the party becomes unelectable at the presidential level because the sum of its parts outweighs its whole.

None of this means the Democrats should get rid of any of these constituencies. They are all key members of the party and deserving of the party's traditional concern and compassion for all Americans. But it *does* mean that the party can no longer bend over backward to accommodate every screaming demand of every one of its parts.

The Republicans do just the opposite. The sum of their parts does not equal the whole. They have great room to grow within their party. They can keep on adding parts until they reach that critical point where the sum of the parts equal the whole. Until that time, they can roll merrily along winning presidential elections with a membership of conservatives and moderates, because those two groups don't exceed the capacity that still exists within the party. The Republicans can still accommodate other organizations and other leaders on various issues. They can add a more liberal block and move to attract the black vote without yet arriving at the point where they simply have too many groups and too many leaders on competing issues and priorities.

The Republicans are also a different kind of a party at this point in American history. They do not base their appeal to the American people on their commitment to improve our lives and our society. It is a matter of record that the Republicans are not the party that produced Social Security for America's older citizens, or Medicare, or student loans for college. Those advancements and so many like them in behalf of the American people were made for them by the Democratic party, which is why Americans repeatedly elect a Democratic Senate and House of Representatives.

But the Republicans have something else that they use as a matter of strategy on their part: our emotions. They are the party of the flag, prayer in schools, and a strong national defense, implying that the Democratic party for some strange un-American reason is opposed to these things.

That campaign stunt by George Bush in visiting a flag factory may have produced belly laughs in some quarters, but that kind of thing plays in Peoria. That's what the Republicans have. They have staked out the emotional issues for themselves, and the elections of Ronald Reagan and George Bush were won in large measure by what I consider the "emotional vote."

A party that can do that doesn't have to worry about its parts exceeding its whole. The Republicans have plenty of room because they don't have that many competing parts, and because they appeal to our emotions rather than worrying about accommodating special interest groups.

The enormous success and popularity of Operation Desert Storm has made that emotional appeal stronger than ever. The Democrats can forget about making an issue out of defense spending. The Cruise missiles—which President Carter authorized after approving a recommendation for their development from the Office of Management and Budget when I was its director—and the Patriot missiles that knocked all of those Iraqi "scuds" out of the skies took care of that issue.

The one issue of concern to all Americans is the state of the economy and our huge budget deficit and national debt. The status of those issues will go far toward deciding the 1992 presidential election, and the party that handles them better will occupy the White House for the following four years.

Even as we put the 1991 recession behind us, the economy and the related subjects of the budget deficit and the debt form an issue that cries out for responsible public debate. Mike Monroney, chairman of the Coalition for Fiscal Restraint, points out that the national debt has tripled since 1981 to $3 trillion today. The budget deficit, which Carter reduced from $79 billion when he took office to $27 billion three years later, is ten times that much today.

In his continuing efforts to hold down taxes while controlling federal spending, Mike, a former vice president of TRW, reminds his audiences that interest payments on the debt cost us $3.2 billion every week.

For us as individuals, he illustrates the budget deficit and national debt in telling terms:

- Every young person entering the work force today will pay $200,000 in *additional* taxes over his or her work life to pay the interest on our national debt.
- Just the interest payments on the debt would have run the entire federal government in 1967.
- If we wanted to wipe out the debt today, every man, woman and child would have to pay the government $11,000.
- Each family of four today pays an average of $2,300 a year in *additional* taxes because of the interest on our national debt.
- Federal spending now exceeds $4,600 for every American, compared to $2,600 in 1980.

The Democrats can perform a valuable national service, even if they lose the 1992 presidential election, by forcing a continuing public debate on this overpowering national problem. To accomplish that, they will have to return to a coalition based more on geography, one that recognizes the roles and interests of various regions of the nation— including the South. But that solution is impossible at the moment, because when you start talking about not being able to meet the demands of certain people in the Democratic party immediately, those folks are going to threaten to join the Republicans or form a third party.

That is the historic progression of coalition government in any party and in any nation where it's been tried. It's the pitfall in coalition government. At some point, the competing voices will start to split the vote—while the opposition walks through the hole in the middle and wins the election.

The Democrats have to do something else, too, concerning the issues, or the party's inability to articulate them effectively. With such a long slump in presidential elections, the Democrats have to resort to a far more daring strategy than they've been willing to employ in recent years. If they don't, they face the growing certainty that they will go from 1964 to at least 1996 with one win in seven presidential elections spanning thirty-two years.

What should that strategy be? One possibility is to admit Bush's outstanding leadership in guiding the world through the Persian Gulf crisis and say to him, "Okay, Mr. President. You were right about that, and we salute you for it. Now let's see if you're right in what you've been saying about the home front. If you are, you'll get reelected. If you're wrong, we'll get elected."

Then the Democrats can do what they didn't do in 1988—identify preemptive targets which will enable them to seize the initiative and wage the campaign on their terms. They can start with the budget crisis and the capital gains controversy. They can say to Bush, "We're going to give you that cut in the capital gains tax, we're going to end the public debate over who's responsible for the deficit by giving you line-item veto authority over the budget, and we're going to give you something else you want—a proposed constitutional amendment requiring a balanced budget."

Then they can add, "We're willing to take our chances and let the voters tell us on election day whether they think you were right about these problems at home the way you were right about the war." With that, the Democrats could guarantee that the campaign would be fought on the issues and on their party's terms, at least more than in 1988.

Will the Democrats have the boldness to switch from their time-worn social laundry list, the one the voters have rejected in five of the last six elections, and employ this—or some other—bold new strategy against the old pilot who is so good at naming his own targets and then attacking them?

Probably not, which helps to explain why George Bush is President. If President Bush is reelected in 1992, the Democrats should start to work the next morning on changing their own attitudes and thus their approach to presidential elections. They should remind themselves that they are all Democrats, and then pledge to move away from these demand factors and leave the 1996 nominee of the party free of single-issue forces.

In other words, they will have to agree to let the nominee be the candidate of *all* the people. They have refused to allow that to happen, even though they have more "star" performers than the Republicans. Their lineup includes such big names as senators Bill Bradley of New Jersey, Sam Nunn of Georgia, Al Gore of Tennessee, John Kerry of Nebraska, and Jay Rockefeller of West Virginia, plus Congressman Dick Gephardt of Missouri and governors Mario Cuomo of New York and Bill Clinton of Arkansas.

There is yet another "star" in the Democratic party who is relatively unknown nationally, but who has labored long and faithfully for the party over the years. He is much better known than was Jimmy Carter in 1975. Thus another Georgia Governor, this one named Zell Miller, has the vision, intelligence, and political know-how to be a real leader during the coming months and years.

Zell, my lifelong friend with whom I shared a double desk in the first grade in Young Harris, Georgia, recently made a speech to the Southern Caucus of the Democratic National Committee in Raleigh. This is absolutely the best speech on the ills and problems of the Democratic party I have ever read, and I commend it to Democrats everywhere for their consideration. He says in simple terms that in order to elect a Democratic President, we must return to our roots in dealing with economic problems as a party and not let only social issues determine our campaign agenda. This speech is truly "must" reading for those who want a Democrat once again in the White House.

It would be one of the greatest ironies if the blueprint and road map leading to a Democratic victory for the presidency was conceived and crafted again by a relatively unknown Georgia Governor.

Then there's Jesse Jackson. The 1992 campaign will be a whole new ball game for him if he decides to run for President again. He'll have to live down the criticism that he's never been elected to anything except "shadow senator" in the District of Columbia, an office that doesn't really exist anyhow. He will have to remind his supporters that they are not the entire party, and that their concerns are not the only concerns facing the American people, black or white. He'll have to point out to them, in convincing terms, that it doesn't do them any good to be on prime-time network TV on the stage at the national convention gaining attention for their own cause if the party is going to lose in November anyhow.

He'll have to convince them that the party has to be able to spotlight together the horrible mess resulting from the credit-card approach of Bush and Reagan which allowed our budget and our national debt to reach historic levels, while promising us just the opposite. That problem—it's not even an issue because it's a fact—has the same deep implications for blacks and whites, and Jesse has to make his supporters understand that they have to rally together with the white members of the party to do something about it as a way of helping their own black brothers and sisters.

Our national economic situation has to be dealt with for the benefit of Americans of every color because it affects all Americans' lives—but you can't be a leader on that subject unless you're concerned about it and helping to shape the national debate about it. And Jesse has to be able to mobilize support on this issue if he is to mobilize support for himself as well.

Jesse can't have it both ways in 1992. He can't help to focus attention on our economic and other problems and their impact on blacks if he is seen by millions of Americans on TV every night as the shouting, preaching candidate of protest. He must show the voters that he has moved above that level in his political maturation and has become a candidate with a statesmanlike knowledge of, and concern for, those things that worry the same voters in Peoria that the Republicans pay attention to.

The Democratic leaders will have to promise themselves and each other that they will work together to form a national party strategy that is just that: one aimed at the nation as a whole and as a general population instead of one that looks like the result of a quilting party for special interest groups.

Epilogue

WHILE WRITING this book, I found myself remembering from time to time the advice of earlier Americans. I'm not one to dwell too much on the past, because I subscribe to the philosophy of another loyal son of the South, Satchel Paige, the baseball Hall of Famer from Alabama, who cautioned us, "Don't look back. Something may be gaining on you."

On the other hand, I am a collector of presidential memorabilia and I gain both knowledge and comfort about ourselves and our nation's future from those who came before us. One man whose words came back to me from time to time during this project was Woodrow Wilson, our beleaguered President during and after World War I.

Wilson had an unshakable faith in America's destiny. He told the people, "Up from the common soil, up from the great heart of the people, rise joyously streams of hope and determination that are bound to renew the face of the earth in glory." I happen to agree with that.

In addition to whatever entertainment value these pages may hold for the reader, I hope they also carry a certain instructive value as a contribution to the history of the years, events, and people they describe. If so, then what Patrick Henry called the "lamp of experience" may provide some measure of insight to those responsible for our nation's future—our citizens in general, our government officials at every level, our business executives, our political parties, the members of America's news media, and those in positions of responsibility in America's judicial system.

During the writing of this book I thought often about a story involving Harry Truman and a dead man, a story that has helped to guide and motivate me throughout my life and my career in public office and private business. The message of the story has remained my personal code of conduct, during my proudest moments and my darkest hours.

It carries a strong and valuable reminder for every American, and especially for those who seek to lead us. We have every reason to want the last word about each of us to be what it was for the dead man in the story.

Truman was on a presidential visit to the Southwest when his travels took him to an old frontier graveyard in New Mexico. One tombstone in particular caught his eye. He stared at it, then said to the reporters covering him, "Boys, I hope that's what history will be able to say about me."

The reporters gathered closer to look at the epitaph on the old tombstone. It said:

> Here lies Jack Williams
> He done his damndest.

Index

About the Authors

BERT LANCE has been president of his hometown bank, the Calhoun First National Bank in Calhoun, Georgia, and the National Bank of Georgia in Atlanta. He was Director of Transportation under Governor Jimmy Carter and became the federal government's Director of Management and Budget, a cabinet-level position, when President Carter took office in 1977.

Since leaving Washington, Mr. Lance has become a widely sought consultant in both business and politics. He operates his own international consulting practice, was chairman of the Georgia Democratic party in the early 1980s and remains a respected political adviser whose advice is sought frequently by prominent Democrats and members of the national news media.

Mr. Lance lives in Calhoun with his wife and grade school sweetheart, LaBelle. They have four grown sons.

BILL GILBERT is a former reporter for the *Washington Post* who has also worked as a public affairs director and press secretary in Washington. He is the best-selling author of thirteen books. He and his wife, Lillian, have a grown son, Dave. They live in Maryland, near Washington.